LEAVES FROM THE TREE OF LIFE
or
Gleanings from the Word of God

by
Rev. L.L. Pickett

"Search the Scriptures," (John v.39.)

"And the leaves of the trees were for the healing of the nations."
(Rev. xxii.2)

SCHMUL PUBLISHING COMPANY
NICHOLASVILLE, KENTUCKY

Copyright © 2018 by Schmul Publishing Co.
All rights reserved. No part of this publication may be reproduced or used in any form or by any means—graphic, electronic, or mechanical, including photocopying, recording, taping, or information storage or retrieval systems—without prior written permission of the publishers.

Churches and other noncommercial interests may reproduce portions of this book without prior written permission of the publisher, provided such quotations are not offered for sale—or other compensation in any form—whether alone or as part of another publication, and provided that the text does not exceed 500 words or five percent of the entire book, whichever is less, and does not include material quoted from another publisher. When reproducing text from this book, the following credit line must be included: "From *Leaves from the Tree of Life* by L.L. Pickett, © 2018 by Schmul Publishing Co., Nicholasville, Kentucky. Used by permission."

Cover image copyright: <a href="https://www.123rf.com/profile_flynt">flynt / 123RF Stock Photo</a>. Used by permission.

Published by Schmul Publishing Co.
PO Box 776
Nicholasville, KY 40340
USA

Printed in the United States of America

ISBN 10: 0-88019-616-5
ISBN 13: 978-0-88019-616-1

Visit us on the Internet at www.wesleyanbooks.com, or order direct from the publisher by calling 800-772-6657, or by writing to the above address.

Contents

	Publisher's Preface	6
	Prefatory	7
1	What God is to Us	9
2	Repentance	14
3	Regeneration	17
4	The Gift of the Holy Ghost	22
5	Some Bible Promises	25
6	Some Bible "Fear Nots"	28
7	Apostasy (No. 1)	31
8	Examples of Apostasy (No. 2)	36
9	How to Prevent Apostasy (No. 3)	43
10	Love (No. 1)	48
11	Love (No. 2)	50
12	Missions (Old Testament, No. 1)	53
13	Missions (New Testament, No. 2)	59
14	Missions (New Testament, No. 3)	67
15	What Christ is to Us	74
16	The Word of God	77
17	The Touch-Stone: A Sermon	79
18	Bible-Reading on Matthew V.3-16 (No. 1, Verses 3, 4.)	88
19	Bible-Reading on Matthew V.3-16 (No. 2, Verses 5, 6.)	90

20	BIBLE-READING ON MATTHEW V.3-16 (NO. 3, VERSE 7.)	93
21	BIBLE-READING ON MATTHEW V.3-16 (NO. 4, VERSE 8.)	95
22	BIBLE-READING ON MATTHEW V.3-16 (NO. 5, VERSE 9.)	97
23	BIBLE-READING ON MATTHEW V.3-16 (NO. 6, VERSES 10-12)	99
24	BIBLE-READING ON MATTHEW V.3-16 (NO. 7, VERSES 13-16)	102
25	ABIDE IN CHRIST	112
26	CONSECRATION	114
27	CHRIST IS THE LIGHT AND THE LIFE	117
28	IS IT RIGHT TO USE TOBACCO?	119
29	WINE AND SOME OF ITS RESULTS	125
30	BACKSLIDING	128
31	FUTURE PUNISHMENT	130
32	SOME BIBLE "COMES" (NO. 1)	133
33	SOME BIBLE "COMES" (NO. 2)	137
34	MINISTERIAL SUPPORT	139
35	SHOUTING	145
36	GIVING (OLD TESTAMENT, NO. 1)	150
37	GIVING (NEW TESTAMENT, NO. 2)	156
38	GIVING (NEW TESTAMENT, NO. 3)	162
39	GOD TURNS AGAINST THE IMPENITENT	169
40	THE JUDGMENT (NO. 1)	172
41	THE JUDGMENT (NO. 2)	174
42	THE RESURRECTION (NO. 1)	176
43	THE RESURRECTION (NO. 2)	178
44	ROMAN CATHOLICISM	180
45	SUPPLEMENTAL NOTE	186
46	THE SCRIPTURES	189
47	SOME BIBLE "WOES"	191
48	ROMANS VI-VIII	194

49	Kingdom of Heaven, of God	206
50	Christian Training of Children	208
51	Infant Baptism	211
52	The Sin of Neglect	220
53	Sin Must Not be Covered, but Confessed	222
54	Dancing	224
55	Mourning for Sin	230
56	The Doctrine of the Lord True	233
57	Drunkenness	235
58	Prayer (No. 1)	242
59	Prayer (No. 2)	245
60	Prayer (No. 3)	247
61	Prayer (No. 4)	249
62	Woman's Ministry	252
63	The Sabbath	258
64	The Holy Spirit	266
65	Supplement to Bible-Reading on the Holy Spirit	271
66	Full Salvation (No. 1)	276
67	Holiness (No. 2)	279
68	Perfect Love (No. 3)	282
69	Sanctification (No. 4)	285
70	Christ as Found in the Old and New Testaments	291
71	Entire Sanctification	297
72	How Holy?	303
73	Sanctification Delivers from Fear	307
74	The Sanctification of the Disciples	314
75	Sanctification the Bible Standard of Salvation	318
76	Encouragements to Spiritual Joy	325

Publisher's Preface

THIS IS A HANDY compendium of many topics that will find wide usage in personal devotional times. Pastors, evangelists, Sunday School teachers, small group leaders will also prove it to be indispensable.

Written by a notable Holiness evangelist from a distinctly unapologetic Holiness point of view, here are timeless issues that have reverberated for centuries. The author addresses such wide-ranging subjects as sanctification, ministerial support, child rearing, tobacco, dancing, missions, wine, giving, alcohol, and a host of other themes.

Here is a comprehensive collection of Holiness beliefs dealing with almost any aspect of the Christian life.

—D. CURTIS HALE
Publisher

Prefatory

We have no apology for sending out this book — not that we think it above criticism, but that, sending it as we do in Jesus' name, we trust it will do good. It doubtless has many imperfections, but there is one feature of the book that we know is good — namely, the scriptures contained in it. We have used the word of God freely and correctly, especially in all those places where the full quotation is indicated, since they were not written, but were cut and pasted.

Some of the readings contain nothing but the scriptures used, with a caption to each passage intending to give the gist of its meaning. Others have brief expositions, in which we have endeavored, without fear or favor of man, to give the real meaning as simply and clearly as we could. Wherein we have reached the truth, may the Holy Spirit graciously apply to every reader; wherein we have erred, may He graciously forgive, and overrule it all to the divine glory.

The method of arrangement adopted can be easily understood: A number of passages were selected bearing on the subject; they were then arranged under captions and numbered. Some were left thus without comment, while others have a brief expository comment based on the Scriptures according to their number in the lesson. If there are seven passages numbered and used in the lesson, there will be found seven numbered paragraphs in the exposition following, unless two or more numbers are commented on in one paragraph, and then the numbers indicate it.

Some of the chapters, prepared for me by other brethren, are not according to this method of arrangement. This, however, will give some diversity to the book, and will thus, no doubt, be pleasing to the reader.

We trust that the reader will study the book prayerfully, and that he may derive help therefrom in the heavenly journey. Will you not also pray that our God may use these pages to the good of some precious souls? When you have read the book, if you can do so, please assist in its circulation— if not otherwise, at least loan it to some friend, if you think he might be helped by it.

Will you, my brother or sister, pray that our God may use both you and me for his glory? My work as an evangelist is heavy; may our God use me to win souls!

And now, my reader, "I commend you to God, and to the word of his grace, which is able to build you up, and to give you an inheritance among all them which are sanctified." (Acts xx.32.)

—L.L. PICKETT
Daingerfield, Tex., December 27, 1888

1
WHAT GOD IS TO US

1. He is our Creator.

   "So God created man in his own image, in the image of God created he him; male and female created he them." (Gen. i.27.)

2. He is our Redeemer.

   "Doubtless thou art our Father, though Abraham be ignorant of us, and Israel acknowledge us not; thou, O Lord, art our Father, our Redeemer; thy name is from everlasting." (Isa. lxiii.16.)

3. He is our Saviour.

   "But hath in due times manifested his word through preaching, which is committed unto me according to the commandment of God our Saviour." (Tit. i.3.) See Titus ii.10.

4. He is also our Preserver.

   "The Lord shall preserve thee from all evil: he shall preserve thy soul. The Lord shall preserve thy going out and thy coming in from this time forth, and even for evermore." (Ps. cxxi.7, 8.) See Psalm xxxvi.6.

5. He is to us a Rock, a Fortress, and a high Tower.

"And he said, the Lord is my rock, and my fortress, and my deliverer; the God of my rock; in him will I trust: he is my shield, and the horn of my salvation, my high tower, and my refuge, my saviour; thou savest me from violence." (2 Sam. xxii.2, 3.) See also Isaiah xxxii.2.

6. He is the Guide of his people.

"I will instruct thee and teach thee in the way which thou shalt go; I will guide thee with mine eye." (Ps. xxxii.8) See Psalm lxxiii.24.

7. He is our Shepherd.

"The Lord is my Shepherd; I shall not want." (Ps. xxiii.1.) See John x.11.

8. More than all else he is our Father.

"Behold, what manner of love the Father hath bestowed upon us, that we should be called the sons of God: therefore the world knoweth us not, because it knew him not." (1 John iii.1.) Romans viii.14-17.

Our God is seen by this lesson from his own word to have come down very near to us, that he might lift us up very near to himself.

1. We here learn that he made us. We are his workmanship. He certainly intended in making us that we should be in harmony with himself, to his own glory and our eternal well-being. The text says God created man in his own image. But sin entered and blighted that image, cursed the highest of earth's creatures, and marred the handiwork of God. But God here undertook for us, perfected a plan of salvation, by which we may be "created

anew in Christ Jesus unto good works" (Eph. ii.10), and he thus became

2. Our Redeemer. To redeem is to buy back, to recover, to rescue, to set free. And since we were under the curse of sin, the bondage of the devil, God himself has bought us back not with "silver and gold," "but with the precious blood of Christ." (1 Pet. i.18, 19.) By this redemption in Christ we are saved from the dominion, power, and pollution of sin; hence, he is

3. Our Saviour. A Saviour is one who saves, and as we are already here lost in sin (Luke xix.10), we must be here saved from sin. Many think they may live in sin while in this world, but that they will be saved from sin when they die, and thereafter in heaven. But God says: "*Now* is the day of salvation." (2 Cor. vi.2.) Christ's name, Jesus, means Saviour; and is given because he came to save his people *from* their *sins*. (Matt. i.21.) He has all power in *earth*, as well as in heaven (Matt. xxviii.18); and can save us from sin as well here as there, for he is able to save unto the uttermost. (Heb. vii.25.) Hence our daily prayer: "Thy will be done in earth, as it is in heaven." (Matt. vi.10.) Saving us from sin here, that we may do his will as it is done there, he will in the end take us to himself in heaven, the final home of the saved.

4. He is our Preserver. In the world we go through many dangers. They beset our path from youth to age; and we would surely fall by the way, but our kind Preserver watches over us, for "the steps of a good man are ordered by the Lord." (Ps. xxxvii.23.) He feedeth the fowls of the air, and to his people he saith: "Are ye not much better than they?" (Matt. vi.26.) Of the righteous it is said: "The law of his God is in his heart; none of his steps shall slide." (Ps. xxxvii.31.) That he may preserve us from all danger God himself becomes

5. Our Rock and our Fortress. He thus takes us into his own divine presence, under his own sheltering care; and

O how safe! If we will but abide there, all is well. "He that dwelleth in the secret place of the Most High shall abide under the shadow of the Almighty. I will say of the Lord, He is my refuge and my fortress: my God; in him will I trust. Surely he shall deliver thee from the snare of the fowler, and from the noisome pestilence." (Ps. xci.1-3.) Here is the Christian's stronghold, that he may dwell continually in the fortress of God's sheltering wing.

6. Our God who preserves also guides us. If we are surrendered implicitly unto God, we may be sure of his guidance; he will open our way before us; he will lead us in all our goings. Our failures in the Christian life, doubtless, come just here. We desire God's blessing, his favor, and his salvation; but we are prone to choose our own ways. We are not always quite willing and ready, without a quibble, to follow our Guide. He guides us (1) by his word; (2) by his providences; (3) by his Spirit.

7. He is also our Shepherd. The shepherd not only guides his flock, but he feeds, shelters, and protects them. Our divine Shepherd, too, so feeds us that we may not want. "He maketh me to lie down in green pastures: he leadeth me beside the still waters." "Thou preparest a table before me in the presence of mine enemies: thou anointest my head with oil; my cup runneth over." (Ps. xxiii.2, 5.) Under the good Shepherd's protection, how safe! how secure our dwelling-place! No harm can come nigh us (Ps. xci.7.) But O unbounded love! To crown it all he announces himself

8. Our Father. "But as many as received him, to them gave he power to become the sons of God." (John i.12.) So he hath taught us to pray, "Our Father who art in heaven." God our Maker, Redeemer, the all-wise, all-powerful One, of his infinite love adopts us into his own family, regenerates our sin-dead natures by his Holy Spirit, and makes us co-heirs with his only begotten Son, "to an inheritance incorruptible, and undefiled, and that fadeth

not away, reserved in heaven" for us. (1 Pet. i.4.) Glory be to God, now and for evermore.

2
REPENTANCE

1. It requires a turning from all sin.

   "Therefore I will judge you, O house of Israel, every one according to his ways, saith the Lord God. Repent, and turn your-selves from all your transgressions; so iniquity shall not be your ruin. Cast away from you all your transgressions, whereby ye have transgressed; and make you a new heart and a new spirit: for why will ye die, O house of Israel? For I have no pleasure in the death of him that dieth, saith the Lord God: wherefrom turn yourselves, and live." (Ezek. xviii.30-32.)

2. It is a stepping-stone to conversion.

   "Repent ye therefore, and be converted, that your sins may be blotted out, when the times of refreshing shall come from the presence of the Lord." (Acts iii.19.)

3. All are commanded to repent.

   "And the times of this ignorance God winked at; but now commandeth all men everywhere to repent." (Acts xvii.30.)

4. John the Baptist preached repentance.

"In those days came John the Baptist, preaching in the wilderness of Judea, and saying, Repent ye: for the kingdom of heaven is at hand." (Matt. iii.1, 2.)

5. Christ preached it in announcing his kingdom.

"From that time Jesus began to preach, and to say, Repent: for the kingdom of heaven is at hand." (Matt. iv.17.)

6. Repentance is preached in Christ's name.

"And that repentance and remission of sins should be preached in his name among all nations, beginning at Jerusalem." (Luke xxi.47.)

7. The repentance of one sinner causeth great joy in heaven.

"I say unto you, that likewise joy shall be in heaven over one sinner that repenteth, more than over ninety and nine just persons, which need no repentance." Likewise, I say unto you, there is joy in the presence of the angels of God over one sinner that repenteth."

8. Backsliders must repent, or God will leave them.

"Remember therefore from whence thou art fallen, and repent, and do the first works; or else I will come unto thee quickly, and will remove thy candlestick out of his place, except thou repent." (Rev. ii.5.)

9. The danger of those who reject this doctrine.

"And whosoever shall not receive you, nor hear you, when ye depart thence, shake off the dust under your feet for a testimony against them. Verily I say unto you, It shall be more tolerable for Sodom and Gomorrah in the day of judgment, than for that city. And they went out, and preached that men should repent." (Mark vi.11, 12.)

10. There is no alternative; it is, repent or die.

"I tell you, Nay: but, except ye repent, ye shall all likewise perish." (Luke xiii.3.)

3
REGENERATION

1. By nature we are dead in sin. Grace quickens.

> "And you hath he quickened, who were dead in trespasses and sins." (Eph. ii.1.) See Ephesians ii.4, 5

2. Accordingly we must be born again, of the Spirit.

> "Jesus answered and said unto him, Verily, verily, I say unto thee, Except a man be born again, he cannot see the kingdom of God." (John iii.3.) See John iii.7, 8.

3. Under the carnal mind we cannot please God. It is enmity to him.

> "For to be carnally minded is death; but to be spiritually minded is life and peace. Because the carnal mind is enmity against God: for it is not subject to the law of God, neither indeed can be. So then they that are in the flesh cannot please God." (Rom. viii.6-8.)

4. God's Spirit regenerates us— without which we are none of his.

"But ye are not in the flesh, but in the Spirit, if so be that the Spirit of God dwell in you. Now if any man have not the Spirit of Christ, he is none of his." (Rom. viii.9.)

5. We must put on this new man, created in righteousness.

"And that ye put on the new man, which after God is created in righteousness and true holiness." (Eph. iv.24.)

6. The new birth is by the will of God, not of man.

"But as many as received him, to them gave he power to become the sons of God, even to them that believe on his name: which were born, not of blood, nor or the will of the flesh, nor of the will of man, but of God." (John i.12, 13.)

7. Begotten of God unto a lively hope by Christ.

"Blessed be the God and Father of our Lord Jesus Christ, which according to his abundant mercy hath begotten us again unto a lively hope by the resurrection of Jesus Christ from the dead." (1 Pet. i.3.)

8. Born of incorruptible seed, by the word of God.

"Being born again, not of corruptible seed, but of incorruptible, by the word of God, which liveth and abideth forever." (1 Pet. i.23.)

9. The Spirit bears witness that we are the children of God.

"The Spirit himself beareth witness with our spirit, that we are the children of God." (Rom. viii.16. R.V.)

1. Man may be spiritually dead while physically alive. He may have no life toward God and heavenly things

while yet thoroughly alive in sin and to the things of earth. So the gospel finds all the world "dead in trespasses and sins." "Having the understanding darkened, being alienated from the life of God through the ignorance that is in them, because of the blindness [or hardness] of their heart: who being past feeling have given themselves over unto lasciviousness, to work all uncleanness with greediness." (Eph. iv.18, 19.) But while by nature we are in such a fearful condition, thank God, grace provides life for the dead! "God, who is rich in mercy, for his great love wherewith he loved us, even when we were dead in sins, hath quickened us together with Christ, (by grace ye are saved;) and hath raised us up together, and made us sit together in heavenly places in Christ Jesus." (Eph. ii.4-6.) Hence

2. We must be born again — that is, born from above by the Spirit of God — into a new and better life. This new heavenly life is wrought in the soul of the believing penitent by the Holy Spirit, which comes, like the unseen wind, in mighty power upon the inmost depths of the soul, and so changes it that old things (habits, ways, customs) pass away and all things become new; so it may truly say: "Things I once loved I now hate; things I once hated I now love." And this new creature in Christ Jesus is a child of God and an heir of the skies. (Rom. viii.16, 17.)

3. A soul dead in sin is under the reign of the carnal or fleshly mind, which is an enemy to God, destructive to peace; and those in bondage thereto cannot please God, for when they would do good evil is present with them; and "they are carnal, sold under sin." Accordingly, in the anguish of bondage, they cry out: "O wretched man that I am! who shall deliver me from the body of this death?" Then the answering shout of victory comes back: "I thank God through Jesus Christ our Lord." So by the Spirit of God, through the merit of Christ, the power of sin is bro-

ken; and the dead soul comes into the divine life, rejoicing with "joy unspeakable and full of glory."

4. In this regenerating power of the Holy Ghost we get from under the yoke of sin in the flesh, so that it is said "ye are not in [subjection to] the flesh, but in [under the influence of] the Spirit, if so be the Spirit of God dwell in you." A deliverance from the slavery of sin is granted to the children of God; for "where the Spirit of the Lord is, there is liberty." To be Christ's we *must* have his Spirit.

5. This demands new living. The "new man," or hidden man of the heart, must control our lives and shape them in righteousness and true holiness for God. Such a one must abandon all sin. He must renounce the world, the flesh, and the devil, so that he will not follow or be led by them. His life must be according to the sacred Scriptures, that it may be pleasing and acceptable to God through Jesus Christ our Lord.

6. The power to become sons of God is given us by faith, which must bring forth "the fruits of righteousness." And this new birth, being spiritual, not of flesh, nor blood, nor of the will of man, but of God, must be sought and obtained as the gift of Heaven. Reader, have you been born again, born of the Spirit, into spiritual life?

7. Begotten of God's mercy in Christ Jesus, the soul rejoices in a lively hope. "Hope maketh not ashamed; because the love of God is shed abroad in our hearts by the Holy Ghost." (Rom. v.5)

8. This seed is said to be incorruptible. Some have said that this teaches the impossibility of apostasy. It certainly cannot so teach; for "when the righteous turneth from his righteousness, and committeth iniquity, he shall even die thereby." (Ezek. xxxiii.18.) The incorruptible seed, the Word of God, liveth and abideth forever. Praise the Lord for the Word, that the world cannot corrupt or devils kill!

9. Thank God for the doctrine of the witness of the Spirit! for he tells us if we are children of God. Hence we

may have this divine life, and may know it for ourselves. Regeneration is life from the dead, and a soul that is alive must know it.

4
THE GIFT OF THE HOLY GHOST

1. The Holy Spirit was in the world before Christ.

   "Cast me not away from thy presence; and take not thy Holy Spirit from me. Restore unto me the joy of thy salvation; and uphold me with thy free Spirit." (Ps. li.11, 12.) See 1 Sam. x.6

2. And the Spirit was given by Christ to his disciples.

   "And when he had said this, he breathed on them, and saith unto them, Receive ye the Holy Ghost." (John xx.22.)

3. But he was promised in an especial manner later.

   "Howbeit when he, the Spirit of truth, is come, he will guide you into all truth: for he shall not speak of himself; but whatever he shall hear, that shall he speak: and he will shew you things to come." (John xvi.13.) See Luke xxiv.49.

4. This further gift of the Spirit was with power from on high.

   "But ye shall receive power, after that the Holy Ghost

is come upon you; and ye shall be witnesses unto me both in Jerusalem, and in all Judea, and in Samaria, and unto the uttermost part of the earth." (Acts i.8.)

5. This induement of power was not limited to the disciples.

"He said unto them, Have ye received the Holy Ghost since ye believed? And they said unto him, We have not so much as heard whether there be any Holy Ghost." "And when Paul laid his hands upon them, the Holy Ghost came on them; and they spake with tongues, and prophesied." (Acts xix.2, 6.)

6. All may receive this baptism of the Spirit.

"For by one Spirit are we all baptized into one body, whether we be Jews or Gentiles, whether we be bond or free; and have been all made to drink into one Spirit." (1 Cor. xii.13.)

7. But the operations of the Spirit will be varied.

"Now there are diversities of gifts, but the same Spirit. And there are differences of administrations, but the same Lord. And there are diversities of operations, but it is the same God which worketh all in all. But the manifestation of the Spirit is given to every man to profit withal.' (1 Cor. xii.4-7.) See 1 Corinthians xii.8-11.

8. The Holy Spirit witnesses to our conversion.

"The Spirit himself beareth witness with our spirit, that we are the children of God." (Rom. viii.16. R.V.)

9. He also witnesses to our sanctification.

"For by one offering he hath perfected forever them that are sanctified. Whereof the Holy Ghost also is a witness to us."

10. The disciples waited in united prayer for the promised baptism.

"These all continued with one accord in prayer and supplication, with the women, and Mary the mother of Jesus, and with his brethren." (Acts. i.14.)

5
SOME BIBLE PROMISES

1. Exceeding great and precious promises.

    "Whereby are given unto us exceeding great and precious promises; that by these ye might be partakers of the divine nature, having escaped the corruption that is in the world through lust." (2 Pet. i.4.)

2. Rest promised to the heavy-laden.

    "Come unto me, all ye that labor and are heavy laden, and I will give you rest. Take my yoke upon you, and learn of me; for I am meek and lowly in heart: and ye shall find rest unto your souls. For my yoke is easy, and my burden is light." (Matt. xi.28-30.)

3. All invited to come— whosoever will.

    "And the Spirit and the bride say, Come. And let him that heareth say, Come. And let him that is athirst come. And whosoever will, let him take the water of life freely." (Rev. xxii.17.)

4. All who come will be accepted.

"Him that cometh to me I will in no wise case out." (John vi.37.)

5. God promises to answer prayer.

"Ask, and it shall be given you; seek, and ye shall find; knock, and it shall be opened unto you: for every one that asketh receiveth; and he that seeketh findeth; and to him that knocketh it shall be opened." (Matt. vii.7, 8.)

6. Salvation promised to faith.

"And brought them out, and said, Sirs, what must I do to be saved? And they said, Believe on the Lord Jesus Christ, and thou shalt be saved, and thy house." (Acts xvi.30, 31.)

7. If we separate ourselves from the world, God will be our Father.

"Wherefore come out from among them, and be ye separate, saith the Lord, and touch not the unclean thing; and I will receive you, and will be a Father unto you, and ye shall be my sons and daughters, saith the Lord Almighty." (2 Cor. vi.17, 18.)

8. A crown of life for such as are faithful till death.

"Fear none of those things which thou shalt suffer: behold, the devil shall cast some of you into prison, that ye may be tried; and ye shall have tribulation ten days: be thou faithful unto death, and I will give thee a crown of life." (Rev. ii.10.)

9. A new heart promised. God's spirit given.

"Then will I sprinkle clean water upon you, and ye shall be clean: from all your filthiness, and from all your idols, will I cleanse you. A new heart also will I give you, and a new spirit will I put within you: and

I will take away the stony heart out of your flesh, and I will give you a heart of flesh. And I will put my Spirit within you, and cause you to walk in my statutes, and ye shall keep my judgments, and do them." (Ezek. xxxvi.25-27.)

10. Full barns promised to the liberal.

"Honor the Lord with thy substance, and with the first fruits of all thine increase: so shall thy barns be filled with plenty, and thy presses shall burst out with new wine." (Prov. iii.9, 10.)

6
SOME BIBLE "FEAR NOTS"

1. Fear not, little flock; victory is yours, the kingdom is sure.

   "Fear not, little flock; for it is your Father's good pleasure to give you the kingdom." (Luke xii.32.)

2. Fear not such as can only kill the body.

   "And fear not them which kill the body, but are not able to kill the soul: but rather fear him which is able to destroy both soul and body in hell." (Matt. x.28.)

3. Fear not threatened want; the Master careth for you.

   "Fear ye not therefore, ye are of more value than many sparrows." (Matt. x.31.)

4. Fear not any man, but fear only.

   "Say ye not, A confederacy, to all them to whom this people shall say, A confederacy; neither fear ye their fear, nor be afraid. Sanctify the Lord of hosts himself; and let him be your fear, and let him be your dread." (Isa. viii.12, 13.)

5. Fear not, O Zion, thy Maker is thy husband.

"Fear not; for thou shalt not be ashamed: neither be thou confounded; for thou shalt not be put to shame: for thou shalt forget the shame of thy youth, and shalt not remember the reproach of thy widowhood any more. For thy Maker is thine husband; the Lord of hosts is his name; and thy Redeemer the Holy One of Israel; the God of the whole earth shall he be called." (Isa. liv.4, 5.)

6. Fear not the reproach of men, ye who know God's law.

"Hearken unto me, ye that know righteousness, the people in whose heart is my law; fear ye not the reproach of men, neither be ye afraid of their revilings." (Isa. li.7.)

7. Fear not: God is with thee; be strong in the Lord.

"Be strong and of a good courage, fear not, nor be afraid of them: for the Lord thy God, he it is that doth go with thee; he will not fail thee, nor forsake thee. And Moses called unto Joshua, and said unto him in the sight of all Israel, Be strong and of a good courage: for thou must go with this people unto the land which the Lord hath sworn unto their fathers to give them; and thou shalt cause them to inherit it. And the Lord, he it is that doth go before thee; he will be with thee, he will not fail thee, neither forsake thee: fear not, neither be dismayed." (Deut. xxxi.6-8.)

8. Fear not: God will strengthen and uphold thee.

"Fear thou not; for I am with thee: be not dismayed; for I am thy God: I will strengthen thee; yea, I will help thee; yea, I will uphold thee with the right hand of my righteousness." "For I the Lord thy God will hold thy right hand, saying unto thee, Fear not; I will help thee." (Isa. xli.10, 13)

7
APOSTASY
No. 1

I. 1. Expressly foretold by the Spirit.

"Now the Spirit speaketh expressly, that in the latter times some shall depart from the faith, giving heed to seducing spirits, and doctrines of devils." (1 Tim. iv.1.)

II. How to fall.
2. Individually, men turn from righteousness, and thus fall.

"But when the righteous turneth away from his righteousness, and committeth iniquity, and doeth according to all the abominations that the wicked man doeth, shall he live? All his righteousness that he hath done shall not be mentioned: in his trespass that he hath trespassed, and in his sin that he hath sinned, in them shall he die." (Ezek. xviii.24.) See Ezekiel xviii.26.

3. We may fall by self-righteousness and other sins.

"Therefore, thou son of man, say unto the children of thy people, The righteousness of the righteous shall not deliver him in the day of his transgression: as for the wickedness of the wicked, he shall not fall thereby in the day that he turneth from his wickedness; neither shall the righteous be able to live for his righteousness in the day he sinneth. When I shall say to the righteous, that he shall surely live; if he trust to his own righteousness, and commit iniquity, all his righteousness shall not be remembered; but for his iniquity that he hath committee, he shall die for it." (Ezek. xxxiii.12, 13.) See Ezekiel xxx.18.

4. By not abiding in Christ, as the branch in the vine.

"If a man abide not in me, he is cast forth as a branch, and is withered; and men gather them, and cast them into the fire and they are burned." "Every branch in me that beareth not fruit he taketh away: and every branch that beareth fruit, he purgeth it, that it may bring forth more fruit." (John xv.6, 2.)

5. By burying his talent, the unfaithful servant was cast out.

"But he that had received one went and digged in the earth, and hid his lord's money." "Take therefore the talent from him, and give it unto him which hath ten talents." "And cast ye the unprofitable servant into outer darkness: there shall be weeping and gnashing of teeth." (Matt. xxv.18, 28, 30.)

6. We may fall by foolishly letting our lamps go out.

"And the foolish said unto the wise, Give us of your oil; for our lamps are gone out." (Matt. xxv.8.)

7. Apostasy is by turning from the holy command-ment.

"For if after they have escaped the pollutions of the

world through the knowledge of the Lord and Saviour Jesus Christ, they are again entangled therein, and overcome, the latter end is worse with them than the beginning. For it had been better for them not to have known the way of righteousness, than, after they have known it, to turn from the holy commandment delivered unto them. But it is happened unto them according to the true proverb, The dog is turned to his own vomit again; and the sow that was washed to her wallowing in the mire." (2 Pet. ii.20-22.)

III. How to get out of Christ.
8. By being spewed out for lukewarmness.

"So then because thou art lukewarm, and neither cold nor hot, I will spew thee out of my mouth." (Rev. iii.16.)

The question whether persons may backslide so far from the experience of religion as to totally apostatize and be lost is sometimes raised. We answer unhesitatingly that we think they can.

1. The Spirit speaketh expressly that some shall depart from the faith. Religiously we act as individuals, and not by communities simply. How can any one "depart from the faith" who has never accepted the faith? In the parable of the sower (Matt. xiii.3-23) Jesus tells us of some who hear the word and anon with joy receive it; yet have they no root (firmness) in themselves, but endure for awhile, and when persecution arises they are offended (turned back). Notice, *they did receive the word* and even *with joy*, and they did *endure for awhile*, but under persecution they fell away. Having tasted the good word of God, it produced joy in their hearts, but they did not abide therein; they departed from the faith.

2. God here tells us plainly: When the righteous *turn away* from their righteousness, and commit iniquity, they

shall die. The sinner is dead, the righteous are quickened (Eph. ii.1, 5), made alive, in Christ, but when they turn from their righteousness, obedience, they die. "The wages of sin is death." (Rom. vi.23.) "The soul that sinneth, it shall die." (Ezek. xviii.20.)

But we are told: "Whosoever is born of God doth not commit sin; for his seed remaineth in him: and he cannot sin, because he is born of God." (1 John iii.9.) Very true, he cannot sin as a Christian. He cannot maintain the divine life and fellowship, and sin. An honest man cannot steal, for when he steals he is no longer honest. A truthful man cannot lie, for when he lies he is no longer truthful. A clean person cannot be filthy, for when he becomes filthy he is no longer clean. A live man cannot be dead, for when he dies he is no longer alive. So whosoever *is born of God* — i.e., is spiritually alive — cannot sin, because if he sins he forfeits his spiritual life, and is no longer a Christian — i.e., alive in Christ, born of God "He that committeth sin is of the devil." (1 John iii.8.)

3. To become self-righteous is to forfeit the spiritual life, since it is maintained in the soul by the same humility and faith necessary to produce it. When one becomes dependent on his own righteousness he thereby surrenders his hold upon Christ, and naturally and necessarily falls into sin; yea, that self-righteousness is sin, and God says all his righteousness shall not be remembered, but, "for his iniquity that he hath committed, he shall die."

4. The fruitless branch is severed from the vine, and dies. So the fruitless branch *"in Christ"* is taken away. (John xv.2.) My brother, are you a fruit-bearing branch in Christ?

5. The servant who buried his talent was cast into outer darkness for his unfaithfulness. He was not an enemy, but an avowed and acknowledged *servant*; still for unfaithfulness he was condemned, and became a castaway.

6. His case was like that of the foolish virgins, who let

their lamps "go out," and were excluded from the feast when the bride-groom came. Are our lamps trimmed and burning, and are our talents employed for the Master?

7. Some have *escaped the pollutions of the world* through a knowledge of Christ, and then afterward *become entangled therein again.* O how plainly this puts the apostasy of the unfaithful! Such, in their lukewarmness, become nauseating to the Almighty, and are

8. *Spewed out of his mouth.*

O reader! beware of the wiles of the devil, and hold fast that which is committed unto thee. Trust in the living God. "Watch and pray, that ye enter not into temptation." "Do justly, love mercy, and walk humbly with thy God." See Numbers vi.24-26.

8
EXAMPLES OF APOSTASY
No. 2

1. **Angels fell from heaven, and are in chains.**

    "And the angels which kept not their first estate, but left their own habitation, he hath reserved in everlasting chains under darkness unto the judgment of the great day." (Jude 6.) See 2 Peter ii.4.

2. **Adam was holy, being made in God's image.**

    "So God created man in his own image, in the image of God created he him; male and female created he them." (Gen. i.27.) See Genesis i.31.

3. **Still he fell so low as to curse with sin all his offspring.**

    "Wherefore, as by one man sin entered into the world and death by sin; and so death passed upon all men, for that all have sinned." (Rom. v.12.) See Romans v.18, 19.

4. **Saul was a new man, by the Spirit of God.**

    "And the Spirit of the Lord will come upon thee, and thou shalt prophesy with them, and shalt be turned into another man." "And when they came thither to the hill, behold, a company of prophets met him; and the Spirit of God came upon him, and he prophesied among them." (1 Sam. x.6, 10.)

5. But God forsook him, and he died a suicide.

"Then said Saul unto his armor-bearer, Draw thy sword, and thrust me through therewith; lest these uncircumcised come and thrust me through, and abuse me. But his armor-bearer would not; for he was sore afraid. Therefore Saul took a sword, and fell upon it." (1 Sam. xxxi.4.) See 1 Samuel xvi.14 and xviii.12.

6. David fell to the double sin of murder and adultery.

"Wherefore hast thou despised the commandment of the Lord, to do evil in his sight? thou hast killed Uriah the Hittite with the sword, and hast taken his wife to be thy wife, and hast slain him with the sword of the children of Ammon." (2 Sam. xii.9.) See 2 Samuel xi.4; also Psalm li.

7. But he was reclaimed, and called God his Rock and Fortress.

"Be thou my strong habitation, whereunto I may continually resort: thou hast given commandment to save me; for thou art my rock and my fortress." (Ps. lxxi.3.)

8. Peter fell so low as to curse and lie.

"And after awhile came unto him they that stood by, and said to Peter, Surely thou also art one of them; for thy speech bewrayeth thee. Then he began to curse and to swear, saying, I know not the man. And immediately the cock crew." (Matt. xxvi.73, 74.)

9. But when reclaimed three thousand were added in a day under his preaching.

> "But Peter, standing up with the eleven, lifted up his voice, and said unto them, Ye men of Judea, and all ye that dwell at Jerusalem, be this known unto you, and hearken to my words." "Then they that gladly received his word were baptized: and the same day there were added unto them about three thousand souls." (Acts ii.14, 41.) See Acts ii.15-40.

10. Hymeneus and Alexander made shipwreck of faith.

> "Holding faith, and a good conscience; which some having put away, concerning faith have made shipwreck; of whom is Hymeneus and Alexander; whom I have delivered unto Satan, that they may learn not to blaspheme." (1 Tim. i.19, 20.)

1. The first example of apostasy was among the angels in heaven's own pure atmosphere. In that holy world it would seem impossible for any pure, unfallen being to go into sin, and stain his character by breaking the law of his God. But there were "angels which kept not their first estate;" and they, with other transgressors, are awaiting their doom, when the wrath of God will overreach the restraining boundaries of mercy and with unquenchable fury sweep the sinners of all worlds and all ages into the lake of fire and brimstone.

2 and 3. Adam, like the angels above mentioned, was created holy, even in God's own image. Was apostasy possible in such a case? Let the blight of earth and the wreck of the race, the groans and sighs, the tears and pains, the heart-ache and anguish, the moanings of the bereaved and universal reign of death over the human family answer the question. By one man— he who was made pure, holy, spotless, the crowning work of his God— by *this* one man sin entered the world and death by sin—

his sin, the sin of an apostate. How fearful! when the angels in glory, and man made in the pure image of his God, fall into sin, and its degrading influence curses their whole being! Ah! sin degrades the highest, brings down the mightiest, and curses the purest of creation.

4 and 5. King Saul is an example of apostasy worthy of note. (1) He was the chosen of the Lord for the ruler of his people Israel, and we would thus infer that he was a good man. (2) The Spirit of the Lord came upon him and converted him — "turned" him "into another man." He was hence a subject of redeeming, saving grace, and was numbered with the prophets of God. But this chosen man of God, this leader of the people, this prophet of the Most High, fell into sins grievous and many. He tried to kill David, brought defeat to the armies of Israel, sought counsel of the witch of Endor, forfeited the kingdom though God himself had appointed him thereto, and to make complete the wreck of his moral character, and cap the climax of his base apostasy, he took his own life — thus thrusting himself a murderer, a suicide, into the presence of his Judge.

6 and 7. David had many excellent traits of moral character, noble signs of spiritual life. He, like Saul, was divinely appointed as king of Israel, the chosen people of God. He went out in God's strength against Goliath, the mighty man of the Philistine, who defied the armies of Israel. He showed a Christian spirit in his refusal to hurt Saul, who sought his life. He relates a thrilling experience in telling how he loves God, who delivered him when the "sorrows of death compassed" him and "the pains of hell gat hold of" him; and how the Almighty took him out of the "horrible pit," and placed his feet upon the rock, putting the "new song" of praise in his mouth. He was looked upon as a man after God's own heart. But this sweet singer, this inspired psalmist, so far forgot his vows, his prayers, and his devotion to God that he basely

murdered Uriah and criminally associated with his wife. "He that committeth sin is of the devil." (1 John iii.8.) And now behold him who has had God as his "sun and shield," who has fed in the pastures of grace, dwelt in the fold of the "Good Shepherd," and abided "under the shadow of the Almighty;" behold him with hands stained with blood and wallowing licentiously in the cess-pools of vice, and say whether or not apostasy— falling from grace— is possible! But some say if there is apostasy it is final, and such can never be saved. That this is a mistake is here seen. The fall of the angels and of Saul seems to have been complete and final. That of Adam and David seemed complete, but not final. David, especially, came back to God, as may be seen in his prayer. See Psalm lxxi. He looks up to God as his Rock, his Fortress, and his strong habitation.

8 and 9. Peter's case, also, illustrates the depths to which one may fall who has known God; and it also shows the power of reclaiming grace to the true penitent. Peter had gone in and out with Christ before the people. He had professed himself a disciple and had preached Jesus to the multitude. He had assisted in miraculously feeding the thousands, had walked to Jesus on the waters, and had heard the voice that stilled the raging of the sea when the storm-king lashed it into fury. He had seen Jesus weep at the grave of Lazarus, and had rejoiced at seeing Lazarus come forth alive. He, with James and John, had been on the Mount of Transfiguration and beheld Jesus with the halo of divine glory upon his brow, while Moses and Elias spake burning words, doubtless in the speech of the glory-world. Peter himself had healed the sick, opened blinded eyes, unstopped deaf ears, and cast out demons. Surely a man of God, a follower of Jesus, one who has seen and used such rich manifestations of heavenly power, will be faithful to the last. "Listen, Peter! Jesus says you will deny him this night." "No, never! Though

all men forsake thee, Lord, I will not. I will be true to death." See Matthew xxvi.35. But the mob came, Christ surrendered to them, and Peter's courage failed him. The temptation was great, and poor Peter acted the miserable coward and denied his Lord, and added to his falsehood and untrueness to his Master the vile sin of cursing and swearing. Jesus looked at him as much as to say, "Poor apostate, how low thou art fallen! Just yesterday preaching my gospel, casting out devils, and healing the sick, while pledging eternal fidelity to me, now thou art denying me, lying and swearing." But that look broke Peter's heart, and the poor, fallen preacher returns a penitent to his God. Only fifty days later, and this same Peter, baptized with the sanctifying power from on high, preached the Pentecost sermon, under which three thousand souls are added to the ranks of the army that shall shake the world, as the conquering Christ leads it on the final and complete victory.

10. Hymeneus and Alexander made shipwreck of the faith. The apostle tells us to hold faith and a good conscience which some, he says, have put away, and having made shipwreck of the faith, he turns them over to Satan, to whom their blasphemies have sold them. Angels fell from heaven, Adam and Eve from the holy precincts of Eden, Saul and David, Peter, Alexander and Hymeneus. So have thousands in all ages. Watch and pray against the wiles of the devil. "Let him that thinketh he standeth take heed lest he fall." (1 Cor. x.12.)

And now, kind reader, may "Grace and peace be multiplied unto you through the knowledge of God, and of Jesus our Lord, according as his divine power hath given unto us all things that pertain unto life and godliness, through the knowledge of him that hath called us to glory and virtue: whereby are given unto us exceeding great and precious promises; that by these ye might be partakers of the divine nature, having escaped the corruption that is in the world through lust. And besides this, giving all diligence, add to your faith virtue; and to virtue, knowledge; and to knowledge, temperance; and to temperance, patience; and to patience, godliness; and to godliness, brotherly kindness; and to brotherly kindness, charity. For if these things be in you, and abound, they make you that ye shall neither be barren nor unfruitful in the knowledge of our Lord Jesus Christ. But he that lacketh these things is blind, and cannot see afar off, and hath forgotten that he was purged from his old sins. Wherefore the rather, brethren, give diligence to make your calling and election sure: for if ye do these things, ye shall never fall: for so an entrance shall be ministered unto you abundantly into the everlasting kingdom of our Lord and Saviour Jesus Christ."

9
HOW TO PREVENT APOSTASY
No. 3

1. By watching and prayer.

   "Watch ye and pray, lest ye enter into temptation. The spirit truly is ready, but the flesh is weak." (Mark xiv.38.) See Mark xiii.33.

2. By putting on the whole armor of God.

   "Finally, my brethren, be strong in the Lord, and in the power of his might. Put on the whole armor of God, that ye may be able to stand against the wiles of the devil." (Eph. vi.10, 11.) See Ephesians vi.12-18.

3. Follow peace with all men, and holiness; lest bitterness spring up.

   "Follow peace with all men, and holiness, without which no man shall see the Lord: looking diligently lest any man fail of the grace of God; lest any root of bitterness springing up trouble you, and thereby many be defiled." (Heb. xii.14, 15.)

4. Our safety is to abide in Christ as the branches in the vine.

> "I am the vine, ye are the branches. He that abideth in me, and I in him, the same bringeth forth much fruit; for without me ye can do nothing. If a man abide not in me, he is cast forth as a branch, and is withered; and men gather them, and cast them into the fire, and they are burned." (John xv.5, 6.)

5. Go on to perfection; lay not again the foundation of repentance.

> "Therefore leaving the principles of the doctrine of Christ, let us go on unto perfection; not laying again the foundation of repentance from dead works, and of faith toward God." (Heb. vi.1.)

6. Faithfulness till death is required of us for the crown.

> "Be thou faithful unto death, and I will give thee a crown of life." (Rev. ii.10.)

7. Be not moved from the faith and hope of the gospel.

> "To present you holy and unblamable and unreprovable in his sight: if ye continue in the faith grounded and settled, and be not moved away from the hope of the gospel." (Col. i.22, 23.)

8. If we are fruitful, nothing can overthrow us.

> "Who shall separate us from the love of Christ? shall tribulation, or distress, or persecution, or famine, or nakedness, or peril, or sword? As it is written, For thy sake we are killed all the day long; we are accounted as sheep for the slaughter. Nay, in all these things we are more than conquerors through him that loved us." (Rom. viii.35-37.) "Every branch in me that beareth not fruit he taketh away." (John xv.2.)

Since so many have fallen, and any one is liable to, it behooves us to consider the way of safety. No Christian ever started his heavenward journey with the intention of falling by the way. Yet how many sad wrecks, strewn along the shores of the past, warn us of danger and bid us "Put on the whole armor of God, that ye may be able to stand against the wiles of the devil."

1. The first safeguard consists in a judicious combination of watchfulness and prayer. Watchfulness without prayer is as a gun without ammunition; prayer without watchfulness is the ammunition without a gun. Watch against evil associations. Bad company will wreck almost any Christian character. Watch against becoming simply a formalist, having a form of godliness without the power. There are thousands who dream of heaven at last, without any real knowledge of heavenly life here! They perhaps belong to the Church, occasionally take the sacraments, and maybe do some good and charitable deeds. Yet they know nothing of the indwelling Comforter, have no real fellowship with Christ, do not seek the daily guidance of the Spirit, and have no conception of that spiritual experience which is described as "the love of God shed abroad in the heart by the Holy Ghost." (Rom. v.5.) See John xiv.16, 17; xvi.7-14.

2. "Be strong in the Lord" means to be bold, courageous, stand firm by the Lord's work and name. When wrong lifts high the hand of rebellion, and the right is ridiculed; when sin is exalted and righteousness is decried among men, then the hearts of many fail, and they tremble as weaklings, refuse to stand up for Jesus, and, being ashamed of him before men, they become backsliders in heart, fall away from Christ, and go into active, open sin. Religious cowards soon become apostates unless they quickly rise to courage in Jesus. Put on the whole Christian armor, "endure hardness as a good soldier of Jesus Christ," and go out "strong in the Lord" to "fight

the good fight of faith, lay hold of eternal life." Thus you may "stand against the wiles of the devil" and be "more than conqueror through him who loved you."

3. An essential to the maintenance of the Christian life is here given. We must be at peace, and we must follow after holiness. Quarreling, envy, and strife are totally subversive of the true spiritual life. To prevent apostasy we should never allow enmity in the heart, but should fight it with the grace of God. Follow holiness— without which "no man shall see the Lord." Many there are who claim to sin every day, and yet profess to be Christians. He is no Christian— Christ-like person— who sins daily. People who expect to sin every day here, and still reach a holy heaven hereafter, have but poor conceptions of the character of God and the work of the gospel. God is holy, and he made man holy. Sin marred the work, and he raised against it a war of extermination which cost the death of his only Son. He tells us definitely to be holy, and says that "without holiness no man shall see" his face in peace. If we would be Christians, then, and not fall away from the Christian life and hope, we must keep up God's standard of holiness. When we pray let us remember: "If I regard iniquity in my heart, the Lord will not hear me." (Ps. lxvi.18.) By seeking to be holy and looking diligently in the way of life we will not fail, or "fall from" (margin), the grace of God. If Paul were like some people, he would have said that it was impossible to fall from grace; but under inspiration he writes: "Follow peace and holiness, looking diligently lest ye fall from grace." He gives the warning, and gives the preventive. Happy the soul that follows his advice!

4. Abide in Christ as the branch in the vine. In this Christ-vine is the place of our strength, nourishment, safety, and fruitfulness. "As the branch cannot bear fruit of itself, except it abide in the vine; no more can ye, except ye abide in me." The secret of strength is to abide in Christ, and the secret of abiding in Christ is

perfect consecration and living faith.

5. If we would escape the fate of the apostate, we must not linger always around our conversion, but leave the beginning point of Christian life and go on unto— not toward, but *unto*— perfection; not absolute, angelic, Adamic or physical perfection, but the perfection of consecration and love, Christian perfection. "Not laying again the foundation of repentance from dead works." That is, if we will go on from conversion to perfect holiness we will not backslide; but if we sit down without going forward we will fall into sin, and have to repent again and be reclaimed from our sins.

6 and 7. Fullness of faith even unto and until death is the way to the crown. If we desire to stand in God's sight holy and unreprovable, without blame, we must not be light, giddy, worthless Christians, but must seek to be grounded and settled in faith and hope, being thereby stablished in holiness.

8. An objector says: "Nothing can separate us from the love of God." Very true: if we are faithful, consecrated, holy, ready to be killed for his sake all the day long, nothing shall separate us from his love, and we will be more than conquerors through his grace. If we turn from our righteousness; if we fail to watch and pray; if we lay off the armor of God; if we reject holiness, and refuse to go on to perfection; if we fail to abide in Christ the Vine, and are moved away from the faith and hope; and if we are unwilling to be wholly the Lord's, and grow careless and lukewarm, we will be taken away by the divine Husbandman as cumberers of the ground; yea, even spewed up by the living God, as nauseating to the Almighty. If we live prayerful, watchful, consecrated, holy, useful lives; if we press the battle for God and the right, and abound in good works, we will come at last with rejoicing, bringing our sheaves, and enter with joy into the presence of our Lord. God grant it may be so!

10
LOVE
No. 1

1. God is love; not God loves, but *is love*.

   "He that loveth not, knoweth not God; for God is love." (1 John iv.8.)

2. Jesus is the gift of God's love to us.

   "For God so loved the world, that he gave his only begotten Son, that whosoever believeth in him should not perish, but have everlasting life." (John iii.16.)

3. In the death of Christ, God commendeth his love to us.

   "But God commendeth his love toward us, in that, while we were yet sinners, Christ died for us." (Rom. v.8.)

4. If we love not God, we'll be accursed at his coming.

   "If any man love not the Lord Jesus Christ, let him be Anathema, Maran atha."

5. If we love God's people, it is a sign of divine life.

   "We know that we have passed from death unto life,

because we love the brethren. He that loveth not his brother abideth in death." (1 John iii.14.)

6. Love is shed abroad in our hearts by the Holy Ghost.

"And hope maketh not ashamed; because the love of God is shed abroad in our hearts by the Holy Ghost which is given unto us."

7. We should have perfect love.

"Herein is our love made perfect, that we may have boldness in the day of judgment: because as he is, so are we in this world. There is no fear in love; but perfect love casteth out fear: because fear hath torment. He that feareth is not made perfect in love." (1 John iv.17, 18.)

8. Worldly love hinders the love of God in us.

"Love not the world, neither the things that are in the world. If any man love the world, the love of the Father is not in him." (1 John ii.15.)

9. We cannot at the same time love God and hate our brother.

"If a man say, I love God, and hateth his brother, he is a liar: for he that loveth not his brother whom he hath seen, how can he love God whom he hath not seen? And this commandment have we from him, That he who loveth God love his brother also." (1 John iv.20, 21.)

10. By love to each other, we have the divine indwelling and perfect love.

"Beloved, if God so loved us, we ought also to love one another. No man hath seen God at any time. If we love one another, God dwelleth in us, and his love is perfected in us." (1 John iv.11, 12.)

11
LOVE
No. 2

1. Love is of God: he first loved us, hence we love him.

> "Beloved, let us love one another: for love is of God; and every one that loveth is born of God, and knoweth God." "We love him, because he first loved us." (1 John iv.7, 19.)

2. We must love God with all our hearts — the first and great commandment.

> "Jesus said unto him, Thou shalt love the Lord thy God with all thy heart, and with all thy soul, and with all thy mind. This is the first and great commandment." (Matt. xxii.37, 38.)

3. To love thy neighbor as thyself is the second commandment.

> "And the second is like unto it, Thou shalt love thy neighbor as thyself. On these two commandments hang all the law and the prophets." (Matt. xxii.39, 40.)

4. Our only indebtedness should be love.

"Owe no man any thing, but to love one another: for he that loveth another hath fulfilled the law. (Rom. xiii.8.)

5. The first and chief fruit of the Spirit is love.

"But the fruit of the Spirit is love." (Gal. v.22.)

6. We must be constrained by Christ's love to live for him.

"For the love of Christ constraineth us; because we thus judge, that if one died for all, then were all dead: and that he died for all, that they which live should not henceforth live unto themselves, but unto him which died for them, and rose again." (2 Cor. v.14, 15.)

7. If we are perfect in love, we love even our enemies.

"But I say unto you, Love your enemies, bless them that curse you, do good to them that hate you, and pray for them which despitefully use you, and persecute you." "Be ye therefore perfect, even as your Father which is in heaven is perfect." (Matt. v.44, 48.)

8. God must be loved supremely, and the same taught to the children.

"And thou shalt love the Lord thy God with all thine heart, and with all thy soul, and with all thy might. And these words, which I command thee this day, shall be in thine heart: and thou shalt teach them diligently unto thy children, and shalt talk of them when thou sittest in thine house, and when thou walkest by the way, and when thou liest down, and when thou riseth up." (Deut. vi.5-7.)

9. In the path of obedience is found perfect love.

"But whoso keepeth his word, in him verily is the love of God perfected: hereby know we that we are in him." (1 John ii.5.)

10. Love is greater than either faith or hope.

"But now abideth faith, hope, love, these three; and the greatest of these is love." (1 Cor. xiii.13. R. V.)

12
MISSIONS (OLD TESTAMENT)
No. 1

1. The universal triumph of Christ foretold.

    "He shall have dominion also from sea to sea, and from the river unto the ends of the earth." (Ps. lxxii.8.)

2. The glorious exaltation of his kingdom.

    "And it shall come to pass in the last days, that the mountain of the Lord's house shall be established in the top of the mountains, and shall be exalted above the hills; and all nations shall flow unto it. And many people shall go and say, Come ye, and let us go up to the mountain of the Lord, to the house of the God of Jacob; and he will teach us of his ways, and we will walk in his paths: for out of Zion shall go forth the law, and the word of the Lord from Jerusalem." (Isa. ii.2, 3.)

3. The heathen, and the uttermost parts, promised to the Son.

    "Ask of me, and I shall give thee the heathen for thine

inheritance, and the uttermost parts of the earth for thy possession." (Ps. ii.8.)

4. The Church must shine with heavenly light.

"Arise, shine; for thy light is come, and the glory of the Lord is risen upon thee. For, behold, the darkness shall cover the earth, and gross darkness the people: but the Lord shall arise upon thee, and his glory shall be seen upon thee. And the Gentiles shall come to thy light, and kings to the brightness of thy rising." (Isa. lx.1-3.)

5. Our prayers should be for the nations, that they may praise God.

"Let the people praise thee, O God; let all the people praise thee. O let the nations be glad and sing for joy: for thou shalt judge the people righteously, and govern the nations upon earth. Selah."

6. God blesses us that the nations may know him through us.

"God be merciful unto us, and bless us; and cause his face to shine upon us; Selah. That thy way may be known upon earth, thy saving health among all nations." "God shall bless us; and the ends of the earth shall fear him." (Ps. lxvii.1, 2, 7.)

7. Christ shall rule the nations, and blot out war.

"And he shall judge among many people, and rebuke strong nations afar off; and they shall beat their swords into plowshares, and their spears into pruning-hooks: nations shall not lift up a sword against nation, neither shall they learn war any more." (Mic. iv.3.)

8. The knowledge of the Lord shall fill the earth.

"They shall not hurt nor destroy in all my holy mountain: for the earth shall be full of the knowledge of the Lord, as the waters cover the sea." (Isa. xi.9.) See Isaiah xi.1-8.

1. This prophecy is truly cheering to the Christian heart. To the humble follower of Jesus, who loves him dearer than all else besides, it is a glorious promise. My brother, rejoice with me; Jesus is our Saviour, and God, the Almighty, has promised that he shall have dominion from sea to sea; yea, from the river to the ends of the earth. Our joy must be commensurate with our devotion to Christ. If we love him truly, we can but be glad at the promise of his triumph.

2. "The mountain of the Lord's house" — that is, the glorious rising of Christ's kingdom shall lift it to the point of eminence from whence all the world shall behold his beauties. Then, as Christ becomes known, and the people see the beauties of his kingdom, they will say, "Come, and let us go up to the mountain of the Lord, to the house of the God of Jacob; and he will teach us of his ways, and we will walk in his paths." Christ said: "I, if I be lifted up from the earth, will draw all men unto me." (John xii.32.) The first missionary promise gives this idea of victory when we are told that the Seed of the woman shall bruise the serpent's head." (Gen. iii.15.) The devil has got the world in trouble by sin; and Christ has undertaken to bruise the serpent's head, to subdue the rebellious, drive out the armies of sin, and exalt his own kingdom of goodness and peace. In the text he is promised dominion by the preaching of the gospel: "For out of Zion [the Church] shall go forth the law, and the word of the Lord from Jerusalem." This "word" and "law" are to exalt Christ above the hills — lifting him up above the nations, that all people shall be drawn unto him, and his triumph shall be complete, his reign universal.

3. Notice here the prominence given to prayer in the

promotion of this kingdom: "Ask of me, and I shall give thee the heathen for thine inheritance, and the *uttermost parts* of the earth for thy possession." How did Christ prepare for his own ministry? By forty days of fasting and prayer. (Matt. iv.2.) True, prayer is not mentioned here, but fasting is, and they are always associated in Scripture. (Matt. xvii.21; Jonah iii.5-10.) Before Jesus chose his disciples he spent a whole night in prayer. (Luke vi.12-16.) So, after his ascension, he promised them an induement of power, for which they tarried in a ten-days' prayer-meeting in Jerusalem. They were commissioned to preach his own everlasting gospel "to every creature," and be witnesses to him unto the uttermost parts of the earth; but while the heathen are to be given him, the condition is, "Ask of me;" hence the disciples, before going out to preach and witness in his name, had to "continue all with one accord" in prayer for ten days. "Thy kingdom come," is the first *petition* in the form for the daily prayer of all his disciples. Thus the triumph of our Saviour, in all the earth, is brought down from the far-off prophetic vision to become the burden of the daily prayer of all his followers.

    4. The Church is called upon to "arise" from her slumbers, and "shine" for the Gentiles (heathens). Not in her own strength may she do this, but under grace; "for thy light is come, and the glory of the Lord is risen upon thee." Christ is the true light, but the Church is his bride; he shines upon the Church, that the Church may reflect his light upon the nations that are covered with darkness, and the people who sit in the shadow of death. He pledges success to his Church in her efforts to shine for him. "The Gentiles [heathens] shall come to thy light, and kings to the brightness of thy rising."

    5. David, with prophetic eye, saw that when the people were greatly revived, so that all the people should praise the Lord, the nations also would be glad and sing for joy.

That is, when there is a revival in the Church, there will be a corresponding missionary activity, and the nations will accept Christ's government.

6. The thought just given is here carried further. "God bless us, and cause his face to shine upon us, *that* [in order that] thy way may be known upon earth, thy saving health [grace] among all nations." *If God shall bless us, the ends of the earth shall fear him.* Is it not here taught that where there is religion in the people of God they will spread the knowledge of it to the nations, so that "the ends of the earth" may fear him? The prayer is even made for a blessing upon us with the idea of missionary progress especially in view; "bless us that thy way may be known," etc. If, then, one claims to love Christ, but still manifests no interests in making known his way "upon earth, his saving health among all nations," that "all the people may praise the Lord, and the nations sing for joy," is not that man's religion vain? Many Church members make loud professions of devotion to Christ and of love to God, and yet when the missionary collection is taken, give a mere pittance— perchance fifty cents, when they should give five dollar, or may be five dollars when it should be fifty, seventy-five, or a hundred. "Wilt thou know, O vain man, that faith without works is dead?" (Jas. ii.20.)

7. Christ is called the Prince of Peace. When his gospel permeates the nations they will bury the tomahawk, their swords shall be beaten into plowshares, and their spears into pruning-hooks. Steps are being taken now to establish terms of arbitration among the nations, instead of war. Amen. Let every Christian help spread the gospel of peace on earth, good-will toward men; and he will thus help bring in the glad time when our Prince of Peace shall "have dominion from sea to sea," when he shall "judge among many people, rebuke strong nations," and they shall "learn war no more." The reign of Christ means universal peace, and it is to be brought about by the

spread of the gospel. *Your missionary activities, brother, are a sure index to your love of Christ, and of peace among me.*

8. When we "fill the earth" with the "knowledge of the Lord," we will see it come to pass that they shall not hurt nor destroy in all his holy mountain. To usher in this glad time we are commissioned by Christ to "go teach all nations" and to "preach the gospel to every creature;" and thus will be fulfilled our daily prayer, "Thy kingdom come, thy will be done in earth, as it is in heaven;" for "the gospel is the power of God unto salvation to every one that believeth."

>Waft, waft, ye winds, his story,
> And you, ye waters, roll,
>Till, like a sea of glory
> It spreads from pole to pole;
>Till o'er our ransomed nature,
> The Lamb for sinners slain,
>Redeemer, King, Creator,
> In bliss returns to reign.

13
MISSIONS (NEW TESTAMENT)
No. 2

1. God loved the world — the whole world, no limit.

    "For God so loved the world, that he gave his only begotten Son, that whosoever believeth in him should not perish, but have everlasting life." (John iii.16.)

2. He commendeth his love toward us.

    "But God commendeth his love toward us, in that, while we were yet sinners, Christ died for us." (Rom. v.8.)

3. Christ's death avails for every one who will accept him.

    "But we see Jesus, who was made a little lower than the angels for the suffering of death, crowned with glory and honor; that he by the grace of God should taste death for every man." (Heb. ii.9.)

4. Hence, there is no respect of persons with God.

    "Then Peter opened his mouth, and said, Of a truth I perceive that God is no respecter of persons: but in every nation he that feareth him, and worketh righteousness, is accepted with him." (Acts x.34, 35.)

5. In salvation there is neither Greek nor Jew; Christ is all.

"And have put on the new man, which is renewed in know-ledge after the image of him that created: where there is neither Greek nor Jew, circumcision nor uncircumcision, Barbarian, Scythian, bond nor free; but Christ is all, and in all." (Col. iii.10, 11.)

6. Paul in debt— owed the gospel to many.

"I am debtor both to the Greeks, and to the Barbarians; both to the wise, and to the unwise. So, as much as in me is, I am ready to preach the gospel to you that are at Rome also." (Rom. i.14, 15.)

7. The middle wall is broken down, and Christ gives peace.

"But now, in Christ Jesus, ye who sometime were far off are made nigh by the blood of Christ. For he is our peace, who hath made both one, and hath broken down the middle wall of partition between us." (Eph. ii.13, 14.)

8. Our daily prayer is for enlargement of Christ's kingdom.

"Thy kingdom come. Thy will be done in earth, as it is in heaven." (Matt. vi.10.)

9. Do we love Christ? Here is his test.

"If ye love me, keep my commandments." "Jesus answered and said unto him, If a man love me, he will keep my words: and my Father will love him, and we will come unto him, and make our abode with him." (John xiv.15, 23.)

10. Take this commandment as a sample of our devotion to him.

"And he said unto them, Go ye into all the world, and preach the gospel to every creature." (Mark xvi.15.) See Matthew xxviii.19, 20.

1. The love of God to man is the foundation-stone of the gospel. But for God's love there would have been no sacrifice for sin, hence no Saviour, consequently no redemption and no gospel. The word "gospel" means "good news." The angel, in telling the shepherds of the birth of Christ, said: "I bring you good tidings" — *i.e.*, good news, the gospel. What is that gospel tidings of good? "Unto you is born this day in the city of David a Saviour, which is Christ the Lord." (Luke ii.10, 11.) And whence the Saviour? From the throne of the universe, the gift of God for the salvation of men, *the first and greatest missionary*. The gift of Christ was for the salvation of the *world*, the whole world; not unconditionally, but by faith, "that whosoever believeth on him might not perish."

2. This love of God was manifested not to those who sought him, or were righteous, but to us who were in sin. Here is the true missionary idea: Carry the gospel to those who have no claims upon you for it. The world had no claim upon God, upon Christ, for salvation; yet "God commendeth his love toward us" by the gift of his Son, Christ commendeth his love by the terrible death of the cross— all this while we were yet sinners. In this we see the gospel's power; it is built on the granite rock of God's eternal love. As long as a soul may be found on the earth who is a slave to sin the love of God reaches out after him, to pour into his ear and heart the gospel, good news of salvation. "God is love," and his love reaches the sin-cursed race of man everywhere. "Every one that loveth is born of God, and knoweth God. He that loveth not, knoweth not God; for God is love." (1 John iv.7, 8.) If,

then, God's love was made manifest in the gift of his Son to the work of the world's salvation, can we consistently lay any claim to the love of God, to Christ-likeness, when we have none of Christ's world-wide love, which is the spirit of Missions? See Romans viii.9. Is not the spirit of Missions the Christ-spirit? and is not the Christ-spirit essential to salvation? May God pity the professed Christian who has no hearty fellowship with Christ in his loving efforts to save the world!

3. The gall of Calvary, the bitterness of death, was tasted by Christ for every man. On the cross, as much as in life, he was "the Son of man." He is called the Son of God, also the *Son of man*, not simply a Jew, not simply the Redeemer of a nation or a class, but the Redeemer of all, in that he hath tasted death for *every* man. Here you see how his loving heart ran out for the race of which he claimed to be "the Son." When we are born again, being so changed by the Spirit that we too become the sons of God (1 John iii.1), is it not expected that we should be like Christ? and since he, by the grace of God, tasted death for every man, should it not be the constant burden of our hearts that "every man" should partake of the benefits of his death, and be saved? True sympathy and fellowship with Christ in his marvelous efforts to save the world should characterize every Christian. What is a Christian, if not a *"Christ-like"* person?

4. Our God is no respecter of persons. How could he be, when he tells us he "*so* loved the world, that he gave his only begotten Son, that *whosoever* believeth on him should not perish, but have everlasting life?" There is left, in the broadness of this redeeming love, no ground for respect of persons. God could not show partiality — respect of persons — and be himself. There are many who call themselves Christians, and still show great respect of persons in the distribution of the gospel. They say: "O I believe in Home Missions, but not in Foreign Missions."

That means, then, that you are different from your God; for while you believe in preaching the gospel to some, and not to others, God is, as of yore, no respecter of persons. "He commendeth his love toward us, in that, while we were yet sinners, Christ died for us," and he *tasted [this] death for every man."*

5. In the natural heart of man, before the transforming power of grace is felt, there is dominant a Pharisee-like "I am holier than thou" respect of persons. Many seem to think themselves princes of God, and entitled to a monopoly of his grace. Hence they glory in the gospel and their hope of heaven, while the nations of the world are allowed to sit in the shadow of death, and the burdens of heathenism wring from the hearts of despairing millions sighs that sweep the earth and groans that rend the heavens. But when the Spirit of Christ takes full possession of the life, so that we are renewed in knowledge after the image of the Creator, then we learn that in spiritual life and the world's redemption "there is neither Greek nor Jew,… bond nor free; but Christ is all, and in all." If Christ truly reigns in the heart, being formed in us the hope of glory, there will be such unutterable longings for his universal triumph, his dominion "from sea to sea, and from the river to the ends of the earth;" and mingled with this we will have such hearty sympathy for all those upon whom the blight of sin has fallen, that we will cry out with the apostle:

6. "I am debtor [in debt] both to the Greeks, and to the Barbarians; both to the wise, and to the unwise. So, as much as in me is [*i.e.*, to the utmost of my ability], I am ready to preach the gospel to you that are at Rome also." It seems strange that a man should avow himself in debt to a people whom he never saw, who entertain no claims against him, and who will persecute him unto death for his zeal in meeting the obligation that he says rests upon him. How came you in debt to them, Paul? "I owe my all

to Christ. He redeemed me, and my life shall be spent in his service. He it is who placed me under obligations to these people, when he said: 'Go ye into all the world, and preach the gospel to every creature.' Measuring their claims upon me by my devotion to him, I find myself in debt to them all; I owe them the gospel of his grace, and to the utmost of my ability the obligation shall be met, for I am willing to spend and be spent for Christ." Accordingly, under the force of this obligation, he says: "As much as in me is, I am ready to preach the gospel to you that are at Rome also." Thus he paid his world-wide debt. But, my brethren, was Paul's a peculiar case, that he should owe the gospel to more men than we? Surely not; but let us remember constantly that we too are "in debt to the Greeks, and Barbarians; to the wise, and to the unwise;" and this obligation is only canceled when we have done our utmost to "teach all nations," and to "preach the gospel to every creature." How many of us will face at the bar of God unsettled accounts, unpaid debts, while souls will be swift witnesses against us, crying out for judgment unto condemnation. "To him that knoweth to do good, and doeth it not, to him it is sin." (Jas. iv.17.)

7. Christ, being the Son of God, the Creator, and the Son of man as a race, a whole, has broken down the middle wall, the conditions separating Jew and Gentile, and has become the Author of peace to all who believe. Through gospel grace, they who were "sometime far off" from God and salvation are "made nigh by the blood of Christ." The gospel is world-wide in its scope; knowing no race, color, or distinction in its mighty efforts to lift up and save the world.

8. According to our present lesson, we find that our Saviour has put into the mouth of each of his followers, as they kneel daily around the throne of grace, to offer as their first petition to their Father in heaven: "Thy king-

dom come." And the second is like unto it: "Thy will be done in earth, as it is in heaven." The petition given first is strictly missionary; while the next deepens the idea by asking not only for the general subjugation of the world to the reign of Christ, but that the last vestige of sin may be swept from the hearts of men, so that perfect holiness may flood earth and sky, and "the knowledge of the glory of the Lord" may fill the earth "as the waters cover the sea." After "Thy kingdom come. Thy will be done in earth," et., comes: "Give us this day our daily bread." Christ's universal reign first; afterward, our daily bread. Men— even Church people— commonly put the bread question first, and the help the Master's cause if they "feel like" they "have it to spare." Men act as though they were "lords of all they survey," while their God is treated as though a beggar of their bounty. But the Bible says, "The earth is the Lord's;" and "Seek ye first the kingdom of God, and his righteousness; and all these [necessary] things shall be added unto you." (Ps. xxiv.1; Matt. vi 33.)

9. "If ye love me, keep my commandments." Here is the idea we have been trying to enforce all through this reading, and the No. 1. It is not arbitrary, but natural. Where love is mutual between Master and subject obedience is easy. God has authority, and uses it, yet he keeps love to the front. We, likewise, should render to God the service of obedience, but that of love is better. "Let every Christian get out of the *must I* of duty into the *may I* of love." (Dr. W.B. Godbey.) Christ has commanded his followers to carry his gospel into all the earth. Duty says, with heavy heart: "*Must I* help?" Love says, with beaming eye and happy heart: "*May I* assist?" The one is trying to escape hell, and— barely does it. The other, through love to Christ, is laboring to advance his kingdom, and when death comes he sweeps in through the gates, washed in the blood of the Lamb, while many saved by his labors are there to receive him. See Luke xvi.9.

10. "Go!" Hear it, all ye disciples of Christ. He has no need of idlers, loitering around, waiting for God to save the heathen "in his own good time," but he calls for such as will "fight the good fight of faith," and "endure hardness as good soldiers." Who will prove himself worthy of the field? The world must be evangelized, my brethren. How we treasure the parting messages of friends, as they go out through the shadows to the next world. Here we have the parting message of our Redeemer, fresh from his conquest over death, in the shadows of the grave and as he was just going up to that land where he is preparing a place for us. Every pulsation of our hearts should send up the shout, in holy love: "We go, Lord, to do or die!" "This world for our Jesus!" should be the motto of every Christian heart.

> All hail the power of Jesus' name!
> Let angels prostrate fall;
> Bring forth the royal diadem,
> And crown him Lord of all.

> Let every kindred, every tribe,
> On this terrestrial ball
> To him all majesty ascribe,
> And crown him Lord of all.

14
MISSIONS (NEW TESTAMENT)
No. 3

1. The gospel is the power God uses to save the people.

> "For I am not ashamed of the gospel of Christ: for it is the power of God unto salvation to every one that believeth; to the Jew first, and also to the Greek. For therein is the righteousness of God revealed from faith to faith: as it is written, The just shall live by faith." (Rom. i.16, 17.)

2. And the nations must be taught the gospel truth.

> "And Jesus came and spake unto them, saying, All power is given unto me in heaven and in earth. Go ye therefore, and teach all nations, baptizing them in the name of the Father, and of the Son, and of the Holy Ghost: teaching them to observe all things whatsoever I have commanded you; and, lo, I am with you always, even unto the end of the world. Amen." (Matt. xxviii.18-20.)

3. "Go or send!" Some invincible logic.

> "For there is no difference between the Jew and the Greek: for the same Lord over all is rich unto all that call upon him. For whosoever shall call upon the name of the Lord shall be saved. How then shall they call on him in whom they have not believed? and how shall they believe in him of whom they have not heard? and how shall they hear without a preacher? and how shall they preach, except they be sent." (Rom. x.12-15.)

4. True followers of the Lord sound the word out to the perishing.

> "So that ye were ensamples to all that believe in Macedonia and Achaia. For from you sounded out the word of the Lord not only in Macedonia and Achaia, but also in every place your faith to Godward is spread abroad; so that we need not to speak any thing." (1 Thess i.7, 8.)

5. We pray, "Thy kingdom come," but what of our works?

> "If a brother or sister be naked, and destitute of daily food, And one of you say unto them, Depart in peace, be ye warmed and filled; notwithstanding ye give them not those things which are needful to the body: what doth it profit? Even so faith, if it hath not works, is dead, being alone. (Jas. ii.15-17.)

6. If we do not love Christ, we will be condemned.

> "If any man love not the Lord Jesus Christ, let him be Anathema, Maran atha." (1 Cor. xvi.22.)

7. We must witness for Christ to the uttermost parts of the earth.

> "But ye shall receive power, after that the Holy Ghost is come upon you: and ye shall be witnesses unto me both in Jerusalem, and in all Judea, and in Samaria,

and unto the uttermost part of the earth." (Acts i.8.)

8. The Spirit of Christ is a spirit of Missions. "Whosoever."

"And the Spirit and the bride say, Come. And let him that heareth say, Come. And let him that is athirst come. And whosoever will, let him take the water of life freely." (Rev. xxii.17.)

9. None are Christ's without his Spirit.

"Now if any man have not the Spirit of Christ, he is none of his." (Rom. viii.9.)

1. When will the Church ever learn that the gospel is the power of God unto salvation — that is, it is the power — the means or agency — that God uses to save the world? Christ would not have purchased gospel privileges for men, at the cost of Gethsemane and Calvary, if he had no use for the gospel in the work of man's redemption. But the scheme that he has inaugurated to save men makes prominent use of the gospel; yea, it is *the* power God has appointed to elevate man from the degradation of sin to the peaceful heights of "righteousness, and peace, and joy in the Holy Ghost." The Church is sitting down in the ashes over the few embers that smolder on her altars, when she should be up, marching through the nations, subduing them to Christ, and with the lighted torch of God's grace kindling the fires of heaven in every land. The gospel creates, renews, and intensifies faith; and the righteousness of God is revealed in the advances of faith. From faith to faith; for the just shall live by faith. Let the gospel, as a faith-producing power, be sent into all the earth; for "whosoever believeth in him shall not perish, but have eternal life."

2. And this is true not of one nation only, for the gospel of Christ is for all nations. "All power is given unto me."

What will you do with it, Lord? "I'll use it to assist you in my work. 'Go ye therefore,' because I have 'all power in heaven and in earth,' 'and teach [make disciples of] all nations.'" The work seems so great, so heavy, Lord! "Go! I have all power; 'and, lo, I am with you alway, even unto the end of the world.'" Here, brethren in Christ, is both our duty and our sufficiency. We must go in Christ's name, to advance his work; and we must trust his "all power" and "I am with you always" for results. Teach "all nations" and "every creature" his gospel, and he will use it to their salvation. But some may say: "O we cannot all *go* as missionaries." Very true, but all can take part, either "*go* or *send*." The apostle gives us some conclusive reasoning on this very phase of the question; and to us who cannot go he makes plain the duty we must perform.

3. He tells us the middle wall is taken down, and there is, in consequence, no difference; for the same Lord who is rich toward one is rich toward all, only bear in mind that they must "call upon him." For "whosoever shall call upon the name of the Lord shall be saved." The nations, like the individual who seeks salvation, must pray fervently to God; but the gospel is the agency that will bring them to their knees before God. He continues his searching questions, and they will reach you soon, reader. "How then shall they call on him in whom they have not believed?" They will not, Paul. "And how shall they believe in him of whom they have not heard?" No way, Paul. "And how shall they hear without a preacher?" I know of no way, Paul. "And how shall they preach, except they be sent?" Here our inspired questioner strikes the closing blow with the added weight of all the previous reasoning, at you and me, kind reader, and we are made to see that, although we may not be able to go, we can and must send, and this is the staple to which all the links in his wonderful chain are fastened. We are the

watchmen upon whom the responsibility falls, and if we fail to send the warning cry, the nations will die in their sins, but their blood will God require at our hands. See Ezekiel xxxiii.6.

4. The apostle called the Thessalonians ensamples — *i.e.,* examples — to all the Christians in Macedonia and Achaia. His reason is given: "For from you sounded out [was sent abroad] the word of the Lord." Paul, then, decides under the Spirit's guidance that the missionary Church is the model Church, the Church to be followed. If we sound out the word of the Lord, we are examples; but if we do not, what? Are we not then to be classed with the Church at Sardis, which had a name to live, but was dead (Rev. iii.1); or with the Laodiceans, who were nauseating to the Almighty, so that he spewed them out for lukewarmness (Rev. iii.14-16)?

5. When we see the world in the rags and filth of sin, and dying of want for lack of the gospel, what is our reward if we, in the midst of such destitution, say unto them, "Depart in peace, be ye warmed and filled;" notwithstanding we give them not the gospel of salvation? If we, surrounded with the wealth of gospel privileges that we enjoy, are satisfied to let the heathen lay at our gates as Lazarus at the gate of the rich man, can we hope to escape the rich man's doom? "And in hell he lifted up his eyes, being in torments." See Luke xvi.9-12, with 19-31. "Faith without works is dead." (Jas. ii.26.)

6. "Anathema," accursed; "Maran atha," the Lord cometh. If any man love not the Lord Jesus, he will be accursed when the Lord cometh. But Jesus says, "If ye love me, he will keep my words." Now see his commandment, hear his words: either "go or send." But you refuse! Then you love him not, and will be accursed at his coming. Thus, brother, your own salvation, as well as that of the heathen, demands your service in the great cause of Missions. And no wonder, since on the spread of the gos-

pel hinges the universal reign of Christ and the consequent glory of God. Love Christ; live and labor for him; or perish with all his enemies, when the foot of his power is placed on the head of his last foe. "He must reign, till he hath put all enemies under his feet." (1 Cor. xv.25.)

7. The disciples of Christ— his followers, his people— are to bear witness for him in all the earth; and for this he gives a special induement of power from on high. By this witnessing to the uttermost parts of the earth the name of Christ is to become familiar to every ear, famous in every nation. The gospel must be preached, lived, testified to, till earth accepts her Saviour, and all nations bow at his cross. "And they overcame him [Satan] by the blood of the Lamb, and by the word of their testimony." Rev. xii.11.)

8. The Spirit is calling, the bride (the Church) is calling; and to these witnesses for Christ must be added every one "that heareth" — *i.e.*, every saved person— and all must say: "Come. Let him that is athirst come. *Whosoever will* let him take the water of life freely." Thus the invitations of the gospel are as broad as the needs of man; and all who love the Lord Jesus in sincerity will bear witness accordingly, till "the earth shall be filled with the knowledge of the glory of the Lord, as the waters cover the sea."

9. In conclusion, "If any man have not the Spirit of Christ, he is none of his." And what is a manifestation of the Spirit of Christ? If we have the Spirit, we will do the will and the work of Christ. We will be self-sacrificing. (Matt. xvi.24.) We will be pure in heart. (Matt. v.8.) We will love our enemies. (Matt. v.44.) We will overcome evil with good, and abhor evil, but righteousness. (Rom. xii.9, 21.) We will spend our all in doing good. (2 Cor. viii.9.) We will find it more blessed to give than to receive. (Acts xx.35.)

Reader, have you the Spirit of Christ? are you living to

bless the world and honor your Saviour? May you abound unto every good work! and may the blessing of God be with you! Amen.

> Jesus shall reign where'er the sun
> Does his successive journeys run;
> His kingdom stretch from shore to shore,
> Till moons shall wax and wane no more.

15
WHAT CHRIST IS TO US

1. His name (Jesus) means Saviour.

   "And she shall bring forth a son, and thou shalt call his name Jesus: for he shall save his people from their sins." (Matt. i.21.)

2. He is our Sun and Shield.

   "For the Lord God is a sun and shield: the Lord will give grace and glory: no good thing will he withhold from them that walk uprightly." (Ps. lxxxiv.11.)

3. He is the Vine; we are the branches.

   "I am the vine, ye are the branches. He that abideth in me, and I in him, the same bringeth forth much fruit; for without me ye can do nothing." (John xv.5.)

4. So we must abide in him, to bear fruit or even to live.

   "If a man abide not in me, he is cast forth as a branch, and is withered; and men gather them, and cast them into the fire, and they are burned. If ye abide in me, and my words abide in you, ye shall ask what ye will, and it shall be done unto you." (John xv.6, 7.)

5. He is the Good Shepherd.

"He shall feed his flock like a shepherd: he shall gather the lambs with his arm, and carry them in his bosom, and shall gently lead those that are with young." (Isa. xl.11.) See John x.11.

6. We are safe while he leads.

"The Lord is my shepherd; I shall not want." (Ps. xxiii.1)

7. Christ is our Strength.

"I can do all things through Christ which strengtheneth me." (Phil. iv.13.)

8. He is our Master, and we are brethren.

"But be not ye called Rabbi: for one is your Master, even Christ; and all ye are brethren." "Neither be ye called masters: for one is your Master, even Christ." (Matt. xxiii.8, 10.)

9. Yea, he is our "All in all."

"Where there is neither Greek nor Jew, circumcision nor uncircumcision, Barbarian, Scythian, bond nor free: but Christ is all, and in all." (Col. iii.11.)

10. Our Wisdom, Righteousness, Sanctification, Redemption.

"But of him are ye in Christ Jesus, who of God is made unto us wisdom, and righteousness, and sanctification, and redemption." (1 Cor. i.30.)

11. He is Alpha and Omega, and the bright and Morning Star.

"I am Alpha and Omega, the beginning and the end, the first and the last." "I Jesus have sent mine angel to testify unto you these things in the churches. I am the root and the offspring of David, and the bright and morning star." (Rev. xxii.13, 16.)

16
THE WORD OF GOD

1. The words of the Lord are pure.

    "The words of the Lord are pure words: as silver tried in a furnace of earth, purified seven times." (Ps. xii.6.)

2. God's word is a light unto my feet, and a light unto my path. (Ps. cxix.105.)

3. Yea, his word is a lamp.

    "For the commandment is a lamp: and the law is light; and reproofs of instruction are the way of life." (Prov. vi.23.)

4. The word has power for God's work.

    "For as the rain cometh down, and the snow from heaven, and returneth not thither, but watereth the earth, and maketh it bring forth and bud, that it may give seed to the sower, and bread to the eater: so shall my word be that goeth forth out of my mouth: it shall not return unto me void, but it shall accomplish that which I please, and it shall prosper in the thing whereto I sent it." (Isa. lv.10, 11.)

5. God's law is perfect, converting the soul.

"The law of the Lord is perfect, converting the soul: the testimony of the Lord is sure, making wise the simple." (Ps. xix.7.)

6. It should be prized above gold and silver.

"The law of thy mouth is better unto me than thousands of gold and silver." (Ps. cxix.72.) See Psalm cxix.14.

7. The preciousness of God's judgments or teachings.

"The fear of the Lord is clean, enduring forever: the judgments of the Lord are true and righteous altogether. More to be desired are they than gold, yea, than much fine gold: sweeter also than honey and the honey-comb. Moreover by them is thy servant warned: and in keeping of them there is great reward." (Ps. xix.9-11.)

8. The word — the depth of its perception and penetration.

"For the word of God is quick, and powerful, and sharper than any two-edged sword, piercing even to the dividing asunder of soul and spirit, and of the joints and marrow, and is a discerner of the thoughts and intents of the heart." (Heb. iv.12.)

9. The word — a hammer to break, a fire to purify.

"Is not my word like as a fire? saith the Lord; and like a hammer that breaketh the rock in pieces? (Jer. xxiii.29.)

17
THE TOUCH-STONE: A SERMON
REV. A. J. JARRELL

"For they that are after the flesh, do mind the things of the flesh; but they that are after the Spirit, the things of the Spirit." (Rom. viii.5.)

DID YOU EVER SEE a touch-stone— a hard, black stone used for testing with a touch the purity of the precious metals. I held one in my hand once, and had my watch tested. It was true to its stamp of eighteen carats. But don't you wish you had a moral touch-stone which you could apply to yourself at any time, and tell exactly the purity of your heart? Sea-captains have instruments by which, in mid ocean, a thousand miles from any landmark, they can tell exactly where they are; only they must have some moments' flash from sun, moon, or star to measure from. Don't you wish you had some instrument by which you could take your spiritual bearings, at any place and at any time, though no sun or moon or star gleam across your path? That touch-stone and that instrument you have in the verse before us — an infallible test of what you are and where you are going in every struggle of life and in the most starless night of all your pilgrimage. And the beauty of this instrument is that anybody can read its register. Listen: "For they that are after the flesh, do mind the things of the flesh; but they that are after the Spirit, the things of the Spirit." "To mind" is to attend to, and delight to attend to; to study about, and take pleasure in studying about; to think of, and love to think of. "They that are after the flesh" think of the flesh, and love to think about it. "They that are after the Spirit," study about the Spirit, and love to study about him. Leave a man free, and he'll go where he wants to go, heed what he wants to heed, and sip just where he wants to sip. Read a man's thoughts, and you read his heart. "As a man thinketh in his heart, so is he." He that knows his own thoughts knows his own heart. His thoughts are the register which his heart makes on the touch-stone. A child knows what he thinks about. A child, therefore, can take his own bearings anywhere, and all the time. But, mark you, it is not the thoughts that flit through the mind like birds through the air. These have no moral quality; neither do they signify any thing, save that Satan's darts may fly anywhere and through any brain. The thoughts that have more quality are those that are invited in — caught and caged and petted and caressed — whose coming always gives delight, and whose departure causes regret; and which always find the house "empty and garnished," and thrown open for their return. An unwilling thought never leaves a stain.

Let us apply this touch-stone. Two men stepped from the cars in Cartersville, Ga., just as my prayer-meeting bell was ringing out its cheerful call. One of these men caught the sound in a moment— he was hungry for it; it was just what he wanted to hear— and into my meeting he came. He just "minded" the thing he loved to "mind." He knew, and we all knew, he was of the Spirit. The other man never heard one stroke of the bell— he was not listening for that— but his eye caught a glimpse of a red light clear across town, and he went where he wanted to go. Each sipped just what he loved to sip. But the cup in one case was whiskey, and in the other it was salvation. Each one knew what he was and where he was going. Two young men rolled into Augusta one evening; one was at St. James' Church that night, and the other was at an abominable skating-rink. One "minded" the things of the Spirit, and he knew it; the other "minded" the things of the flesh, and he knew it. Two young ladies go into their father's library in the evening. One instinctively reaches for a love story. The other seizes the memoirs of the saintly Mrs. Fletcher. Each one reads what she loves to read, and each one pores over her volume, forgetful of the hours. But one is "minding" the things of the Spirit, and she knows it; the other is "minding" the things of the flesh, and she knows it. I had two young ladies— members of my Church— one poor, working for four dollars per month; the other "well to do" in the world, and rarely had a wish ungratified. One of these, out of her wages, helped a widowed niece to buy bread, dressed herself neatly, and always had an offering ready when I took collections, and if she was absent from Church, she was at my door next day with her contribution. The other spent in personal adornments all that was her own. Each spent her money where she loved to spend it. But one "minded" the flesh, and the other the Spirit. In one of my Churches I had great difficulty in getting my people to prayer-meeting. Warnings and entreaties, tears and sighs, were alike largely in vain. But, three nights successively— the gloomiest and the bitterest of winter— with the slush shoe-mouth deep on the sidewalks— a traveling "juggler-show" was held in the opera-house. There was hardly standing-room for the crowds of Methodists and Baptists and Presbyterians. The melting snow could not chill their ardor. They were simply going where they loved to go, and slush could not keep them back.

Apply the touch-stone. "Adam, where art thou?" What do you think most about, and love most to think about? Where do you go most, and love most to go? When left perfectly free, which way does the current of your thoughts run? Where do you delight most to have it run? These are not idle questions. Each one weighs a ton. Do you mind the things of the flesh or the things of the Spirit, which?

But I cannot afford to be misunderstood here. It is not minding the things of the flesh that makes us carnal, though that would be the inevitable result if we were ever so spiritual; but it is the carnal mind in us that makes us "mind the things of the flesh." This is the line of truth the Holy Spirit is trying to hammer into our dull understandings. The death is not in the doing or the thinking, but it is in the carnal mind that makes us want to think and do them. Hence, that terrible masked battery that Paul suddenly uncovers: *"To be carnally minded is death."* No matter what you do or don't do; no matter what you think or don't think, *"to be carnally minded is death."* I wish I could chisel that verb *"to be"* so deep into the heart of the Church that the "wear and tear" of a hundred years' warfare could never efface a single letter. For six thousand years God has been trying to turn our thoughts inward— to character, and not conduct first; to *"being,"* and not merely "doing"— as the transcendent concern of man. His voice has rung down the ages: "Make the tree good, and then the fruit will be good." Still we go on beating and cutting the branches to make them bring good fruit. O in what living light God writes that word "*be!*" "Except ye *be* converted." "*Be* ye perfect." "*Be* ye holy." "*Be* not conformed." "*Be* ye transformed." "To *be* or *not to be*," is the question in a deeper sense than Hamlet ever dreamed of. Our deeds, our words, our thoughts. our outward lives, supremely important as they are, borrow all their supremacy from the character within, from which they spring. The one great, overmastering question for us is, What *are we*? not merely, *What do we*? "To be carnally minded is death." Am I understood?

God always has the "ax at the *root* of the tree;" man at the *branches*. "To be carnally minded is death." This is the Master's way of declaring the great issues of life. "Is it wrong to go to the theater?" No more wrong than it was in John Bunyan to go to Bedford jail— if you go there against your will, and have no heart for it while you are there— but there is death in the carnal mind that wants to go there; no harm in a ball-room, but there is death in the desire for the ball-room. And I am so glad God has not left it to men to settle the grade of evil there is in the carnal mind. Good men differ and dispute whether there is any evil in it at all, and the best of men hardly realize how deadly it is; but God has declared that it is always "death," no matter where found, and no matter how modified.

It is death to all love of God in the heart. Here we reach bed-rock in the investigation. This foundation God has laid— "the carnal mind is enmity against God." It is enmity, the very soul and spirit of hate, toward him. Whatever else it may do, it can never love him.

So it is, likewise, death to all religious joy in the soul. Who ever heard of a carnal mind being troubled with "joy unspeakable and full of glory?" Who ever knew a carnal man to "rejoice evermore, pray without ceasing, and in every thing give thanks?" Who ever saw such a one with streaming eyes and beaming face singing:

> O the rapturous height Of that holy delight;
> Which I feel in the life-giving blood!
> Of my Saviour possessed, I am perfectly blessed,
> As if filled with the fullness of God!

If such a song were heard, from such a source, there would be "silence in heaven" again "by the space of half an hour."

More than this, the carnal mind is death to all usefulness in the Church. But I employ that word "usefulness" intelligently and in a scriptural sense. I mean only such things as bring glory to God and everlasting good to man. A lower order of usefulness, falsely so called, demands a carnal mind. Any other would be unfitted for the work. But I mean that usefulness of which Christ spake when he said: "Herein is my father glorified, that ye bear much fruit." I mean that which Paul meant when he said: "Ye have your fruit unto holiness, and the end everlasting life." To all such usefulness the carnal mind is sure and certain death. Imagine, if you can, a carnal man with tears begging a sinner to flee from the wrath to come, or weeping "between the porch and the altar" at the languishing state of Zion, or planning and pushing a glowing prayer-meeting to triumphant success. Who ever knew a leader of the "German" to lead an "altar service?" The "German" don't lead that way [sic]. The devil would drop it in an hour if it did. Figs may fall from thistles, and grapes from thorns, but usefulness never yet sprung from a carnal mind. Nothing but death ever comes from that.

"But to be spiritually minded is life and peace." Of course it is. A spiritual mind completes our union with Him who is life, and there must be life, "and that more abundantly." Put one hand on my heart, and the other on my wrist, and you will find the beats are the same, not a peculiarity in one that is not in the other. If the heart beats sixty beats to the minute, the wrist beats sixty; if the heart misses one beat in ten, the wrist does the same; if one is strong, the other is strong; if one is feeble, the other is feeble. The connection is complete by the artery, and the life-tide flows through both; and flow it will until "heart and flesh shall fail," unless that connection is broken. A surgeon may hack that arm from shoulder to wrist, he may saw that bone in a dozen pieces; but until that artery is broken, or injured, the beating will still go on. Lay one hand on the heart of a spiritually-minded man, and reverently lift the other to the "Heart that was pierced." The throbs are the same. One is on the great white throne, the other in the turmoil of earthly strife; but the connection is complete, and neither the distance nor the turmoil and strife can vary one heart-throb. Twelve legions of devils may march between us and our "Life," but the pulse will not abate one jot. In a telegraph office on the coast of New Foundland, and in another at Queenstown, Ireland, is a little shuttle-like instrument, into which a patient watcher sits looking at the sparks that flash back and forth in the shuttle. There is no click to that battery, but Europe and America are talking to each other across three thousand miles of water. These instruments are connected, and that is enough — no matter what the distance. The ocean may be stirred from shore to shore; forty tempests may double-quick back and forth across that connecting line, but the operator will not miss one flashing spark. Every dragon of the deep may gnaw away at that connecting line, but until it is broken they can never intercept a solitary message. All day long — and all night too — these distant continents commune with each other, without the click of a battery or the whisper of a human breath. There is union there, and there is union here; and this union is through the indwelling Spirit. "I in them, and thou in me, that they may be made perfect in one." The Marys can still sit at Jesus' feet, and receive, all day long — and all night too —

the flashes of his love and tenderness. He is "far above all principalities and powers," but the weeping Magdalenes can still hear him say, "Mary!" and they can still clasp his feet and cry, "Rabboni." O if there is life anywhere, if there is life in heaven, as surely as there is life in God, just so surely is there life in a spiritual mind!

"And peace." How could it be otherwise when the lies throbbing on the bosom of the Prince of peace? "Lo, I am with you alway, even unto the end of the world." And shall we be disturbed while this sweet voice is ringing in our ears, "My peace I give unto you?" and shall we ever get uneasy until we find him getting uneasy? Shall we repeat the folly of the apostles, wringing their hands over a little gale, while the Master was lying right by their side? "These things I have spoken unto you, that in me ye might have peace." "Let not your heart be troubled, neither let it," — do you hear? don't let it — "be afraid."

What will you do with that carnal mind? "Not carnal?" Better take your bearings. The captain of the ill-fated steam-ship "Atlantic," a few years ago, was so sure he was in no danger that he went into his cabin to sleep at ten o'clock at night. Howbeit he had not taken his bearings. In less than an hour he had run on the rocks of New Foundland, and his noble ship sunk to rise no more. What will you do with that carnal mind? "Restrain it?" Yes, when you have restrained a lightning-bolt. "Tame it?" Know this: "That every kind of beasts and of birds, and of serpents, and of things in the sea, is tamed, and hath been tamed of mankind; but the" carnal mind "can no man tame." What will you do with it? "Bring it into subjection?" "It is not subject to the law of God, neither indeed can be." Here we reach bed-rock again. Millions have tried the experiment of subjection, but the subjection was always on the wrong side. It will dominate you to your grave, if it does not sink you into hell. What will you do with it? There is but one thing that can be done;

and that is to destroy it. Nothing short of extermination can ever give you perfect peace or perfect life. There is no other help on earth, and there is none in heaven but this. You may dream of "suppression" if you will; but it is the same old dream, and it will have the same old awakening. "Hard gospel?" I think it is inexpressibly glorious. To have the last chain stricken from me, and I walk the earth a free-man, and mount the skies an heir of glory— hallelujah! this is all I want, and the least that God has promised!

18
BIBLE-READING ON MATTHEW V.3-16
No. 1 (Verses 3, 4.)

I. 1. Conviction for sin; poverty of spirit.

"Blessed are the poor in spirit: for theirs is the kingdom of heaven." (Matt. v.3.)

2. Pride is destructive; humility is profitable.

"Pride goeth before destruction, and a haughty spirit before a fall. Better it is to be of a humble spirit with the lowly, than to divide the spoil with the proud." (Prov. xvi.18, 19.)

3. God favors the broken spirit, the contrite heart.

"The sacrifices of God are a broken spirit: a broken and a contrite heart, O God, thou wilt not despise." (Ps. li.17.)

4. The Lord is near to the broken-hearted, the contrite in spirit.

"The Lord is nigh unto them that are of a broken heart; and saveth such as be of a contrite spirit." (Ps. xxxiv.18.)

5. God dwells with the humble and revives them.

"For thus saith the high and lofty One that inhabiteth eternity, whose name is Holy; I dwell in the high and holy place, with him also that is of a contrite and humble spirit, to revive the spirit of the humble, and to revive the heart of the contrite ones." (Isa. lvii.15.)

II. 6. Our God blesses and comforts the mourner.

"Blessed are they that mourn: for they shall be comforted." (Matt. v.4.)

7. Christ gives the garment of praise for the spirit of heaviness.

"To proclaim the acceptable year of the Lord, and the day of vengeance of our God; to comfort all that mourn; to appoint unto them that mourn in Zion, to give unto them beauty for ashes, the oil of joy for mourning, the garment of praise for the spirit of heaviness; that they might be called Trees of righteousness, The planting of the Lord, that he might be glorified." (Isa. lxi.2, 3.)

8. Humble yourselves, and God will lift you up.

"Be afflicted, and mourn, and weep: let your laughter be turned to mourning, and your joy to heaviness. Humble yourselves in the sight of the Lord, and he shall lift you up." (Jas. iv.9, 10.)

9. Joy shall supplant the sorrow of God's people.

"Verily, verily, I say unto you, That ye shall weep and lament, but the world shall rejoice; and ye shall be sorrowful, but your sorrow shall be turned into joy." (John xvi.20.)

19
BIBLE-READING ON MATTHEW V.3-16
No. 2 (Verses 5, 6.)

III. 1. Jesus pronounces his blessings on the meek.

"Blessed are the meek: for they shall inherit the earth." (Matt. v.5.)

2. The delight of the meek; their inheritance.

"But the meek shall inherit the earth; and shall delight themselves in the abundance of peace." (Ps. xxxvii.11.)

3. God himself will teach and guide the meek.

"The meek will be guide in judgment: and the meek will he teach his way." (Ps. xxv.9.)

4. God gave judgment in behalf of the meek.

"Thou didst cause judgment to be heard from heaven; the earth feared, and was still, when God arose to judgment, to save all the meek of the earth. Selah." (Ps. lxxvi.8, 9.)

5. He lifts up the meek, but casts down the wicked.

"The Lord lifteth up the meek: he casteth the wicked down to the ground." (Ps. cxlvii.6.)

6. The joy of the meek shall increase in the Lord.

"The meek also shall increase their joy in the Lord, and the poor among men shall rejoice in the Holy One of Israel." (Isa. xxix.19.)

7. The Lord shall reprove with equity in behalf of the meek.

"But with righteousness shall he judge the poor, and reprove with equity for the meek of the earth: and he shall smite the earth with the rod of his mouth, and with the breath of his lips shall he slay the wicked." (Isa. xi.4.)

IV. 8. The hungering and thirsting soul shall be filled.

"Blessed are they which do hunger and thirst after righteousness: for they shall be filled." (Matt. v.6.)

9. The disciples filled with the Holy Ghost.

"And they were all filled with the Holy Ghost, and began to speak with other tongues, as the Spirit gave them utterance." "And when they had prayed, the place was shaken where they were assembled together; and they were all filled with the Holy Ghost, and they spake the word of God with boldness." (Acts ii.4; iv.31.)

10. Our God will fill the lips of the perfect with rejoicing.

"Behold, God will not cast away a perfect man, neither will he help the evil doers: till he fill thy mouth with laughing, and thy lips with rejoicing." (Job viii.20, 21.)

11. Christ is the Bread that satisfies the soul.

"And Jesus said unto them, I am the bread of life: he that cometh to me shall never hunger; and he that believeth on me shall never thirst." (John vi.35.)

20
BIBLE-READING ON MATTHEW V.3-16
No. 3 (Verse 7.)

V. 1. Christ promises mercy to the merciful.

"Blessed are the merciful: for they shall obtain mercy." (Matt. v.7.)

2. We must forgive that we may be forgiven.

"For if ye forgive men their trespasses, your heavenly Father will also forgive you: but if ye forgive not men their trespasses, neither will your Father forgive your trespasses." (Matt. vi.14, 15.)

3. If we in mercy help the poor, God will also help us.

"Blessed is he that considereth the poor: the Lord will deliver him in time of trouble. The Lord will preserve him, and keep him alive; and he shall be blessed upon the earth: and thou wilt not deliver him unto the will of his enemies." (Ps. xli.1, 2.)

4. God will not forget our labor of love in his name.

"For God is not unrighteous to forget your work and labor of love, which ye have shewed toward his name, in that ye have ministered to the saints, and do minister." (Heb. vi.10.) See Matthew xxv.40.

5. He shall have no mercy who shows none.

"For he shall have judgment without mercy, that hath showed no mercy; and mercy rejoiceth against judgment." (Jas. ii.13.)

6. He shall cry himself who stoppeth his ears against the poor.

"Whoso stoppeth his ears at the cry of the poor, he also shall cry himself, but shall not be heard." (Prov. xxi.13.)

7. God will deliver him to the tormentors, who will not forgive.

"And his lord was wroth, and delivered him to the tormentors, till he should pay all that was due unto him. So likewise shall my heavenly Father do also unto you, if ye from your hearts forgive not every one his brother their trespasses." (Matt. xviii.34, 35.)

8. To oppress the poor is to reproach our Maker.

"He that oppresseth the poor reproacheth his Maker: but he that honoreth him hath mercy on the poor." (Prov. xiv.31.)

9. The practice of mercy is good for the soul; but evil troubleth.

"The merciful man doeth good to his own soul: but he that is cruel troubleth his own flesh. The wicked worketh a deceitful work: but to him that soweth righteousness shall be a sure reward." (Prov. xi.17, 18.)

21
BIBLE-READING ON MATTHEW V.3-16
No. 4 (Verse 8.)

VI. The pure in heart shall see God.

"Blessed are the pure in heart: for they shall see God." (Matt. v.8.)

2. Clean hands and a pure heart necessary to see God.

"Who shall ascend into the hill of the Lord? or who shall stand in his holy place? He that hath clean hands, and a pure heart; who hath not lifted up his soul unto vanity, nor sworn deceitfully." (Ps. xxiv.3, 4.) See Psalm xv.2.

3. Our eyes should be closed to evil, that we may see the King.

"He that walketh righteously, and speaketh uprightly; he that despiseth the gain of oppressions, that shaketh his hands from holding of bribes, that stoppeth his ears from hearing of blood, and shutteth his eyes from seeing evil; he shall dwell on high; his place of defense shall be the munitions of rocks: bread shall be given unto him; his waters shall be sure. Thine eyes shall see the King in his beauty: they shall behold the land that is very far off." (Isa. xxxiii.15-17.)

4. Heart-purity is holiness; without it we cannot see God.

"Follow peace with all men, and holiness, without which no man shall see the Lord." (Heb. xii.14.)

5. The children of God should purify themselves.

"And every man that hath this hope in him purifieth himself, even as He is pure." (1 John iii.3.) See 1 John iii.1, 2.

6. To perfect holiness, cleanse from all filthiness of flesh and spirit.

"Having therefore these promises, dearly beloved, let us cleanse ourselves from all filthiness of the flesh and spirit, perfecting holiness in the fear of God." (2 Cor. vii.1.)

7. Flee lust; follow righteousness, faith, charity.

"Flee also youthful lusts: but follow righteousness, faith, charity, peace, with them that call on the Lord out of a pure heart." (2 Tim. ii.22.) See 1 Timothy i.5.

8. Many shall be purified, and made white, but *tried*.

"Many shall be purified, and made white, and tried; but the wicked shall do wickedly: and none of the wicked shall understand; but the wise shall understand." (Dan. xii.10.)

9. Jesus' blood cleanseth from all sin.

"But if we walk in the light, as he is in the light, we have fellowship one with another, and the blood of Jesus Christ his Son cleanseth us from all sin." (1 John i.7.) See Luke i.73-75; 1 Thessalonians v.23; Hebrews xiii.12.

22
BIBLE-READING ON MATTHEW V.3-16
No. 5 (Verse 9.)

VII. The peace-makers are called the *children of God*.

"Blessed are the peace-makers: for they shall be called the children of God." (Matt. v.9.)

1. Christ, the Son of God, is the *Prince of Peace*.

"The mighty God, The everlasting Father, The Prince of Peace." (Isa. ix.6.)

2. Our peace-maker with God is Christ.

"For he is our peace, who hath made both one, and hath broken down the middle wall of partition between us." (Eph. ii.14.)

3. The angels which announced Christ's birth sung peace on earth.

"Glory to God in the highest, and on earth, peace, good will toward men." (Luke ii.14.)

4. God gives healing and peace, but not to the wicked.

"I create the fruit of the lips; Peace, peace to him that

is far off, and to him that is near, saith the Lord; and I will heal him. But the wicked are like the troubled sea, when it cannot rest, whose waters cast up mire and dirt. There is no peace, saith my God, to the wicked." (Isa. lvii.19-21.)

5. We must follow peace with all men.

"Follow peace with all men, and holiness, without which no man shall see the Lord." (Heb. xii.14.)

6. Our part must always be done for peace with every one.

"If it be possible, as much as lieth in you, live peaceably with all men." (Rom. xii.18.)

7. Though others hate us, we must still love them.

"But I say unto you, Love your enemies, bless them that curse you, do good to them that hate you, and pray for them which despitefully use you, and persecute you." (Matt. v.44.)

8. Do good for evil. Leave vengeance with God.

"Bless them which persecute you: bless, and curse not." "Dearly beloved, avenge not yourselves, but rather give place unto wrath: for it is written, Vengeance is mine; I will repay, saith the Lord. Therefore if thine enemy hunger, feed him; if he thirst, give him drink: for in so doing thou shalt heap coals of fire on his head. Be not overcome evil, but overcome evil with good." (Rom. xii.14, 19-21.)

23
BIBLE-READING ON MATTHEW V.3-16
No. 6 (Verses 10-12)

VIII. God's blessing on those who are persecuted for righteousness.

> "Blessed are they which are persecuted for righteousness' sake: for theirs is the kingdom of heaven. Blessed are ye, when men shall revile you, and persecute you, and shall say all manner of evil against you falsely, for my sake. Rejoice, and be exceeding glad: or great is your reward in heaven: for so persecuted they the prophets which were before you." (Matt. v.10-2.)

1. The world hated and persecuted Christ the Lord even unto death.

> "If the world hate you, ye know that it hated me before it hated you." "Remember the word that I said unto you, The servant is not greater than his lord. If they have persecuted me, they will also persecute you: if they have kept my saying, they will keep yours also. (John xv.18, 20.) See Matthew xxvii.35.

2. It also hated his disciples because they were like him.

"I have given them thy word; and the world hath hated them, because they are not of the world, even as I am not of the world." (John xvii.14.)

3. The prophets in olden times were persecuted.

"Which of the prophets have not your fathers persecuted? and they have slain them which shewed before of the coming of the Just One; of whom ye have been now the betrayers and murderers." (Acts vii.52.)

4. The apostles gave blessing for persecution.

"Even unto this present hour we both hunger, and thirst, and are naked, and are buffeted, and have no certain dwelling-place; and labor, working with our own hands: being reviled, we bless; being persecuted, we suffer it." (1 Cor. iv.11, 12.)

5. Stony-ground hearers are offended at persecution.

"And these are they likewise which are sown on stony ground; who, when they have heard the word, immediately receive it with gladness; and have no root in themselves, and so endure but for a time: afterward, when affliction or persecution ariseth for the word's sake, immediately they are offended." (Mark iv.16, 17.)

6. Persecutions are promised to those who forsake all for Christ.

"And Jesus answered and said, Verily I say unto you, There is no man that hath left house, or brethren, or sisters, or father, or mother, or wife, or children, or lands, for my sake, and the gospel's, but he shall receive a hundred-fold now in this time, houses, and brethren, and sisters, and mothers, and children, and lands, with persecutions; and in the world to come eternal life.

7. Paul took pleasure in persecutions for Christ's sake.

"Therefore I take pleasure in infirmities, in reproaches, in necessities, in persecutions, in distresses for Christ's sake: for when I am weak, then am I strong." (2 Cor. xii.10.)

8. If we exercise patience under persecutions, we prove worthy of the kingdom.

"So that we ourselves glory in you in the churches of God, for your patience and faith iin all your persecutions and tribulations that ye endure: which is a manifest token of the righteous judgment of God, that ye may be counted worthy of the kingdom of God, for which ye also suffer." (2 Thess. i.4, 5.)

24
Bible-Reading on Matthew V.3-16
No. 7 (Verses 13-16)

IX. The people just described are the salt of the earth.

"Ye are the salt of the earth: but if the salt have lost his savor, wherewith shall it be salted? it is thenceforth good for nothing, but to be cast out, and to be trodden under foot of men." (Matt. v.13.)

1. Have the salt of grace in yourselves, and peace one with another.

"Salt is good: but if the salt have lost his saltiness, wherewith will ye season it? Have salt in yourselves, and have peace one with another." (Mark ix.50.)

X. God's people the light of the world; they must shine.

"Ye are the light of the world. A city that is set on a hill cannot be hid. Neither do men light a candle, and put it under a bushel, but on a candlestick; and it giveth light unto all that are in the house. Let your light so shine before men, that they may see your good works, and glorify your Father which is in heaven." (Matt v.14-16.)

1. We must be blameless to shine in the world for God.

"That ye may be blameless and harmless, the sons of God, without rebuke, in the midst of a crooked and perverse nation, among whom ye shine as lights in the world." (Phil. ii.15.)

2. We were darkness, but now light in the Lord.

"For ye were sometime darkness, but now are ye light in the Lord: walk as children of light." (Eph. v.8.)

3. Christ is the true Light, the Source of all light.

"Then spake Jesus again unto them, saying, I am the light of the world: he that followeth me shall not walk in darkness, but shall have the light of life." (John viii.12.)

4. Let Zion shine in the Divine light and glory.

"Arise, shine; for thy light is come, and the glory of the Lord is risen upon thee. For, behold, the darkness shall cover the earth, and gross darkness that people: but the Lord shall arise upon thee, and his glory shall be seen upon thee." (Isa. lx.1, 2.)

5. God's light is not understood by the world.

"And the light shineth in darkness; and the darkness comprehended it not." (John i.5.) See 1 Corinthians ii.14.

6. He who walketh in darkness (sin) has no fellowship with God.

"This then is the message which we have heard of him, and declare unto you, that God is light, and in him is no darkness at all. If we say that we have fellowship with him, and walk in darkness, we lie, and do not the truth." (1 John i.5, 6.)

I. This section of our lesson teaches the doctrine of conviction for sin. It is the first step in the Christian life. The natural heart of man is estranged from God, filled with sin, the root of which is pride. Poverty of spirit expresses that condition of mind that follows or accompanies a realization of the ruin wrought by sin. It is a fact that sin works the ruin of soul and body here, and then sinks the whole man into hell at last. But man is blinded to this ruin in his natural estate, and hence the Bible call is: "Awake thou that sleepest, and arise from the dead, and Christ shall give thee light." (Eph. v.14.) While sin makes the man a pauper in fact, the impenitent sinner does not realize it; hence he is haughty, and independent in spirit. In this condition he is without God and without hope, a stranger to grace and an alien from the common-wealth of Israel. But the gospel alarm sounds in his ear, the Spirit awakens his guilty soul, and the poor sin-curse wretch trembles at the thought of his impending doom. He feels that he is lost, that the wrath of God hangs over him, while hell opens wide beneath him to engulf him forever. Where can be found a more terrific description of true conviction for sin than David gives in his experience? "The sorrows of death compassed me, and the pains of hell gat hold upon me; I found trouble and sorrow." (Ps. cxvi.3.) See Psalm cxvi.1-9.

II. After this deep conviction is produced, mourning over the follies, the wreck and ruin wrought by sin, is naturally the next step of the soul toward a Christian life. Poverty of spirit is but a realization by the soul of its sin-beggared condition, while mourning for the sin that defied God and cursed the soul is a natural— yea, a necessary— result. Mourning is the anguish of soul felt by an individual on account of some sorrow. What can more powerfully stir the soul's deepest anguish than a consciousness of having defied God, offended heaven, and paved the way to eternal damnation by one's own sins.

To a truly-awakened soul mourning is perfectly natural. It were idle to urge the man or woman standing at the open grave of father loved, or a mother dear, not to weep. Their weeping is uncontrollable, their anguish heart-breaking. So, when the soul is thoroughly aroused to its ruin by sin, when it is made to *feel* the condemnation that its sins have brought down upon its own head, it mourns, not by proxy, not because exhorted, but spontaneously, as naturally as water runs downhill. "Blessed are they that mourn." Thank God! "they shall be comforted." Christ Jesus promises to give "the oil of joy for mourning, the garment of praise for the spirit of heaviness;" and that which he hath promised he is able to perform.

III. As we see now, this lesson is progressive. The first thing taught is conviction— poverty of spirit. This is followed next in order by mourning, expressive of deep sorrow for sin. We now reach the third step of the soul seeking God, and here the surrender is made, and the soul is converted. "Blessed are the meek" — that is, the submissive. The sinner is a rebel under the Divine government; he is not subject to God's holy law. But when the Spirit of God operating on his heart breaks his stubborn, rebellious will, shows him his lost estate, and makes him in deep conviction realize his certain doom; and when in this awakened condition he mourns in true penitence over his sins, he becomes ready soon to surrender, to lay down the arms of his rebellion, and to submissively accept the yoke of Christ's government. When the soul reaches this point of surrender, being no longer in the attitude of rebellion against God, mercy reaches him, and grace transforms him. He is no longer a rebel, a traitor, an insurrectionist, but a member of the "household of faith," a child of God, an heir of the skies; being "born, not of blood, nor of the will of the flesh, nor of the will of man, but of God." (John i.13.) At the point of surrender to God the soul of the believer is born again, and thus starts out on its heaven-ward journey. We see signs of life clearly manifest in the next stage of progress.

IV. Hungering and thirsting after righteousness (holiness) implies spiritual life. The sinner is represented as dead (Eph. ii.1-5), the new birth being necessary to bring him to life. Who ever saw a dead man hunger and thirst? So the unconverted man, dead in sin and transgression, must be born again, made alive spiritually, before he will hunger and thirst after righteousness— *i.e.,* holiness. The sinner in impenitence has no life, no appetite for spiritual things; but when awakened he trembles as a guilty culprit at the bar of his judge, knowing that unless mercy reaches him his doom is certain and eternal. Then it is the Saviour speaks peace to his soul, God is reconciled, heavenly light floods his mind, and divine life springs up in his soul. His fear ceases, the shadows flee away, he loves the things of God, and hates the sins of his former life. Being alive in Christ, born of the Spirit (John iii.7, 8), he has an appetite for spiritual food, his soul yearns for God, he hungers and thirsts after righteousness. "As the hart panteth after the water brooks, so panteth my soul after thee, O God." (Psalm xlii.1.) Thank God! Jesus promises, "he shall be filled;" Barnabas "was a good man, and *full of the Holy Ghost and of faith.*" (Acts xi.24.) "And they were all *filled* with the Holy Ghost."

V. In this part of our lesson we see the practical side of the Christian life brought out. Heretofore we have had simply the experimental development of the Master's teaching. He now sets forth a practical test which corroborates and confirms the experimental doctrines before taught. One may claim to be poor in spirit, to mourn for sin, to meekly surrender to Christ, to be born again, yea, to hunger and thirst after righteousness; but if he is cruel, vindictive, unmerciful, his pretensions to Christ-likeness are vain. Men may be merciful to each other, to their companions, to their children, to the poor; yea, to the dumb brutes that perish in helplessness on their hands. This writer has no doubt that thousands will fail of mercy in God's great judgment-day because of their cruelty to the poor dumb brutes. Horses, hard-worked and unfed; cattle, hard-driven and unsheltered; dogs, cats, and other defenseless creatures will stand up as swift witnesses against cruel, unmerciful men in the last great day. "He shall have judgment without mercy, that hath showed no mercy; and mercy rejoiceth against judgment."

VI. Heart-purity is the experimental culmination of this lesson. The steps heretofore taken were but leading up to this. We have (1) conviction; this is followed (2) by true penitence, mourning for sin; we have (3), surrender to God, meekness; here spiritual life is kindled in the soul, and we have consequently (4) hungering and thirsting after righteousness; this shows life, and this life must bear the practical fruit of (5) mercy; then the triumph is gained, the hungering and thirsting soul is filled with all the fullness of God, the remains of the carnal mind are destroyed, the last vestige of sin is purged away and the sanctified believer rejoices (6) in purity of heart. This precious triumph of grace brings the believer into such intimate relation to his adorable Redeemer that he sees God here by faith, and will see him with all the blood-washed in glory when the storms of life shall have all swept by. St. Paul says: "We know that all things work together for good to them that love God." (Rom. viii.28.) Not we "hope," but we *"know"* — that is, we can see the hand of God in every thing. It is the happy privilege of every child of God to be so fully sanctified unto God, so thoroughly cleansed from sin, from doubts and fears and unbelief, that he may see God in all the dispensations of his providence. Though adversity comes, though trials multiply, though sorrows accumulate, though distresses abound, though bereavements settle down upon him, though the wing of the death-messenger shadow the home, though the starlight of earth's fondest hopes seems to go out in the gloom of the midnight darkness, yet the purified, trusting heart looks up through the darkness by the eye of faith, and sees streaming down from the throne of God the undimmed light of his eternal glory, and amidst it all he raises the victorious shout of his triumph: "Glory to God in the highest, on earth peace, good will toward men." "Though he slay me, yet will I trust him." "Bless the Lord, O my soul: and all that is within me, bless his holy name."

VII. Peace-making is twofold: (1) between God and man; and (2) between man and man. Christ is called the Prince of Peace. (Isa. ix.6.) The angels in announcing his coming sung: "On earth peace, good will toward men." "Being justified by faith, we have peace with God through our Lord Jesus Christ." (Rom. v.1.) Thus when a sinner is reconciled to God, peace is made between the offended God and the rebellious offender, man. He who wins souls from sin to God is a peace-maker in the highest sense. Making peace between man and man is a high and holy work— one that every Christian should be ready for. But this will easily follow where the life abounds in the great work of soul-winning. The greater work of reconciling men to God will well prepare one for the lesser work of reconciling men to men. In order to succeed as peace-makers, my brethren, the love of God must abound in our own hearts. It must be that perfect love that enmity cannot quench. It must not be overcome of evil, but must overcome evil with good. Peace-makers are called "the children of God," but the successful peace-maker must have heart-purity, or perfect love. "Love your enemies, do good to them that hate you," etc., "that ye may be the children of your Father, which is in heaven." Christ is our Peace-maker in heaven, and we must carry forward his work of peace-making on earth. We will thus be like him, being also children of our heavenly Father.

VIII. Persecution for righteousness' sake is as yet rather

scarce, because of the fewness of suitable subjects. The qualification for it has been given by the Master in the preceding part of the sermon. The steps, as before mentioned, are: Conviction, mourning, meekness, hungering and thirsting after righteousness, mercifulness, heart-purity, peace-making. In the stages here given the soul develops into the righteousness (true holiness of heart and life) that invites the opposition of the devil and the persecution of the world. Some one has said that a person is hardly fit to do good service for the Lord till he is so spiritual, so holy, that the world thinks him crazy— *i.e.,* "cranky." They said of Christ, "He hath a devil"— that is: "He is a fanatic; he is crazy, cranky." No Christian should be fanatical, or cranky; but all the followers of the lowly Christ should be so separated from the world, so devoted to God and good works, that the persecutions of the holy, the righteous, may be theirs. If any one say evil of me, and it is true, I need not get mad at him, but must correct my own life; but if evil be said of me that is false, it being a persecution for righteousness, I may rejoice and be exceeding glad, for the Master will place it all to my credit in glory, and great will be my reward, praise the Lord.

IX. Salt is to save, also to season or flavor. So God's people, by living holy lives, though persecuted by the world, will nevertheless save it. The old world perished not till Noah reached the ark, nor did Sodom perish till Lot escaped. It is by the holy living and diligent service of the Church of God that the world is to be saved. "If the salt have lost his savor, wherewith shall it be salted? it is *thenceforth good for nothing.*" A Church without religion— true spirituality, vital godliness, holiness— is about the deadest thing to be found. Some Churches spend their time nursing their respectability. Being too stingy to support themselves, and taking but little stock in the salvation of the world, they spend their strength on suppers, fairs, raffles, grab-bags and other like substitutes for religion and works, vainly dreaming that their miserable frolics are acceptable to God. "Woe to them that go down to Egypt for help." (Isa. xxx.1.) Such Churches die quickly of dry-rot, and failing in their God-given mission of saving men, they are cast out and trodden under foot by the world.

X. There are two means of receiving light. (1) Directly, from its source; (2) indirectly, by reflection. Christians are not the source of light, but simply its reflection. Christ is "the true Light, that lighteth every man that cometh into the world." Christians are lights only as they show Christ-likeness. The sun gives light; the moon reflects it. So Christ gives light, and the Christian— Christ-like person— reflects it to the world. A mirror (looking-glass) needs a good, smooth, unbroken surface, and the quicksilver preparation. If the surface be cracked and broken, the mirror will be untrue, or a like result will follow if the quicksilver be rubbed from the glass. The smooth surface of the mirror represents a consistent walk and conversation in the Christian, and the preparation of mercury represents the grace of God in the heart of the believer. If the life be ungodly, its influence for good is broken, and there is no heavenly light, no reflection of Christ if there be not in the heart the grace of God. "Ye are the light of the world." Let the Church of God catch divine inspiration and measure to her great responsibility. Let her shine with Christ-likeness among men. Notice that the light is not simply for a few at home, but for the "world." As wide as the fall, as deep as the curse of sin must the light shine for salvation. Let no man call himself a Christian who will not make earnest, persistent effort to carry abroad the good news of salvation, to "preach the gospel to every creature," that the light may shine in the dark places of earth, and the world may be brought to the light of the knowledge of the glory of God. "Neither do *men* light a candle, and put it under a bushel." As though he had said: "I appoint you to be the light of the world, and even man is not foolish enough to light a candle to hide it away; how much less am I?" From this hear his conclusion: "Let your light" therefore "so shine before men, that they may see your good works, and glorify your Father which is in heaven." We must let our light shine, it was given us for that purpose; and *we must either use it or lose it*. While Christ is in heaven representing us, he has left us on earth to represent him.

25
ABIDE IN CHRIST

1. We must abide in Christ, that we may bear fruit.

   "Abide in me, and I in you. As the branch cannot bear fruit of itself, except it abide in the vine; no more can ye, except ye abide in me." (John xv.4.)

2. In him we may bear *much* fruit; without him, *none*.

   "I am the vine, ye are the branches. He that abideth in me, and I in him, the same bringeth forth much fruit; for without me ye can do nothing." (John xv.5.)

3. If we abide in him, we have power in prayer.

   "If ye abide in me, and my words abide in you, ye shall ask what ye will, and it shall be done unto you." (John xv.7.)

4. But if we abide not in him, we are cast forth.

   "If a man abide not in me, he is cast forth as a branch, and is withered; and men gather them, and cast them into the fire, and they are burned." (John xv.6.)

5. If we are fruitful, we glorify the Father.

"Herein is my Father glorified, that ye bear much fruit; so shall ye be my disciples." (John xv.8.)

6. Christ is received by faith (Rom. v.1.), and so we abide in him.

"As ye have therefore received Christ Jesus the Lord, so walk ye in him: rooted and built up in him, and stablished in the faith, as ye have been taught, abounding therein with thanksgiving." (Col. ii.6, 7.)

7. If we would abide in him, we must keep his commandments.

"If ye keep my commandments, ye shall abide in my love; even as I have kept my Father's commandments, and abide in his love." (John xv.10.)

8. He gives the Spirit, that we may know of the abiding.

"And he that keepeth his commandments dwelleth in him, and he in him. And hereby we know that he abideth in us, by the Spirit which he hath given us." (1 John iii.24.)

9. Obeying the will of God, we continue to abide in Christ forever.

"And the world passeth away, and the lust thereof: but he that doeth the will of God abideth forever." (1 John ii.17.)

10. If we abide in Christ, we have him and the Father for our refuge.

"Whosoever transgresseth, and abideth not in the doctrine of Christ, hath not God. He that abideth in the doctrine of Christ, he hath both the Father and the Son." (2 John 9.)

26
Consecration

1. Consecration of self to God is required.

"For Moses had said, Consecrate yourselves to-day to the Lord, even every man upon his son, and upon his brother; that he may bestow upon you a blessing this day." (Ex. xxxii.29.)

2. The priests were consecrated to God's work.

"These are the names of the sons of Aaron, the priests which were anointed, whom he consecrated to minister in the priest's office." (Num. iii.3.)

3. David called the people to consecrate their service — property.

"Moreover, because I have set my affection to the house of my God, I have of mine own proper good, of gold and silver, which I have given to the house of my God, over and above all that I have prepared for the holy house, even three thousand talents of gold, of the gold of Ophir, and seven thousand talents of refined silver, to overlay the walls of the houses withal; the gold for things of gold, and the silver for the things of silver, and for all manner of work to be made by the hands of artificers. And who then is willing to consecrate his service this day unto the Lord?" (1 Chron. xxix.3-5.)

4. Our bodies must be consecrated — living sacrifices.

"I beseech you therefore, brethren, by the mercies of God, that ye present your bodies a living sacrifice, holy, acceptable unto God, which is your reasonable service." (Rom. xii.1.)

5. This demand is just, for we belong to God.

"What! know ye not that your body is the temple of the Holy Ghost which is in you, which ye have of God, and ye are not your own? For ye are bought with a price: therefore glorify God in your body, and in your spirit, which are God's." (1 Cor. vi.19, 20.)

6. Consecration regulates every point in life for God.

"Whether therefore ye eat, or drink, or whatsoever ye do, do all to the glory of God." (1 Cor. x.31.)

7. All our doings, word or deed, must be in Jesus' name.

"And whatsoever ye do in word or deed, do all in the name of the Lord Jesus, giving thanks to God and the Father by him." "And whatsoever ye do, do it heartily, as to the Lord, and not unto men." (Col. iii.17, 23.)

8. Our members must be surrendered to God, to glorify him.

"Yield yourselves unto God, as those that are alive from the dead, and your members as instruments of righteousness unto God." (Rom. vi.13.)

9. Then we may be dead unto sin, but alive unto God.

"Likewise reckon ye also yourselves to be dead indeed unto sin, but alive unto God through Jesus Christ our Lord." (Rom. vi.11.)

27
CHRIST IS THE LIGHT AND THE LIFE

1. He is the Way, the Truth, and the Life.

    "Jesus saith unto him, I am the way, the truth, and the life: no man cometh unto the Father, but by me." (John xiv.5.)

2. He is the Resurrection and the Life.

    "Jesus said unto her, I am the resurrection, and the life: he that believeth in me, though he were dead, yet shall he live." (John xi.25.)

3. He gives his people eternal life.

    "And I give unto them eternal life; and they shall never perish, neither shall any man pluck them out of my hand." (John x.28.)

4. The crown of eternal life is only for the faithful.

    "Be thou faithful unto death, and I will give thee a crown of life." (Rev.ii.10.)

5. If we overcome by Christ, we shall eat of the tree of life.

"He that hath an ear, let him hear what the Spirit saith unto the churches; To him that overcomeths will I give to eat of the tree of life, which is in the midst of the paradise of God." (Rev. ii.7.)

6. Jesus proclaims himself the Light of the world.

"Then spake Jesus again unto them, saying, I am the light of the world: he that followeth me shall not walk in darkness, but shall have the light of life." (John viii.12.)

7. If we walk in his light, his blood cleanseth us from all sin.

"If we walk in the light, as he is in the light, we have fellowship one with another, and the blood of Jesus Christ his [God's] Son cleanseth us from all sin. (1 John. i.7.)

8. Such as walk in darkness have no fellowship with the light.

"This the is the message which we have heard of him, and declare unto you, that God is light, and in him is no darkness at all. If we say that we have fellowship with him, and walk in darkness, we lie, and do not the truth." (John i.5, 6.)

9. Our light and life are in him.

"In him was life; and the life was the light of men." (John i.4.)

28
IS IT RIGHT TO USE TOBACCO?

We answer, No!
I. Christians should live only for Christ.
1. Even our eating and drinking must glorify God.

"Whether therefore ye eat, or drink, or whatsoever ye do, do all for the glory of God." (1 Cor. x.31.)

2. Do all, both word and deed, in Jesus' name.

"And whatsoever ye do in word or deed, do all in the name of the Lord Jesus, giving thanks to God and the Father by him." (Col. iii.17.)

3. Let us follow the disciples as they followed Christ.

"And ye became followers of us, and of the Lord, having received the word in much affliction, with joy of the Holy Ghost." (1 Thess. i.6.)

II. We should not waste the money spent for tobacco.
1. All things belong only to God.

"The earth is the Lord's, and the fullness thereof; the world, and they that dwell therein." (Ps. xxiv.1.)

2. We must lay up our money as treasure in heaven.

"Lay not up for yourselves treasures upon earth, where moth and rust doth corrupt, and where thieves break through and steal: but lay up for yourselves treasures in heaven, where neither moth nor rust doth corrupt, and where thieves do not break through nor steal: for where your treasure is, there will your heart be also." (Matt. vi.19-21.)

3. We should be faithful in money's use.

"And I say unto you, Make to yourselves friends of the mammon of unrighteousness; that, when ye fail, they may receive you into everlasting habitations. He that is faithful in that which is least is faithful also in much: and he that is unjust in the least is unjust also in much. If therefore ye have not been faithful in the unrighteous mammon, who will commit to your trust the true riches? And if ye have not been faithful in that which is another man's, who shall give you that which is your own?" (Luke xvi.9-12.)

III. Tobacco is filthy, hence should not be used.
1. Should be cleansed of all filthiness of flesh, etc.

"Having therefore these promises, dearly beloved, let us cleanse ourselves from all filthiness of the flesh and spirit, perfecting holiness in the fear of God." (2 Cor. vii.1.)

IV. Let us be fit temples for God's indwelling.
1. The Christian is the temple of the Holy Ghost.

"Know ye not that ye are the temple of God, and that the Spirit of God dwelleth in you?" (1 Cor. iii.16.)

We object to the use of tobacco, because
I. *Christians must be Christ-like.* Does any one think Christ would chew, smoke, or snuff tobacco? if not, ought

any follower of his to do so? What! a *Christian* do what Christ could not do! If it were wrong for Christ to use it, he would not do it; and if he would not, should his followers, who claim to have renounced the world, the flesh, and the devil, that they might take up their cross daily, and follow Christ? (Matt. xvi.24.)

1. Is our position, here assumed, unreasonable, or in any wise too strong? Let the inspired pen answer: *"Whether therefore ye eat, or drink, or whatsoever ye do, do all to the glory of God."* That is, do all in imitation of Christ; follow the divine pattern; consult the will, the glory, the honor of God in every thing. Does chewing, smoking, dipping, glorify God? Does the habit show Christ-likeness in any way? does it commend your Saviour to men, and indicate to the world that you have "been with Jesus," and have learned of him? Does *slavery* to such a weed show the spirit of Christian freedom? Can you ask God to bless your example before others, especially the young, while using the filthy weed? Christ says: "Ye are the light of the world." Can your light *shine* with undimmed luster through clouds of tobacco-smoke and pools of spittle? Can you lay your tobacco down on God's altar, offer thanks for the "precious weed," and pray his richest blessing to attend your example in its use? Answer these questions, one by one, not "to get around them," but with honesty as at the bar of God, in examination on my text. "Whether ye *eat, or drink*, or whatsoever ye do, *do all to the glory of God.*"

2. This text simply confirms, corroborates, and strengthens the other just noticed. "Do all in the name [that is, in the spirit, in harmony with the name] of Jesus." You cannot gamble, or drink whisky in the name of Jesus; you cannot raffle (notwithstanding some backslidden Churches, sold out to the devil root and branch, do such things) in the holy name of Jesus. Then, I ask, can you use an expensive, filthy, nauseating, disgusting weed to

the glory of God, *in the name of Jesus?* Answer as at God's judgment bar, brother, and you will be sure to quit, "once for all."

3. The disciples were but men, yet they followed Christ and bade us follow them. Reader, how do you think Paul and Peter would have looked with cigars, James and John with pipes, Philip and Bartholomew with chews; and "Mary, the mother of Jesus," and the other Mary, with brush and box? Let us follow them, as they followed Christ.

II. *Tobacco-using is very wasteful; therefore wrong.* It is estimated that the tobacco bill of the United States—this Christian (?) nation, this land of Bibles—is $600,000,000 per year. Spell it out: *six hundred millions of dollars a year!* Here is a great waste, and each user of the weed is responsible not simply for the part that he spends, but for his influence in countenancing and patronizing this enormous waste of money, that might feed the hungry, clothe the naked, house the homeless, and send the gospel to the uttermost parts of the earth; thus hastening the triumph of Christ in all the world. The Bible confirms the idea here set forth.

1. "The earth is the Lord's." Who can have the impudence to stand up in the presence of the "Lord of all the earth," and try to justify this wholesale waste of God's funds? Who can ask God to smile his approval, while thousands of men and women are taken from employments that would elevate mankind, glorify God, and bless the world; to spend their time and strength in cultivating, preparing, and handling a filthy, poisonous narcotic, the use of which pollutes the pure air, stains the earth, and—alas, how often!—besmears the sanctuary of the living God, the holy temple of his worship? "Honor the Lord with thy substance." (Pro. iii.9.)

2. "Lay up for yourself treasure in heaven." Our country spends $3,000,000 (*three millions*) annually to spread

the gospel among the nations which know not our Christ; albeit his last words were "Go teach all nations," "preach the gospel to every creature." As people we owe all to the gospel of Christ, who became poor that we might be rich (2 Cor. viii.9), and at times we profess great love for him, but we respond to his parting words with $3,000,000, and then form a filthy habit, create an unnatural appetite, and spend $600,000,000 a year on it! $3,000,000 to save the world for which Christ bled and died, and $600,000,000 in chewing, dipping, and burning incense to the devil; and this is not left for worldlings and sinners, but in the mighty procession of incense-burners may be seen deacons, stewards, elders, class-leaders, singers, shouters, and preachers of the gospel of self-denial! (Mark viii.34.) Homes with barefoot, thinly-clad, untaught children; with few or no books, papers, etc.; with poorly-spread tables; with debts unpaid, and accumulating; with the daily cry of "poverty," "hard times," etc.; with no money for pastoral support, and nothing for Missions, are yet spending from ten to fifty dollars a year for tobacco, while professing undying love for Christ. These things are not as they should be— *they are not Christ-like*. They do not increase the bank account in the skies; they lay up no treasure in heaven. We write with a heavy heart.

3. Christ requires faithfulness in the use of money. He bids us so use it here that souls may be saved by it, who will welcome us to the happy home above— the God-built mansions. "Make to yourselves friends of the mammon of unrighteousness; that, when ye fail [die], they [the friends made by using your money for God] may receive you into everlasting habitations"— that is, they will bid you welcome to the heavenly home. *Tobacco-spent money will produce no such results.*

III. *Tobacco is filthy and unhealthful.* Religion claims the whole being, body as well as soul. "Present your *bodies* a living sacrifice, holy, acceptable unto God... And be not conformed to this world." (Rom. xii.1, 2.)

1. We must "cleanse ourselves from all filthiness of the flesh and spirit, perfecting holiness in the fear of God." Tobacco is notoriously filthy. All who wish to be Christlike should cleanse themselves from it. See 1 John iii.1-3. It is unhealthful. How many sallow-faced, sickly women; lean, feeble, weakly men; spindling, diseased children owe all their ailments to tobacco, either used by themselves, or inherited from their parents. Consumptive, coughing women, their lungs full of snuff; feeble, diseased men, tobacco-poison coursing through every vein; emaciated, scrofulous children, death gnawing their puny lives away through inherited tobacco-poison— may God save the people!

IV. Temples of the Holy Ghost. What a glorious privilege! "Be pure," "cleanse yourselves," "be ye holy." "If a man love me, he will keep my words: and my Father will love him, and we will come unto him, and make our abode with him." (John xiv.23.)

1. If we are temples for God to dwell in, how important that we should be pure! Yet, many professing Christians pollute and defile their bodies with this nauseating narcotic, till they become a living stench.

Finally: Let each one resolve henceforth to follow Christ in all things. Live pure, earnest, holy, spiritual lives. Keep a tender conscience, sensitive to every motion of the Holy Spirit; and may we meet in that bright world where there is nothing unclean! Amen.

29
WINE AND SOME OF ITS RESULTS

1. New wine was given from God as a blessing.

   "Honor the Lord with thy substance, and with the first-fruits of all thine increase: so shall thy barns be filled with plenty, and thy presses shall burst out with new wine." (Pro. iii.9, 10.)

2. But fermented wine brings woe and sorrow; look not upon it.

   "Who hath woe? who hath sorrow? who hath contentions? who hath babbling? who hath wounds without a cause? who hath redness of eyes? They that tarry long at the wine; they that go to seek mixed wine. Look not thou upon the wine when it is red, when it giveth his color in the cup, when it moveth itself aright. At the last it biteth like a serpent, and stingeth like an adder." (Pro. xxiii.29-32.)

3. It is a mocker, and deceives the unwise.

   "Wine is a mocker, strong drink is raging: and whosoever is deceived thereby is not wise." (Prov. xx.1.)

4. Even the good man, Noah, was deceived by wine.

"And Noah began to be a husbandman, and he planted a vineyard: and he drank of the wine, and was drunken; and he was uncovered within his tent." (Gen. ix.20, 21.)

5. Wine and strong drink caused both priest and prophet to err.

"But they also have erred through wine, and through strong drink are out of the way; the priest and the prophet have erred through strong drink, they are swallowed up of wine, they are out of the way through strong drink; they err in vision, they stumble in judgment." (Isa. xxviii.7.)

6. Hell hath enlarged herself for such as are inflamed with wine.

"Woe unto them that rise up early in the morning, that they may follow strong drink; that continue until night, till wine inflame them! And the harp and viol, the tabret and pipe, and wine, are in their feasts: but they regard not the work of the Lord, neither consider the operation of his hands. Therefore my people are gone into captivity, because they have no knowledge: and their honorable men are famished, and their multitude dried up with thirst. Therefore hell hath enlarged herself, and opened her mouth without measure: and their glory, and their multitude, and their pomp, and he that rejoiceth, shall descend into it." (Isa. v.11-14.)

7. Woe to them that are mighty to drink wine, which justify the wicked!

"Woe unto them that are mighty to drink wine, and men of strength to mingle strong drink: which justify the wicked for reward, and take away the righteousness of the righteous from him!" (Isa. v, 22, 23.)

30
BACKSLIDING

1. There were some who left their first love.

   "Nevertheless I have somewhat against thee, because thou hast left thy first love." (Rev. ii.4.)

2. Backsliders in heart are filled with their own ways.

   "The backslider in heart shall be filled with his own ways: and a good man shall be satisfied from himself." (Prov. xiv.14.)

3. The backslider must repent and do his first works.

   "Remember therefore from whence thou art fallen, and repent, and do the first works; or else I will come unto thee quickly, and will remove thy candlestick out of his place, except thou repent." (Rev. ii.5.)

4. The lukewarm, cold backslider God will spew out.

   "I know thy works, that thou art neither cold nor hot: I would thou wert cold or hot. So then because thou art lukewarm, and neither cold nor hot, I will spew thee out of my mouth." (Rev. iii.15, 16.)

5. The backslider sins against his God.

"O Lord, though our iniquities testify against us, do thou it for thy name's sake: for our backslidings are many; we have sinned against thee." (Jer. xiv.7.)

6. Great men knew the way of the Lord, but broke his yoke.

"I will get me unto the great men, and will speak unto them; for they have known the way of Lord, and the judgment of their God: but these have altogether broken the yoke, and burst the bonds. Wherefore a lion out of the forest shall slay them, and a wolf of the evenings shall spoil them, a leopard shall watch over their cities: every one that goeth out thence shall be torn in pieces: because their transgressions are many, and their backslidings are increased." (Jer. v.5, 6.)

7. God's people prone to backsliding from him.

"And my people are bent to backsliding from me: though they called them to the Most High, none at all would exalt him." (Hosea xi.7.)

8. Our God will save the returning backslider.

"O Israel, return unto the Lord thy God; for thou hast fallen by thine iniquity." "I will heal their backsliding, I will love them freely: for mine anger is turned away from him." (Hosea xiv.1, 4.)

9. He pleads with the backsliders to return, and promises to heal them.

"Return, ye backsliding children, and I will heal your backslidings. Behold, we come unto thee; for thou art the Lord our God." (Jer. iii.22.)

31
FUTURE PUNISHMENT

1. The wicked will be turned down to hell.

   "The wicked shall be turned into hell, and all the nations that forget God." (Ps. ix.17.)

2. If we escape eternal punishment, we must part with every sin.

   "And if thy right eye offend thee, pluck it out, and cast it from thee: for it is profitable for thee that one of thy members should perish, and not that thy whole body should be cast into hell. And if thy right hand offend thee, cut it off, and cast it from thee: for it is profitable for thee that one of thy members should perish, and not that thy whole body should be cast into hell." (Matt. v.29, 30.)

3. As life is eternal, so punishment is everlasting.

   "And these shall go away into everlasting punishment: but the righteous into life eternal." (Matt. xxv.46.)

4. There shall be weeping and gnashing of teeth.

"So shall it be at the end of the world: the angels shall come forth, and sever the wicked from among the just, and shall cast them into the furnace of fire: there shall be wailing and gnashing of teeth." (Matt. xiii.49, 50.)

5. Hypocrites receive as their doom the damnation of hell.

"Woe unto you, scribes and Pharisees, hypocrites! for ye devour widows' houses, and for a pretense make long prayer: therefore ye shall receive the greater damnation." "Ye serpents, ye generation of vipers, how can ye escape the damnation of hell?" (Matt. 14, 33.)

6. To the sinner shame and everlasting contempt.

"And many of them that sleep in the dust of the earth shall awake, some to everlasting life, and some to shame and everlasting contempt." (Dan. xii.2.)

7. Eternal life, the gift of God, but death the wages of sin.

"For the wages of sin is death; but the gift of God is eternal life through Jesus Christ our Lord." (Rom vi.23.)

8. God bids us shun this eternal death in sin.

"Say unto them, As I live, saith the Lord God, I have no pleasure in the death of the wicked; but that the wicked turn from his way and live: turn ye, turn ye from your evil ways; for why will ye die, O house of Israel?" (Ezek. xxxiii.11.)

9. An impassable gulf— this life, probation— lies between heaven and hell.

"And it came to pass, that the beggar died, and was carried by the angels into Abraham's bosom: the rich man also died, and was buried; and in hell he lifted up his eyes, being in torments, and seeth Abraham afar off, and Lazarus in his bosom. And he cried and said, Father Abraham, have mercy on me, and send Lazarus, that he may dip the tip of his finger in water, and cool my tongue; for I am tormented in this flame. But Abraham said, Son, remember that thou in thy life-time receivedst thy good things, and likewise Lazarus evil things: but now he is comforted, and thou art tormented. And beside all this, between us and you there is a great gulf fixed: so that they which would pass from hence to you cannot; neither can they pass to us, that would come from thence, (Luke xvi.22-26.)

32
SOME BIBLE "COMES"
No. 1

1. *Come* into the ark— God's invitation to Noah.

   "And the Lord said unto Noah, Come thou and all thy house into the ark; for thee have I seen righteous before me in this generation." (Gen. vii.1.)

2. The day *cometh*.

   "Behold, the day of the Lord cometh, cruel both with wrath and fierce anger, to lay the land desolate; and he shall destroy the sinners thereof out of it." (Isa. xiii.9.)

3. The day that *cometh* shall burn as an oven.

   "For, behold, the day cometh, that shall burn as an oven; and all the proud, yea, and all that do wickedly, shall be stubble: and the day that cometh shall burn them up, saith the Lord of hosts, that it shall leave them neither root nor branch." (Mal. iv.1.)

4. Who may abide in the day of his *coming*?

   "But who may abide the day of his coming? and who

shall stand when he appeareth? for he is like a refiner's fire, and like fullers' soap. (Mal. iii.2.)

5. God's redeemed shall *come* with singing unto Zion.

"Therefore the redeemed of the Lord shall return, and come with singing unto Zion; and everlasting joy shall be upon their head: they shall obtain gladness and joy; and sorrow and mourning shall flee away." (Isa. li.11.)

6. He who redeemed us from sin shall *come* to Zion.

"And the Redeemer shall come to Zion, and unto them that turn from transgression in Jacob, saith the Lord." (Isa. lix.20.)

7. *Come*, let us join to the Lord in a perpetual covenant.

"They shall ask the way to Zion with their faces thitherward, saying, Come, and let us join ourselves to the Lord in a perpetual covenant that shall not be forgotten." (Jer. l. 5.)

8. The Lord God will *come* with strong arm.

"Behold, the Lord God will come with strong hand, and his arm shall rule for him: behold, his reward is with him, and his work before him." (Isa. xl. 10.)

9. They which were ready to perish shall *come* and worship.

"And it shall come to pass in that day, that the great trumpet shall be blown, and they shall come which were ready to perish in the land of Assyria, and the outcasts in the land of Egypt, and shall worship the Lord in the holy mount at Jerusalem." (Isa. xxvii.13.)

10. Yea, all flesh shall come to worship the Lord.

"And it shall come to pass, that from one new moon

to another, and from one Sabbath to another, shall all flesh come to worship before me, saith the Lord." (Isa. lxvi.23.)

1. "Come into the ark" is God's invitation to all who are in danger, to all the homeless, shelterless, suffering, sin-cursed wanderers of the earth.

2, 3, and 4. These verses declare the coming of God's great day of wrath and judgment, which shall burn with the fierceness of his anger, against all manner of wickedness. The sinner will reap the reward of his doing in the fiery wrath of his God, whose coming then is not to call men to mercy and salvation, but to judgment unto condemnation.

5 and 6. Here the redeemed of the Lord come into his presence with joy and gladness, and with songs and shouts of victory. He is their Defense, and they rejoice in his protection; their Shepherd, they glory in his guidance; their Comforter, they are happy in the smiles of his love, and their sorrow and sighing flee far away. He comes into his Zion— the Church of the living God— and abides with such as turn from transgression. His presence is the security, the comfort, and the strength of Zion.

7. Here is the invitation that shall go from lip to lip, till all shall come into the covenant fold of the Lord of hosts.

8. The Lord omnipotent will come with stretched-out arm. He shall rule the people, govern among men, and save his redeemed. He shall carry forward his work and distribute his rewards.

9 and 10. The needy shall come with such as are ready to perish, and our God shall supply them. All people shall come before him with prayers and songs to his grace, while the hosts of heaven and earth join in his praise "and crown him Lord of all."

All hail the power of Jesus name!
  Let angels prostrate fall;
Bring forth the royal diadem,
  And crown him Lord of all.

33
SOME BIBLE "COMES"
No. 2

1. Jesus says: "*Come* unto me,... I will give you rest."

   "Come unto me, all ye that labor and are heavy laden, and I will give you rest. Take my yoke upon you, and learn of me; for I am meek and lowly in heart: and ye shall find rest unto your souls." (Matt. xi.28, 29.)

2. God wills that all should *come* to repentance.

   "The Lord is not slack concerning his promise, as some men count slackness; but is longsuffering to us-ward, not willing that any should perish, but that all should come to repentance." (2 Pet. iii.9.)

3. Whosoever will *come* may do so.

   "And the Spirit and the bride say, Come. And let him that heareth say, Come. And let him that is athirst come. And whosoever will, let him take the water of life freely." (Rev. xxii.17.)

4. All who *come* will be received.

   "All that the Father giveth me shall come to me; and

him that cometh to me I will in no wise cast out." (John vi.37.)

5. Let all who thirst *come* to Jesus and drink.

"In the last day, that great day of the feast, Jesus stood and cried, saying, If any man thirst, let him come unto me, and drink." (John vii.37.)

6. But some *will not come*.

"And ye will not come to me, that ye might have life." (John v.40.)

7. The Son of man *came* not to destroy, but to save.

"For the Son of man is not come to destroy men's lives, but to save them. And they went to another village." (Luke ix.56.)

8. He *came* to save that which was lost.

"For the Son of man is come to seek and to save that which was lost." (Luke xix.10.)

9. The resurrection is *coming*.

"Marvel not at this: for the hour is coming in the which all that are in the graves shall hear his voice, and shall come forth; they that have done good, unto the resurrection of life; and they that have done evil, unto the resurrection of damnation." (John v.28, 29.)

10. God's wrath *cometh* upon the disobedient.

"Mortify therefore your members which are upon the earth; fornication, uncleanness, inordinate affection, evil concupiscence, and covetousness, which is idolatry: for which things' sake the wrath of God cometh on the children of disobedience." (Col. iii.5, 6.)

34
MINISTERIAL SUPPORT

1. The minister's mission— he is an ambassador for God.

"Now then we are ambassadors for Christ, as though God did beseech you by us: we pray you in Christ's stead, be ye reconciled to God." (2 Cor. v.20)

2. As God's messenger, he must keep knowledge and do his work.

"For the priest's lips should keep knowledge, and they should seek the law at his mouth: for he is the messenger of the Lord of hosts." (Mal. ii.7.)

3. The Church should pray for more ministers of God.

"Therefore said he unto them, The harvest truly is great, but the laborers are few: pray ye therefore the Lord of the harvest, that he would send forth laborers into his harvest." (Luke x.2.)

4. Under God's call, the minister *must* preach. Necessity is on him.

"For though I preach the gospel, I have nothing to

glory of: for necessity is laid upon me; yea, woe is unto me, if I preach not the gospel!" (1 Cor. ix.16.)

5. But who shall fight another's battles at his own expense?

"Who goeth a warfare any time at his own charges? who planteth a vineyard, and eateth not of the fruit thereof? or who feedeth a flock, and eateth not of the milk of the flock?" (1 Cor. ix.7.)

6. The minister in the temple lives of the things of the temple.

"Do ye not know that they which minister about holy things live of the things of the temple? and they which wait at the altar are partakers with the altar?" (1 Cor. ix.13.)

7. God also ordains that the minister live by his ministry.

"Even so hath the Lord ordained that they which preach the gospel should live of the gospel." (1 Cor. ix.14.)

8. The Saviour teaches that the workman is entitled to his living.

"Nor scrip for your journey, neither two coats, neither shoes, nor yet staves: for the workman is worthy of his meat." (Matt. x.10.)

9. Simple justice rewards the laborer. He is worthy of it.

"For the Scripture saith, Thou shalt not muzzle the ox that treadeth out the corn. And, The laborer is worthy of his reward." (1 Tim. v.18.)

10. The laborer's hire withheld brings down Divine vengeance.

"Behold, the hire of the laborers who have reaped

down your fields, which is of you kept back by fraud, crieth: and the cries of them which have reaped are entered into the ears of the Lord of Sabaoth. (Jas. v.4.)

In many places our ministers are not properly supported. Some people pauperize their preachers. They fail to pay them just and living salaries for their services, and instead dole out niggardly pittances (which they call "giving") to their pastor, as though he were a beggar. This system is curse with a curse, because it robs God, dishonoring him whose representative the minister is.

1. The preacher is a minister or representative of God, an ambassador of heaven, and consequently a wrong or injustice done him in his ministerial capacity is an insult to Almighty God. The minister or ambassador of any government is supposed to be supported by the government he represents. Our text calls the preacher the ambassador of Christ. If, then, you stint him, you rob and insult Christ. Do not the Scriptures bear out this idea? "All tithe of the land is the *Lord's*." "The tenth shall be holy unto the *Lord*." (Lev. xxvii.30, 32.) "Honor the *Lord* with thy substance," etc. (Prov. iii.9, 10.) "Will a man rob *God*? Yet ye have robbed me." (Mal. iii.8-12.) Now, God doesn't say, "Honor the preacher with thy substance; will a man rob the preacher?" but, "Will a man rob God?" He makes the preacher of the gospel his minister, and ordains for the minister to be supported in his name. Hence the way that many beggarize the minister, by failing to pay— not give— him a just support is a mockery of heaven, an insult to Deity.

2. The minister— "the messenger of the Lord of hosts" — "should keep knowledge." This requires two things: 1. Suitable libraries, books, periodicals, etc., for study. This necessitates heavy expense, which must

be provided. 2. Time to study. This he cannot have without he is properly cared for in all the needs of himself and family.

3. This sets forth the source of supply. We must pray *the Lord* to send forth laborers. Ministers of the gospel must be called of God, and not of man. When we recognize a divine call to the ministry all we assume here is established. His support, then, will measure our obedience to God; the amount of our gifts, according to the requirements of the case and our ability, will be the expression of our devotion to God who sent and is represented by the minister. If a merchant seeks a clerk, or a farmer a laborer, the fact of seeking the man implies a willingness to support him— to pay him for his services. So, the prayer for more laborers implies a readiness to provide for their support when the petition is answered and they are sent. And to refuse then to provide for them is a breach of trust, a sin against Heaven.

4. This text tightens the lines we have drawn. The preacher loses himself in his mission; necessity is laid upon him, and he cries out: "Woe is unto me, if I preach not the gospel!" With him it is not a matter of choice. You have prayed for laborers; God has heard your cry, and lays it upon him to answer your call. He *must go*, or reject the call of the Lord of the harvest; to do which is to sin against God, and brings judgment upon his own soul. But he answers the call, and enters the vineyard of his Lord and yours. You rejoice in his labors, but refuse him just support, and pauperize him among men. He is greatly wronged; Heaven is highly insulted; and the "woe" that he escaped falls upon your head. "Ye are cursed with a curse: for ye have robbed me," saith the Lord of the harvest.

5. This text illustrates the subject. No man must be left to feed himself while fighting the battles of his country. No laborers shall plant and till a vineyard,

and lack for fruit. Nor shall he who keeps the flock perish for milk. So also,

6. They which minister about holy things live of the things of the temple, and they which wait at the altar are partakers with the altar. So God here associates his ministers with his own altar. If your substance then is laid on God's altar in consecration to his service, there will be no trouble about the pay of your preacher, for God says he is partaker with the altar. While there is any thing on God's altar his servant shall be supplied. But, brother, "the earth is the Lord's" (Ps. xxiv.1); and if you withhold from God, you see at once the force of Malachi's searching question, "Will a man rob God?"

7. The Lord hath ordained — provided, arranged, required — that they which preach the gospel should live of the gospel. There are those who do not believe in supporting preachers. Which is the better authority — they or their God? They who oppose the support of the ministry oppose the God who ordained it, and such as slight and neglect it do so not simply to the man, but to God who sent him.

8. But here the minister is represented as a workman who is *worthy* of his support. The preacher should be devoted to his work and diligent in his every duty. Then he should be paid like men in other vocations. His pay is not for his preaching on Sunday, but for his week-day time as a student to qualify himself for his ministry, and as a pastor devoting himself to the work of the Church.

9. Stewards and other collectors for the ministry sometimes beg for a "little something to keep the preacher and his family from suffering." Such a statement puts the minister of the Church of God on the plane of a pauper, and is an insult to his manhood, to the Church of which he is a member, and to the great God whom he represents. When a given Church fails to pay a faithful man of God a living salary for his services such act brands

as dishonest each and every member of that Church who has not cleared his or her skirts of the crime by a *faithful* and *liberal effort* to meet the obligation. And when this is done by all, the minister will never be brought to want or be classed as a mendicant.

10. Withholding the laborer's reward, of which he is worthy, is a fraud; and his cry will enter into the ears of the Lord. Judgment will come to your house, and condemnation will rest upon your soul.

May God's people learn lessons of faithfulness! and may the spirit of liberality to our ministers— and all other good causes— rest upon us all! Amen!

35
SHOUTING

1. Let the righteous be glad and shout out for joy.

   "Be glad in the Lord, and rejoice, ye righteous: and shout for joy, all ye that are upright in heart." (Ps. xxxii.11.)

2. The upright in heart shall glory, trusting in the Lord.

   "The righteous shall be glad in the Lord, and shall trust in him; and all the upright in heart shall glory." (Ps. lxiv.10.)

3. David shouted, singing the "new song" at his conversion.

   "I waited patiently for the Lord; and he inclined unto me, and heard my cry. He brought me up also out of a horrible pit, out of the miry clay, and set my feet upon a rock, and established my goings. And he hath put a new song in my mouth, even praise unto our God: many shall see it, and fear, and shall trust in the Lord." (Ps. xl. 1-3.)

4. God gave Jericho to the Israelites while they were shouting.

"And it came to pass at the seventh time, when the priests blew with the trumpets, Joshua said unto the people, Shout; for the Lord hath given you the city." "So the people shouted when the priests blew with the trumpets: and it came to pass, when the people heard the sound of the trumpet, and the people shouted with a great shout, that the wall fell down flat, so that the people went up into the city, every man straight before him, and they took the city." (Josh. vi.16, 20.)

5. The angels shouted at the advent of the Saviour.

"And suddenly there was with the angel a multitude of the heavenly host praising God, and saying, Glory to God in the highest, and on earth peace, good will toward men." (Luke ii.13, 14.)

6. So the disciples shouted as Jesus went up to Jerusalem.

"And when he was come nigh, even now at the descent of the mount of Olives, the whole multitude of the disciples began to rejoice and praise God with a loud voice for all the mighty works that they had seen; saying, Blessed be the King that cometh in the name of the Lord: peace in heaven, and glory in the highest." (Luke xix.37, 38.)

7. Jesus defends their shouting in his answer to the carping Pharisees.

"And some of the Pharisees from among the multitude said unto him, Master, rebuke thy disciples. And he answered and said unto them, I tell you that, if these should hold their peace, the stones would immediately cry out." (Luke xix.39, 40.)

8. David describes the shouting as being with triumph and clapping of hands.

"O clap your hands, all ye people; shout unto God with the voice of triumph." (Ps. xlvii.1.)

9. How the multitude shout in heaven "Alleluia!"

"And the four and twenty elders and the four beasts fell down and worshiped God that sat on the throne, saying, Amen: Alleluia. And a voice came out of the throne, saying, Praise our God, all ye his servants, and ye that fear him, both small and great. And I heard as it were the voice of a great multitude, and as the voice of many waters, and as the voice of mighty thunderings, saying, Alleluia: for the Lord God omnipotent reigneth. Let us be glad and rejoice, and give honor to him: for the marriage of the Lamb is come, and his wife hath made herself ready." (Rev. xix.4-7.)

Shouting is a noisy demonstration of exultant joy in God. It comes from a sense of God's mercy and love being realized in the heart.

1. David says: "Let the righteous [those who are right with God] be glad" in the Lord and "shout for joy." If we are right with God, we have reason to be glad, and our joy in the Lord is naturally expressed in the loud voice of praise.

2. The upright in heart (those whose hearts are running up after God, heavenward) shall glory, or rejoice, or feel jubilant and happy. And why? Because they trust (have confidence, faith, reliance, rest) in God. If God is the object of our soul's affection and trust, in him we will surely rejoice as our strong Tower.

3. A beautiful figure of David's conversion is given us in the One Hundredth and Sixteenth Psalm. "The sorrows of death compassed me, and the pains of hell gat hold upon me: I found trouble and sorrow," etc. See Psalm cxvi.3-9. The new song— a song of redemption, of praise— was given to him from on high— "put in his mouth." It

was *new*: he could sing before, but not the exultant song of praise. It produces great results too. "Many shall see it, and fear, and shall trust in the Lord." I have seen the new convert arise praising God, and the congregation would melt down under the sense of the Divine presence.

4. That was a wonderful victory of faith when they Israelites marched around Jericho that last time, and at God's word they raised their shouts of victory even before the walls fell. They shouted under Divine command and purely by faith. The faith that could shout in advance— on credit, as it were, before there was a crack in the walls— was a faith that pleased God and wrought the victory. "By faith the walls of Jericho fell down." (Heb. xi.30.) This shouting was surely well pleasing unto God, for it was by his command, and was crowned with blessing.

5. When Christ was born and the angels announced his advent there appeared "a multitude of the heavenly host praising God [shouting], and saying, Glory to God in the highest, and on earth peace, good will toward men." That shout of praise was a spark from heaven to kindle the fires of joy in the hearts of men and send the triumphant songs and shouts of redemption around this earth of ours. Glory be to God, that song is echoing with heavenly melody on earth yet! "Salvation's rolling on."

6. The disciples raised their glad shouts as Jesus was going up to Jerusalem. But then, as now, there were the Pharisees— cold, formal, lifeless— who opposed shouting. They demanded that Jesus stop it (or perhaps they would "leave the meeting"). But Jesus said: "If these should hold their peace, the stones would immediately cry out." Divine power was present, and God was glorified in the praise of his people. He will never rebuke true heart-felt shouts of praise, because he is glorified thereby.

7.. We sometimes see people in meetings where revival power is manifest and shouts of newborn souls rend the air, crying out: "Excitement! excitement!" To such we would recommend the exhortation of the Psalmist: "*O clap your hands, all ye people*; shout unto God with the voice of triumph." He could see no objection to shouting with the voice and clapping the hands, and that it be general with "all the people," which is surely very extensive excitement.

8. Finally inspiration lifts the veil, and we get a glimpse of the redeemed, the righteous, the holy ones before God's throne in heaven; and lo! they are shouting there. The vast multitude "as the voice of many waters, and as the voice of mighty thunderings, saying Alleluia: for the Lord God omnipotent reigneth." Let all the people of God on earth join in the mighty refrain; yea, "let every thing that hath breath praise the Lord." Amen! and "praise ye the Lord."

36
GIVING (OLD TESTAMENT)
No. 1

1. God's ownership— the earth is his.

   "The earth is the Lord's, and the fullness thereof; the world, and they that dwell therein." (Ps. xxiv.1.)

2. He demands a tithe (tenth) for holy uses.

   "And all the tithe of the land, whether of the seed of the land, or of the fruit of the tree, is the Lord's: it is holy unto the Lord." "And concerning the tithe of the herd, or of the flock, even of whatsoever passeth under the rod, the tenth shall be holy unto the Lord." (Lev. xxvii.30, 32.)

3. This was not a new law with Moses. Abraham paid tithes.

   "And Melchizedek king of Salem brought forth bread and wine: and he was the priest of the most high God. And he blessed him, and said, Blessed be Abram of the most high God, possessor of heaven and earth: and blessed be the most high God, which hath delivered thine enemies into thy hand. And he gave him tithes of all." (Gen. xiv.18-20.)

4. His grandson, Jacob, also practiced this rule.

"And Jacob vowed a vow, saying, If God will be with me, and will keep me in this way that I go, and will give me bread to eat, and raiment to put on, so that I come again to my father's house in peace; then shall the Lord be my God: and this stone, which I have set up for a pillar, shall be God's house: and of all that thou shalt give me I will surely give the tenth unto thee." (Gen. xxviii.20-22.)

5. God calls those robbers who withhold the tithe.

"Will a man rob God? Yet ye have robbed me. But ye say, Wherein have we robbed thee? In tithes and offerings. Ye are cursed with a curse: for ye have robbed me, even this whole nation." (Mal. iii.8, 9.)

6. He promises abundant reward to such as bring him the tithes.

"Bring ye all the tithes into the store-house, that there may be meat in mine house, and prove me now herewith, saith the Lord of hosts, if I will not open you the windows of heaven, and pour you out a blessing, that there shall not be room enough to receive it. And I will rebuke the devourer for your sakes, and he shall not destroy the fruits of your ground; neither shall your vine cast her fruit before the time in the field, saith the Lord of hosts." (Mal. iii.10, 11.)

7. God will prosper us with plenty if we honor him with our means.

"Honor the Lord with thy substance, and with the first-fruits of all thine increase: so shall thy barns be filled with plenty, and thy presses shall burst out with new wine." (Prov. iii.9, 10.)

8. Liberal scattering brings a rich increase.

"There is that scattereth, and yet increaseth; and there is that withholdeth more than is meet, but it tendeth to poverty. The liberal soul shall be made fat: and he that watereth shall be watered also himself." (Prov. xi.24, 25.)

9. A time when more was given than was needed.

"And they spake unto Moses, saying, The people bring much more than enough for the service of the work, which the Lord commanded to make. And Moses gave commandment, and they caused it to be proclaimed throughout the camp, saying, Let neither man nor woman make any more work or the offering of the sanctuary. So the people were restrained from bringing. For the stuff they had was sufficient for all the work to make it, and too much." (Ex. xxxvi.5-7.) See Exodus xxxv.20-29.

Too many people feel themselves burdened in meeting the demands upon them, financially, in religious and benevolent directions. They feel that they are poorer by all they give, and think it rather an imposition that they are called upon so often to help in the "collections." Let us study the word of God on this question a little.

1. The earth upon which we live belongs to God. The ground which produces all we eat, the sunshine and rain, the day for labor, and the night for rest, are all the Lord's. Of all we eat and wear, or use and enjoy, there is nothing that does not come from God. So we too are the Lord's. He made us, and to him belong. It seems but reasonable, then, since all we are and have belong to God, that, if he has an interest in the earth, we should care for it; if he

has a cause, we should assist I propagating it. But does he make such demands upon us? Listen:

2. All the tithe— literally, tenth— is holy unto the Lord. Concerning the herd, the tenth shall be holy unto the Lord. Here God, who says the earth is his, claims his rents, and says the tenth shall be holy unto him. It must be devoted to his work, to the advancement of his kingdom, the promotion of his glory in the earth. God does not here appear as a beggar asking alms, but as a landlord with authority, demanding his rights. *The tenth shall be holy unto the Lord*. Mark you: holy unto the *Lord*, not the priest or Levite, but the Most High.

3. Melchizedek was the priest of God, and being without priestly lineage, genealogy, or descent, he was typical of Christ. When Abram returned from the slaughter of the kings, bringing with him the goods of the Sodomites, together with the people who were carried away captives, he paid to Melchizedek, the priest of God and type of Christ, the tithe of the goods taken. Then the king of Sodom told him to give him his people and keep the goods, but Abram refused, saying: "I will not take any thing that is thine,… save only that which the young men have eaten, and the portion of the men which went with me;… let them take their portion." (Gen. xiv.23, 24.) Well, Abram, while making exceptions, why do you not mention the tithe you paid the priest? You are inconsistent to mention even the small amount eaten by the young men, and still not mention the tenth you gave to Melchizedek. Abram replies: "The tithe was not the king's. These wicked Sodomites have withheld their tithes from the Lord, and as God had given the things into my hands in battle, it became my duty to pay to God that which was his, and return to the king of Sodom his own, with the exceptions I named."

4. Jacob also recognized this law of the tithe as the will of God when he vows: "If God will be with me,… of all

thou shalt give me I will surely give the tenth unto thee." As though he had said: "Lord, I know that thou dost require the tithe, and with thy blessing on me I will certainly meet the obligation." Now, here is Abraham recognizing God's tithe law, and his grandson, Jacob, consenting to it as an obligation, long before it was enacted as a law for the Jews by Moses. Yet there are those who contend that the tithe was simply a Mosaic law and is not now in force, but we here find it before Moses as the law of religious giving. Has any Christian met his obligation who falls below it? *Surely not.*

5. "*Will a man rob God?*" How searching the question! how stunning the interrogation! Will a man rob God? It seems that all our nature— yea, all people— would rise up quickly and answer vehemently, "No! a thousand times, *No!*" but place your hand to your lips, for God speaks: "*Yet ye have robbed me.*" How, Lord? "In tithes and offerings. Ye are cursed with a curse." Why, Lord? O why? "*For ye have robbed me!*" So the stinginess which man calls a necessity, and thinks but prudent economy, God calls *robbery*. Awake, ye people, and bring in the tithes to God's house.

6. God promises prosperity to us if we bring in all the tithes. We have known preachers to use this passage: "Will a man rob God?" "bring ye all the tithes in," etc., in revival meetings and urge the people to pray, talk to sinners, and in many ways seek to promote the revival: all of which was right, and very important, but it had no connection with the text whatever. It refers exclusively to the payment to God's cause of a tenth of our income. And such preaching as we have mentioned from this text is a fearful *perversion of God's word*. Many believe themselves unable to pay a tenth to God; but the fact is that he is poorer who does not, for God here pledges his blessing upon him who brings in the tithe, and challenges men to the test.

7. This shows that if God is settled with the first, and our substance is used to his glory, he will reward us with plenty, even full barns. The wine here promised as a blessing was harmless— a new, unfermented wine. When it ferments, "moveth itself aright," etc. (Prov. xxiii.31, 32), it becomes a curse, is not to be "looked upon"— i.e., favorably. In other words, keep from it, hate it, abhor it.

8. The figure here is of sowing and reaping. The man who keeps his seed, thinking himself too poor to plant, will soon realize that "there is that withholdeth more than is meet, but it tendeth to poverty." So it is here applied to giving: "The liberal soul shall be made fat." "Give, and it shall be given unto you."

9. That was a wonderful day when the people found the joy of giving, and their willing offerings made more than was needed. When the Church of God gets this spirit everywhere the gospel will spread through all the earth, and salvation's chorus will rend the skies. Heaven will rejoice, earth will shout the victories of our conquering Christ, and while all hell is draped in mourning we will "Crown him Lord of all." Our "God loveth a cheerful giver." To him be glory forever. Amen.

37
GIVING (NEW TESTAMENT)
No. 2

1. Christ commended the payment of tithes as a duty.

"But woe unto you, Pharisees! for ye tithe mint and rue and all manner of herbs, and pass over judgment and the love of God: these ought ye to have done, and not to leave the other undone." (Luke xi.42.)

2. Levites received tithes: but One yet higher did likewise.

"And verily they that are of the sons of Levi, who receive the office of the priesthood, have a commandment to take tithes of the people according to the law, that is, of their brethren, though they come out of the loins of Abraham: but he whose descent is not counted from them received tithes of Abraham, and blessed him that had the promises. And without all contradiction the less is blessed of the better." (Heb. vii.5-7.)

3. Christ, who liveth in an unchangeable priesthood, receiveth tithes.

"But this man, because he continueth ever, hath an unchangeable priesthood." "And here men that die receive tithes; but there he receiveth them, of whom it is witnessed that he liveth. And as I may so say, Levi also, who receiveth tithes, paid tithes in Abraham."

4. Thus, by Bible rule, we should give regularly.

"Now concerning the collection for the saints, as I have given order to the Churches of Galatia, even so do ye. Upon the first day of the week let every one of you lay by him in store, as God hath prospered him, that there be no gatherings when I come." (1 Cor. xvi.1, 2.)

5. God loveth a cheerful (willing, liberal, anxious) giver.

"Every man according as he purposeth in his heart, so let him give; not grudgingly, or of necessity: for God loveth a cheerful giver." (2 Cor. ix.7.)

6. According as we sow, so we reap, whether bountifully or sparingly.

"But this I say, He which soweth sparingly shall reap also sparingly; and he which soweth bountifully shall reap also bountifully." (2 Cor. ix.6.)

7. It is more blessed to give than to receive.

"I have shewed you all things, how that so laboring ye ought to support the weak, and to remember the words of the Lord Jesus, how he said, It is more blessed to give than to receive." (Acts xx 35.)

8. Give, and it shall be given unto you.

"Give, and it shall be given unto you; good measure, pressed down, and shaken together, and running over, shall men give into your bosom. For with the same measure that ye mete withal it shall be measured to you again." (Luke vi.38.)

9. We should lay up our treasures in heaven

"Lay not up for yourselves treasures upon earth, where moth and rust doth corrupt, and where thieves break through and steal: but lay up for yourselves treasures in heaven, where neither moth nor rust doth corrupt, and where thieves do not break through nor steal: for where your treasure is, there will your heart be also." (Matt. vi.19-21.).

1. The Master said these Pharisees tithed all manner of herbs, even including "mint and rue." They show their hypocrisy, however, by simply attending to these outward, formal acts of duty and obedience, while the great underlying principles of Christian character— "judgment and the love of God" — were passed over. "These ought ye to have done, and not to leave the other undone." The tithes, he tells us, *ought* to have been paid, but no ceremonial or outward performance of duty can for once take the place of "judgment and the love of God." Get the heart right in the sight of God, and then neglect not to "bring in all the tithes," for the Master has said: "These ought ye" to do.

2 and 3. Here the Apostle Paul shows the imperishability of the tithe law of giving. He separates it from the perishable features of the Mosaic law, and connects with it, by the Melchizedek lineage, with the undying priesthood of Christ. "The sons of Levi... take tithes of the people according to the [Mosaic] law." "But he whose descent is not counted from them [not in their lineage, not dependent on them] received tithes of Abraham, and blessed him." He was greater, too, than Abraham, being the type of Christ. Melchizedek, representing the heavenly and eternal priesthood of Christ, received the tithes

of the Gentile Sodomites, thus showing that Christ, in his universal reign, should receive the tithes of the Gentiles as well as the Jews. For, let it be remembered, "The earth is the Lord's," and "All the tithe shall be *holy* unto *him*." The abolition of the Jewish ceremonial law can in nowise affect the permanency of this law of tithes, since Christ, who received the tithes from the Sodomites through Melchizedek by Abraham, "abideth a priest forever." His, the "unchangeable priesthood," received an installment of tithes on that memorable occasion, which has passed into history, and from which Paul's inspired pen draws a lesson for every Gentile, as well as Jewish, convert. "Here men that die receive tithes" — that is, they are paid to mortal men in Jesus' name. "But there he receiveth them, of whom it is witnessed that he liveth." When paid here to men in his name he receives them as to himself and gives us credit in the account books of heaven. "Lay up for yourselves treasure in heaven."

4. "Upon the first day of the week." This teaches regularity in giving. Many object to the frequency of collections, but we are here taught to lay aside for the Master's work something every Sunday. It is probable that in a farming community, where the income is computed annually instead of weekly, the apportionment could not be made every "first day of the week." Still, if the amount is regularly set apart for religious uses "as God hath prospered" us— that is, according to Bible system, the tenth— we will always have an offering when the collection is taken.

5. "God loveth a cheerful giver." Cheerful— free, willing, liberal, anxious— giver. "God loveth" such a one. Why not? It is like himself; besides, this spirit of free, loving, liberal giving commends itself to even the hard and unkind. But how few *"cheerful givers"* may be found! Men may give meagerly from force of circumstances or a sense of duty who know nothing of giving with *delight*, with

warm heart, with cheerful countenance. Give systematically, regularly, "as God hath prospered," till the heart catches the heavenly glow, and the love of God for the "cheerful giver" becomes our abiding heritage.

6. As we sow— sparingly, bountifully— so will we reap. This is the universal law, and we are not surprised that it applies here. This is a life of sowing; eternity brings the day of reaping. He who said, "Lay up your treasure in heaven," "God loveth a cheerful giver," now tells us: "Sow as you purpose in your heart; but as you sow, so will you reap." Alas! how very few have learned this lesson. Wastefulness abounds, and men are called liberal who continually "rob God" (Mal. iii.8-12), and who will perish in the sin of "covetousness, which is idolatry." (Col. iii.5.) How short will be the "cash account" in the bank of heaven with many who talk glibly and sing lustily of robes and crowns and unfading riches in glory. Heaven is at the end of a life of faithfulness, and its treasures are to be laid up by self-denial, liberality, and good works.

7. Jesus said: "It is more blessed to give than to receive." God gives, man receives. The greater blessing is in the God-like spirit of giving. We must labor to support the weak. How happy must have been Jesus and his disciples when they were privileged to feed the "five thousand men, besides women and children," who had followed them till overcome by weariness and hunger. See Matthew xiv.15-21. O that all the people might learn the blessedness of giving! So many complain of the burdens they have to carry in supporting the Church, in helping the poor, or in other works of mercy and charity; whereas they should rather rejoice at the privilege of thus doing good to others while at the same time laying up for themselves imperishable treasures in glory, "where neither moth nor rust doth corrupt," nor thieves break through and steal.

8. "Give, and it shall be given unto you, for with the

same measure that ye mete shall it be measured unto you." Here is, in other words, the lesson learned above on sowing and reaping. Our liberality will always return into our own bosoms, while our stinginess will return with its waste and barrenness to our own hearts. "There is that scattereth, and yet increaseth; and there is that withholdeth more than is meet, but it tendeth to poverty." (Pro. xi.24.)

9. Earthly treasures are uncertain, perishable, insecure; moth and rust corrupt them, thieves steal them. Heavenly treasures are sure, safe, unfading; thieves cannot steal nor moth and rust corrupt them; hence it is the part of wisdom to lay up our treasures in heaven, while folly is clearly manifest in the prevalent custom of living— in the management of business affairs especially— as if this were the real life while heaven were but a myth, a vague uncertainty. Let us use this world simply to increase our treasures in the skies, to make to ourselves riches enduring, eternal at God's right hand.

If we are liberal; if, like our Master, we go about doing good; if we "sow beside all waters; if we abound unto every good work— we will thus "lay up in store for ourselves a good foundation against the time to come, that we may lay hold on eternal life." (1 Tim. vi.19.)

> That man may *last*, but never *lives*,
> Who much receives, but nothing gives,
> Whom none can love, whom none can thank,
> Creation's blot, creation's blank.
>
> But he who marks, from day to day,
> In generous acts his radiant way,
> Treads the same path the Saviour trod,
> The path to glory and to God.

38
GIVING (NEW TESTAMENT)
No. 3

1. The love of money is a snare, even the great root of evil.

> "But they that will be rich fall into temptation and a snare, and into many foolish and hurtful lusts, which drown men in destruction and perdition. For the love of money is the root of all evil: which while some coveted after, they have erred from the faith, and pierced themselves through with many sorrows." (1 Tim. vi.9, 10.)

2. We may not trust in money, but must use it for good.

> "Charge them that are rich in this world, that they be not high-minded, nor trust in uncertain riches, but in the living God, who giveth us richly all things to enjoy; that they do good, that they be rich in good works, ready to distribute, willing to communicate; laying up in store for themselves a good foundation against the time to come, that they may lay hold on eternal life." (1 Tim. vi.17-19.)

3. We may make friends for eternity out of our money.

"And I say unto you, Make to yourselves friends of the mammon of unrighteousness; that, when ye fail, they may receive you into everlasting habitations." (Luke xvi.9.)

4. If unfaithful in the use of money, how will we get heavenly riches?

"He that is faithful in that which is least is faithful also in much; and he that is unjust in the least is unjust also in much. If therefore ye have not been faithful in the unrighteousness mammon, who will commit to your trust the true riches? And if ye have not been faithful in that which is another man's, who shall give you that which is your own?" (Luke xvi.10-12.)

5. Let giving be done for God's eye, and reward, only.

"But when thou doest alms, let not thy left hand know what they right hand doeth: that thine alms may be in secret: and thy Father which seeth in secret himself shall reward thee openly." (Matt. vi.3, 4.) See Matthew vi.1, 2.

6. Christ became poor — gave all — for us.

"For ye know the grace of our Lord Jesus Christ, that, though he was rich, yet for your sakes he became poor, that ye through his poverty might be rich." (2 Cor. viii.9.) See Mark viii.34-38.

7. Helping the poor is but lending unto God.

"He that hath pity upon the poor lendeth unto the Lord; and that which he hath given will he pay him again." (Prov. xix.17.) Luke xiv.13, 14.

8. We must abound in liberality. It is a grace.

"How that in a great trial of affliction, the abundance

of their joy and their deep poverty abounded unto the riches of their liberality." "Therefore, as ye abound in every thing, in faith, and utterance, and knowledge, and in all diligence, and in all diligence, and in your love to us, see that ye abound in this grace also." (2 Cor. viii.2, 7.)

9. Our money should be consecrated to the Lord. Who will do so?

> "Moreover, because I have set my affection to the house of my God, I have of mine own proper good, of gold and silver, which I have given to the house of my God, over and above all that I have prepared for the holy house, even three thousand talents of gold, of the gold of Ophir, and seven thousand talents of refined silver, to overlay the walls of the houses withal: the gold for things of gold, and the silver for things of silver, and for all manner of work to be made by the hands of artificers.
>
> "And who then is willing to consecrate his service this day unto the Lord?" (1 Chron. xxix.3-5.)

1. "They that will be rich." It speaks of such as have their hearts set on getting rich. The love of money, covetousness, is the ruin of many even though they fail in the accumulation of riches. Many condemn "the rich" who may be more covetous, stingy, close-fisted than the rich men they curse so bitterly. Money, like fire, is a good *servant*, but a bad master. "The love of money is the root of all [kinds of] evil." When money is *loved* it becomes an idol, is thus no longer a servant, as it should always be, but becomes master, and in this capacity it has caused, at different places and times, all kinds of evil— sin. Make money a servant, use it for the glory of God, lay it up as treasure in heaven, make friends of it who will receive

you into everlasting habitations when earth fails you. With this use of money before us we can see the importance of Paul's words: "Be not slothful in business; fervent in spirit; serving the Lord." Fervency of spirit must not supplant, but regulate and control, diligence in business, that in it all we may *serve the Lord*. Some people boast that they "care nothing about making money, except a good living;" forgetful of the fact that there are hungry ones to be fed, naked ones to be clothed, homeless orphans and widows to be sheltered, thousands of poor and sick Lazaruses in the earth; besides whole nations raising their piteous wail from the dark and cheerless night of their heathen bondage and superstition, while no other sun can light them than the "Sun of righteousness," no other Christ can save them than the Christ of Calvary, whose gospel must be preached "in all the world," "to every creature." We must not love money, but must love Christ and make and use money to advance his kingdom.

2. "The rich" must "be not high-minded, nor trust in uncertain riches, but in the living God." They must "do good," "be rich in good works, ready to distribute;" "laying up in store for themselves a good foundation." This corroborates the testimony we have just given, viz.: that *we must be the master of money, using it for God; instead of being its servant, used by it for the devil.*

3. "Mammon of unrighteousness" means money; and we are here told to use it for good, that friends may be made of it for eternity. The case of the rich man and Lazarus follows in this chapter (Luke xvi.) in illustration of the text. The rich man is not charged with murder, theft, adultery, or any other crime; but simply that he spent his wealth in costly living, thinking that his money was his own and that he had a right to use it as he pleased. Lazarus lay in need at his gate, feeding on the crumbs which fell from his table; while he, a respected and highly-

esteemed Church-member, spent his wealth upon himself, dressing in "purple and fine linen and faring sumptuously every day." His selfishness and stinginess sent him to hell. He might and should have made a friend of the "mammon of unrighteousness" who would with Christ's sanction have received him "into everlasting habitations." Beware, O reader, that you make not his fearful mistake! Thousands, even in the Church, are doing it.

4. But you say this is too small a matter to judge a man's Christian character by! Hear the Master: "If you have not been faithful in the unrighteous mammon [money], who will commit to your trust the true riches?" for "he that is faithful in that which is least is faithful also in much; and he that is unjust in the least in unjust also in much." Here the Great Teacher makes our use of money in his name a test of the faithfulness we have toward him. After this lesson, with the case of the Pharisees, "who were covetous" and "derided him," he gives us the illustrative case of Dives and Lazarus— the rich man being an example of one who, "unfaithful in that which was least," was not intrusted by the Master with "the true riches." He is not alone in the roll of unfaithful stewards who will be "cast into outer darkness" because of their "covetousness, which is idolatry."

5. "Let not thy left hand know what thy right hand doeth: that thine alms may be in secret." The meaning is: *Do not give to be seen of men*, give only for the glory of God and the good man. A man who would only give five dollars alone with the collector, but would make it twenty dollars or fifty dollars in a great congregation, is giving to be seen of men, and thus loses the heavenly reward. But this Scripture has been abused. There are times when giving should be done in public— namely, when public collections are being taken— for we are to "let our light so shine that others may *see* our good works and *glorify our Father* which is in heaven." Suppose I, who claim to

be a Christian, am in a congregation where a collection is taken for Missions, and I refuse to give, saying: "I'll do my giving privately." My influence is against the success of the work— a stumbling-block, whereas, I should "let my light shine" to the glory of God. "Pray to thy Father in secret" does not mean that there shall be no public prayers. So "give in secret" does not mean that there shall be no public gifts, but simply that by both prayers and alms *only God's will and glory shall be consulted*.

6. "Our Lord Jesus Christ, though he was rich, yet for your sakes he became poor, that ye through his poverty might be rich." Giving is kept prominently before every Bible-reader. God *gave* his Son," Christ *gave* his riches and his life. "God loveth a cheerful *giver*," and "it is more blessed to *give* than to receive." All this divine giving was through "grace" — unmerited favor, love. This example of Christ is intended to stir the devotion of every heart that has feeling. Christ, through grace, descended from the highest riches to the deepest poverty, that we through his poverty might ascend to the heavenly and eternal riches. But still, if we catch not his spirit of liberality, how can we live with him in his glory? O may we too learn the Christ-like spirit of self-denial! and, true to the Master, may we go about "doing good," that others may share with us the riches of the heavenly inheritance!

7. "He that hath pity upon the poor lendeth unto the Lord." Brother, how would it suit you to lend unto the Lord? Take with you as much as you feel willing to deposit in his bank, and with it help the poor, the sick, the suffering, the needy. God will pay you both here and hereafter, for "godliness is profitable unto all things, having promise of the life that now is, and of that which is to come." (1 Tim. iv.8.)

8. We are to "abound in this grace" of liberality, as well as knowledge, faith, diligence, and love to each other. Many pray for more faith, more knowledge, more love

who ought to be praying day and night for more of "this grace" of true, abounding, untiring liberality. He must have but little access to the throne of grace who is daily "robbing God" of his tithes and offerings. There are those who think it cheaper and easier to serve God with songs and shouts and "talks" than with hard-earned dollars and cents. They had much rather hear a shout than a missionary collection, and would rather "give in an experience" of their conversion years ago than settle an honest bill of "quarterage" or "salary" due their pastor. If any reader thinks this writer opposed to "shouting," let him consult other pages of this book; but he readily admits that shouting, singing, etc., comes with poor grace upon his ears from a "close-fisted," stingy Church-member whose profession of experimental religion is a libel upon the grace of the Lord Jesus Christ, who "became poor that we might be rich," and who fails not to tell us that as we sow so will we reap.

9. David's affection was set upon the house of his God, and his abundant offering indicated it. So, when our hearts are set upon the kingdom of Christ and the glory of God in the earth, our offerings will show it to all who know us. Let each one "consecrate his service this day unto the Lord," and as the spirit of Christly giving and true consecration burns in the hearts of the Church she will move out through all the earth on a swelling tidal-wave of salvation, and then the hosts of the Lord, on shouting-ground, will rend heaven and earth with the high praises of our Redeemer, while heavenly glory floods earth and sky. Amen, and praise ye the Lord!

39
GOD TURNS AGAINST THE IMPENITENT

1. Resisting much reproof brings sudden destruction.

"He, that being often reproved hardeneth his neck, shall suddenly be destroyed, and that without remedy." (Prov. xxix.1.)

2. God's wrath rises against such as despise his words.

"And the Lord God of their fathers sent to them by his messengers, rising up betimes, and sending; because he had compassion on his people, and on his dwelling-place: but they mocked the messengers of God, and despised his words, and misused his prophets, until the wrath of the Lord arose against his people, till there was no remedy." (2 Chron. xxxvi.15, 16.)

3. Those belie the Lord who say that evil shall not visit the ungodly.

"For the house of Israel and the house of Judah have dealt very treacherously against me, saith the Lord. They have belied the Lord, and said, It is not he; neither shall evil come upon us; neither shall we see sword nor famine." (Jer. v.11, 12.)

4. Some refuse to hear, and make their hearts as adamant.

> "But they refused to hearken, and pulled away the shoulder, and stopped their ears, that they should not hear. Yea, they made their hearts as an adamant stone, lest they should hear the law, and the words which the Lord of hosts hath sent in his Spirit by the former prophets: therefore came a great wrath from the Lord of hosts. Therefore it is come to pass, that as he cried, and they would not hear; so they cried, and I would not hear, saith the Lord of hosts." (Zech. vii.11-13.)

5. God says: "I have called, and ye refused."

> "Because I have called, and ye refused; I have stretched out my hand, and no man regarded; but ye have set at naught all my counsel, and would none of my reproof." (Prov. i.24, 25.)

6. He says to such: "I also will laugh at your calamity."

> "I also will laugh at your calamity; I will mock when your fear cometh; when your fear cometh as desolation, and your destruction cometh as a whirlwind; when distress and anguish cometh upon you." (Prov. i 26, 27.)

7. Their prayers then will bring no answer.

> "Then shall they call upon me, but I will not answer; they shall seek me early, but they shall not find me: for that they hated knowledge, and did not choose the fear of the Lord: they would none of my counsel: they despised all my reproof." (Prov. i.28-30.)

8. God leaves them to destruction in their own way.

> "Therefore shall they eat of the fruit of their own way,

and be filled with their own devices. For the turning away of the simple shall slay them, and the prosperity of fools shall destroy them." (Prov. i.31, 32.)

9. **But those who hear God shall dwell safely.**

"But whoso hearkeneth unto me shall dwell safely, and shall be quiet from fear of evil. (Prov. i.33.)

40
THE JUDGMENT
No. 1

1. It is certain as death, but after death.

   "And as it is appointed unto men once to die, but after this the judgment" (Heb. ix.27.)

2. All must be judged, both good and bad.

   "For we must all appear before the judgment seat of Christ: that every one may receive the things done in his body, according to that he hath done, whether it be good or bad." (2 Cor. v.10.)

3. There will be a separation of the good and the evil.

   "When the Son of man shall come in his glory, and all the holy angels with him, then shall he sit upon the throne of his glory: and before him shall be gathered all nations: and he shall separate them one from another, as a shepherd divideth his sheep from the goats: and he shall set the sheep on his right hand, but the goats on the left." (Matt. xxv.31-33.)

4. In the judgment each one will receive according to his works.

"For the Son of man shall come in the glory of his Father with his angels; and then he shall reward every man according to his works." (Matt. xvi.27.)

5. The dead will stand before God in judgment.

"And I saw the dead, small and great, stand before God; and the books were opened: and another book was opened, which is the book of life: and the dead were judged out of those things which were written in the books, according to their works." (Rev. xx.12.)

6. A fiery stream will issue forth before the judge.

"A fiery stream issued and came forth from before him: thousand thousands ministered unto him, and ten thousand times ten thousand stood before him: the judgment was set, and the books were opened." (Dan. vii.10.)

7. It will be a day of wrath. Can we then stand?

"And the kings of the earth, and the great men, and the rich men, and the chief captains, and the mighty men, and every bond man, and every free man, hid themselves in the dens and in the rocks of the mountains; and said to the mountains and rocks, Fall on us, and hide us from the face of him that sitteth on the throne, and from the wrath of the Lamb: for the great day of his wrath is come; and who shall be able to stand?" (Rev. vi.15-17.)

8. The doom of all who are not written in the book of life.

"And whosoever was not found written in the book of life was cast into the lake of fire." (Rev. xx.15.)

41
THE JUDGMENT
No. 2

1. It is Christ's judgment-seat.

    "But why dost thou judge thy brother? or why dost thou set at naught thy brother? for we shall all stand before the judgment-seat of Christ." (Rom. xiv.10.)

2. Christ is appointed Judge of the living and the dead.

    "And he commanded us to preach unto the people, and to testify that it is he which was ordained of God to be the Judge of quick and dead." (Acts x.42.)

3. He will judge the world in righteousness.

    "Because he hath appointed a day, in the which he will judge the world in righteousness by that man whom he hath ordained; whereof he hath given assurance unto all men, in that he hath raised him from the dead." (Acts xvii.31.)

4. The judgment will be on gospel principles.

    "In the day when God shall judge the secrets of men by Jesus Christ according to my gospel." (Rom. ii.16.)

5. Every secret will then be brought to judgment.

"For God shall bring every work into judgment, with every secret thing, whether it be good, or whether it be evil." (Eccles. xii.14.)

6. Be sure your sin will then be exposed.

"But if ye will not do so, behold, ye have sinned against the Lord: and be sure your sin will find you out." (Num xxxii.23.)

7. The unjust will go from judgment to punishment.

"The Lord knoweth how to deliver the godly out of temptation, and to reserve the unjust unto the day of judgment to be punished." (2 Pet ii.9.)

8. God, the Judge, is strong.

"Therefore shall her plagues come in one day, death, and mourning, and famine; and she shall be utterly burned with fire: for strong is the Lord God who judgeth her." (Rev. xviii.8.)

9. The issues of that day are final.

"And these shall go away into everlasting punishment: but the righteous into life eternal." (Matt. xxv.46.)

42
THE RESURRECTION
No. 1

1. The doctrine taught in the Old Testament.

    "And many of them that sleep in the dust of the earth shall awake, some to everlasting life, and some to shame and everlasting contempt." (Dan. xii.2.)

2. The Pharisees believed, but the Sadducees denied.

    "For the Sadducees say that there is no resurrection, neither angel, nor spirit: but the Pharisees confess both." (Acts xxiii.8.)

3. Christ taught the doctrine of the resurrection.

    "Marvel not at this: for the hour is coming, in the which all that are in the graves shall hear his voice, and shall come forth; they that have done good, unto the resurrection of life; and they that have done evil, unto the resurrection of damnation." (John v.28, 29.)

4. He declared its power to be in himself.

    "Jesus said unto her, I am the resurrection, and the

life: he that believeth in me, though he were dead, yet shall he live: and whosoever liveth and believeth in me shall never die. Believest thou this?" (John xi.25, 26.)

5. Jesus himself rose from the dead.

"And the angel answered and said unto the women, Fear not ye: for I know that ye seek Jesus, which was crucified. He is not here: for he is risen, as he said. Come, see the place where the Lord lay. And go quickly, and tell his disciples that he is risen from the dead; and, behold, he goeth before you into Galilee; there shall ye see him: lo, I have told you." (Matt. xxviii.5-7.)

6. So he is called the first-fruits of the resurrection.

"But now is Christ risen from the dead, and become the first-fruits of them that slept. For since by man came death, by man came also the resurrection of the dead." (1 Cor. xv.20, 21.)

7. On this doctrine and fact hinges our faith.

"For if the dead rise not, then is not Christ raised: and if Christ be not raised, your faith is vain; ye are yet in your sins." (1 Cor. xv.16, 17.)

8. It is the body that is to be raised all immortal.

"So also is the resurrection of the dead. It is sown in corruption, it is raised in incorruption: it is sown in dishonor, it is raised in glory: it is sown in weakness, it is raised in power: it is sown a natural body, it is raised a spiritual body. There is a natural body, and there is a spiritual body." (1 Cor. xv.42-44.)

43
THE RESURRECTION
No. 2

1. The resurrection is by Christ, as death by Adam.

   "For since by man came death, by man came also the resurrection of the dead." (1 Cor. xv.21.)

2. By the resurrection death loses its sting, and the grave its victory.

   "So when this corruptible shall have put on incorruption, and this mortal shall have put on immortality, then shall be brought to pass the saying that is written, Death is swallowed up in victory. O death, where is thy sting? O grave, where is thy victory?" (1 Cor. xv.54, 55.)

3. It is God who redeems us from death and the grave.

   "I will ransom them from the power of the grave; I will redeem them from death: O death, I will be thy plagues; O grave, I will be thy destruction: repentance shall be hid from mine eyes." (Hos. xiii.14.)

4. He will swallow up death in victory.

"He will swallow up death in victory; and the Lord God will wipe away tears from off all faces; and the rebuke of his people shall he take away from off all the earth: for the Lord hath spoken it," (Isa. xxv.8.)

5. **The dead in Christ shall rise first.**

"For the Lord himself shall descend from heaven with a shout, with the voice of the archangel, and with the trump of God: and the dead in Christ shall rise first." (1 Thess. iv.16.)

6. **The remaining believers shall then be changed.**

"Then we which are alive and remain shall be caught up together with them in the clouds, to meet the Lord in the air: and so shall we ever be with the Lord." (1 Thess iv.17.)

7. **Paul had the resurrection hope.**

"And have hope toward God, which they themselves also allow, that there shall be a resurrection of the dead, both of the just and unjust." (Acts xxiv.15.)

8. **The Christian's death is but a sleep; God will awake him.**

"For if we believe that Jesus died and rose again, even so them also which sleep in Jesus will God bring with him." (1 Thess. iv.14.)

9. **The redeemed, awaking in Christ's likeness, will be satisfied.**

"As for me, I will behold thy face in righteousness: I shall be satisfied, when I awake, with thy likeness." (Ps. xvii.15.)

44
ROMAN CATHOLICISM

1. The pope exalteth himself above God.

    "Who opposeth and exalteth himself above all that is called God, or that is worshiped; so that he as God sitteth in the temple of God, showing himself that he is God." (2 Thess. ii.4.)

2. He is called the man of sin, the son of perdition.

    "Let no man deceive you by any means: for that day shall not come, except there come a falling away first, and that man of sin be revealed, the son of perdition." (2 Thess. ii.3.)

3. He shall be consumed by the spirit of the gospel.

    "And then shall that Wicked be revealed, whom the Lord shall consume with the spirit of his mouth, and shall destroy with the brightness of his coming." (2 Thess. ii.8.)

4. He worked signs by Satanic power; they were lying wonders.

    "Even him, whose coming is after the working of

Satan with all power and signs and lying wonders, and with all deceivableness of unrighteousness in them that perish; because they received not the love of the truth, that they might be saved. And for this cause God shall send them strong delusion, that they should believe a lie: that they all might be damned who believed not the truth, but had pleasure in unrighteousness." (2 Thess. ii.9-12.)

5. Catholicism forbids to marry, commands abstinence from meats.

"Now the Spirit speaketh expressly, that in the latter times some shall depart from the faith, giving heed to seducing spirits, and doctrines of devils; speaking lies in hypocrisy; having their conscience seared with a hot iron; forbidding to marry, and commanding to abstain from meats, which God hath created to be received with thanksgiving of them which believe and know the truth." (1 Tim. iv.1-3.)

6. Rome full of abominations, and drunk with the blood of the martyrs.

"And upon her forehead was a name written, MYSTERY, BABYLON THE GREAT, THE MOTHER OF HARLOTS AND ABOMINATIONS OF THE EARTH. And I saw the woman drunken with the blood of the saints, and with the blood of the martyrs of Jesus." (Rev. xvii.5, 6.)

7. Her pictures and images break the second commandment.

"Thou shalt not make unto thee any graven image, or any likeness of any thing that is in heaven above, or that is in the earth beneath, or that is in the water under the earth: thou shalt not bow down thyself to them, nor serve them: for I the Lord thy God am a jealous God, visiting the iniquity of the fathers upon the children unto the third and fourth generation of them that hate me." (Ex. xx.4, 5.)

8. Christ claims spiritual supremacy; Rome, temporal.

"Jesus answered, My kingdom is not of this world: if my kingdom were of this world, then would my servants fight, that I should not be delivered to the Jews: but now is my kingdom not from hence." (John xviii.36.) "For the kingdom of God is not meat and drink; but righteousness, and peace, and joy in the Holy Ghost." (Rom. xiv.17.)

We believe it high time that the people of this land of gospel light and Christian freedom were awakened to the real character of this "mother of harlots and abominations," the fallen apostate Church of degenerate Rome. St. Paul told the people of his day, "The mystery of iniquity doth already work" (2 Thess. ii.7), and he so graphically portrayed the pope as the "man of sin, the son of perdition," that we open this Bible-reading with his wonderful prophecy.

1. "Who opposeth and exalteth himself above... God," and "sitteth in the temple of God, showing himself that he is God." What could be a deeper sin, a more heinous sacrilege, a more abominable blasphemy, than for a mortal man to assume the prerogative of God and set his authority above that of his Maker, even demanding credence for and obedience to his traditions above the written word of God?

2. "Let no man deceive you;" the "man of sin, the son of perdition," must be revealed. Many were looking for the "day of Christ," but Paul said the apostasy should first come, and the son of perdition should "exalt himself above all that is called God." The pope claims the right to sell indulgences, grant pardons, depose kings, degrade dignitaries, rule the nations, and

even shut heaven against the poor unfortunates who chance to incur his displeasure.

3. But "that Wicked shall be revealed, whom the Lord shall consume with the spirit of his mouth, and shall destroy with the brightness of his coming." The spirit of the Lord's mouth is the gospel of God accompanied by the Holy Ghost. Romanism has been an uncompromising foe to a free gospel. Not only are her members forbidden to hear the gospel of Protestant pulpits, but the Bible itself is excluded from the deluded followers of pagan Rome. The Bibles she has burned would make the largest collection of books, doubtless, on earth; while her martyrs, if turned loose in unbroken phalanx upon the heathenism of the world to-day, would subdue its mighty forces and bring down its hoary locks to the dust before the advancing, conquering Christ. The gospel of Christ has already broken the power of "the man of sin;" the sun of the Reformation that rose in the days of Luther is advancing to the high noon of heavenly light, and the last remnants of Romish superstition shall be dispelled, for the Lord shall destroy that Wicked "with the brightness of his coming." Amen.

4. But that Wicked came in Satan's strength with "power and signs and lying wonders." Many miracles have been attributed to the *"saints"* (?) of Rome. They have claimed the healing of all manner of diseases, infirmities, etc. even going so far as to raise the dead! So "God shall send them strong delusion, that they should believe a lie," and thus they perish, "because they received not the love of the truth, that they might be saved." For proof of these delusions see the Catholic countries of the world to-day — Italy, Spain, Mexico, the South American and a number of European States. Poverty, immorality, fanaticism, licentiousness, ignorance, and infidelity — all blended in a heterogeneous

mass, that degrades man, defies God, and shuts out the light and hope of a true and heavenly spirituality.

5. This fearful apostasy from the faith, "forbidding to marry, and commanding to abstain from meats" is clearly applicable to Romanism. Her priests are all forced into vows of celibacy, and this in turn produces a horde of iniquitous, licentious leaders of the corrupt, degenerate, and apostate Church (?).

6. St. John here brings to light a fearful prophetic description of the fallen hierarchy which carries in bold characters the names given by the inspiration of God: "Babylon the great, the mother of harlots and abominations of the earth;" "the woman drunken with the blood of the saints, and with the blood of the martyrs of Jesus." Who can count the thousands of martyrs who have perished in the dungeon, on the gibbet, and at the stake through the heartless demands of this implacable foe of freedom and of Christ. Ridley, Cranmer, Latimer, and others of learning, of greatness, and of fame, besides the uncounted multitudes of humble followers of Jesus, whose blood has made drunken this "mother of harlots and abominations of the earth."

7. The second of the Ten Commandments forbids the making of images to worship them, yet the churches of Romanism are filled with pictures and images before which the poor deluded follower prostrates himself, while angels weep in sorrow and devils rejoice with exceeding great joy.

8. Jesus says: "My kingdom is not of this world." The kingdom of God is "righteousness, and peace, and joy in the Holy Ghost." The pope claims universal temporal power. Dr. Brownson, a Catholic, speaks as follows: "The people need governing, and must be governed. They must have a master, and this master is the Pope of Rome, whom the Almighty God has placed us under to obey." ("Essays," pp. 380, 383.) *The Catholic*, September, 1871, says:

"If the American Government is to be sustained and preserved at all, it must be by the rejection of the principles of the Reformation and the acceptance of the Catholic principles— i.e., the government of the pope." "The time is not far away when the Roman Catholics, at the order of the pope, will refuse to pay their school-tax, and will send bullets to the breasts of the Government agents rather than pay it." "The order can come any day from Rome. It will come as quickly as the click of the trigger, and it will be obeyed, of course, as coming from God Almighty himself." (From a newspaper report of a conversation of Monsignor Capel.) The above quotations are from the circular letter of "The Committee of One Hundred," Boston, Mass., 1888.

Romanism is a standing, uncompromising foe to civil and religious freedom, seeking with base and hellish intrigue to subjugate this and all other lands where the people have an open Bible and a free pulpit, an unhampered press and free speech, to the galling chains of papal bondage. She is planting her schools far and near, and, strange to say, is actually educating thousands of youths from Protestant families. Father, your noble son had better die in ignorance than become entangled in the foul meshes of Romanism; and mother, your lovely daughter had better go untaught through the highway of Bible holiness to heaven than be subjected to the wily influences of the scheming propagandists of the "man of sin, the son of perdition" "who opposeth and exalteth himself above all that is called God," and "whom the Lord shall consume with the spirit of his mouth, and destroy with the brightness of his coming."

45
SUPPLEMENTAL NOTE
From Bishop Newton

THE TRUE CHRISTIAN WORSHIP is the worship of *the one only God, through the one only Mediator, the man Christ Jesus*; and from this worship the Church of Rome has most notoriously departed, by substituting other mediators, and invocating and adoring saints and angels: nothing is apostasy in idolatry be not. And are not the members of the Church of Rome guilty of idolatry in the worship of images, in the adoration of the host, in the invocation of angels and saints, and in the oblation of prayers and praises to the Virgin Mary; as much, or more, than to God blessed forever? This is the grand corruption of the Christian Church; this is the *apostasy*, as it is emphatically called, and deserves to be called, which was not only predicted by St. Paul, but by the Prophet Daniel likewise. If the apostasy be rightly charged upon the Church of Rome, it follows of consequence, that the *man of sin* is the pope; not meaning any pope in particular, but the *pope* in general, as the chief head and supporter of this apostasy. He is properly the *man of sin*, not only on account of the scandalous lives of many popes, but by reason of their most scandalous doctrines and principles; dispensing with the most necessary duties, and granting, or rather selling, pardons and indulgences to the most abominable crimes... He [the pope] is the great adversary of God and man; persecuting and destroying, by *croisades* [sic], inquisitions, and massacres, those Christians who prefer the word of God to the authority of men. The *heathen emperor* of Rome may have slain his thousands of innocent Christians; but the *Christian Bishop* of Rome has slain his ten thousands. *He exalteth himself above all that is called God or is worshiped*; not only above inferior magistrates, but likewise above bishops and primates; not only above bishops and primates, but likewise above kings and emperors; deposing some, obliging them to kiss his toe, to hold his stirrup, treading even upon the neck of a king, and kicking off the imperial crown with his foot; nay, not only kings and emperors, but likewise above Christ and God himself: *making the word of God of none effect by his traditions*; forbidding what God has commanded; as marriage, the use of Scriptures, etc., and also commanding, or allowing what God has forbidden, as idolatry, persecution, etc. (Clarke's Commentary, 2 Thess. ii.)

The inscription upon her forehead is exactly the portraiture of the Latin Church. This Church is, as Bishop Newton well expresses it, a mystery of iniquity. This woman is also called *Babylon the Great*; she is the exact antitype of the ancient Babylon in her idolatry and cruelty; but the ancient city called Babylon is only a drawing of her in miniature. This is, indeed, *Babylon* THE GREAT. "She affects the style and title of our Holy Mother *the* Church; but she is, in truth, the mother of harlots and abominations of the earth." "*Drunken with the blood of the saints.*" …How exactly the cruelties exercised by the Latin Church against all it has denominated heretic correspond with this description, the reader need not be informed. (Clarke's Commentary, Rev. xvii.5, 6.)

46
THE SCRIPTURES

1. They were written for our learning and comfort.

"For whatsoever things were written aforetime were written for our learning, that we through patience and comfort of the Scriptures might have hope." (Rom. xv.4.)

2. They contain the word of God, which worketh effectually.

"For this cause also thank we God without ceasing, because, when ye received the word of God which ye heard of us, ye received it not as the word of men, but, as it is in truth, the word of God, which effectually worketh also in you that believe." (1 Thess. ii.13.)

3. We may not take from or add to the Scriptures.

"For I testify unto every man that heareth the words of the prophecy of this book, If any man shall add unto these things, God shall add unto him the plagues that are written in this book: and if any man shall take away from the words of the book of this prophecy, God shall take away his part out of the book of life, and out of the holy city, and from the things which are written in this book." (Rev. xxii.18, 19.) See Deuteronomy iv.2.

4. Make the Scriptures the test of every doctrine.

"These were more noble than those in Thessalonica, in that they received the word with all readiness of mind, and searched the Scriptures daily, whether those things were so." (Acts xvii.11.)

5. The word is a better witness than one risen from the dead.

"And he said unto him, If they hear not Moses and the prophets, neither will they be persuaded, though one rose from the dead." (Luke xvi.31.)

6. Let the word of God dwell in you richly.

"Let the word of Christ dwell in you richly in all wisdom; teaching and admonishing one another in psalms and hymns and spiritual songs, singing with grace in your hearts to the Lord." (Col. iii.16.)

7. We should meditate day and night in the Scriptures.

"This book of the law shall not depart out of thy mouth; but thou shalt meditate therein day and night, that thou mayest observe to do according to all that is written therein: for then thou shalt make thy way prosperous, and then thou shalt have good success." (Josh. i.8.)

8. The word of God is the sword of the Spirit.

"And take the helmet of salvation, and the sword of the Spirit, which is the word of God." Eph. vi.17.)

47
Some Bible "Woes"

1. Woe to the indifferent and careless in Zion!

    "Woe to them that are at ease in Zion, and trust in the mountains of Samaria." (Amos vi.1.)

2. Woe to the Christian who cannot raise the world's antagonism!

    "Woe unto you, when all men shall speak well of you! for so did their fathers to the false prophets." (Luke vi.26.)

3. Woe to such as plan wickedly!

    "Woe to them that devise iniquity, and work evil upon their beds! when the morning is light, they practice it, because it is in the power of their hand." (Micah ii.1.)

4. Woe to the city of falsehood and blood!

    "Woe to the bloody city! it is all full of lies and robbery; the prey departeth not." (Nah. iii.1.)

5. Woe to them which gather evil gains!

"Woe to him that coveteth an evil covetousness to his house, that he may set his nest on high, that he may be delivered from the power of evil!" "Woe to him that buildeth a town with blood, and establisheth a city by iniquity!" (Hab. ii.9, 12.)

6. Woe to the one that giveth drink to his neighbor!

"Woe unto him that giveth his neighbor drink, that puttest thy bottle to him, and makest him drunken also, that thou mayest look on their nakedness! Thou art filled with shame for glory: drink thou also, and let thy foreskin be uncovered: the cup of the Lord's right hand shall be turned unto thee, and shameful spewing shall be on thy glory." (Hab. ii.15, 16.)

7. Woe to the filthy, polluted, oppressing city!

"Woe to her that is filthy and polluted, to the oppressing city! She obeyed not the voice; she received not correction; she trusted not in the Lord; she drew not near to her God." (Zeph. iii.1, 2.)

8. Woe to the unfaithful pastors! they destroy God's flock.

"Woe be unto the pastors that destroy and scatter the sheep of my pasture! saith the Lord. Therefore thus saith the Lord God of Israel against the pastors that feed my people; Ye have scattered my flock, and driven them away, and have not visited them: behold, I will visit upon you the evil of your doings, saith the Lord." (Jer. xxiii.1, 2.)

9. Woe to them that go to Egypt, and not the Lord, for help!

Woe to them that go down to Egypt for help; and stay on horses, and trust in chariots, because they are many; and in horsemen, because they are very strong; but they look not unto the Holy One of Israel, neither seek the Lord! (Isa. xxxi.1.)

10. Woe to the rebellious ones, which trust in Pharaoh and Egypt!

"Woe to the rebellious children, saith the Lord, that take counsel, but not of me; and that cover with a covering, but not of my Spirit, that they may add sin to sin: that walk to go down into Egypt, and have not asked at my mouth; to strengthen themselves in the strength of Pharaoh, and to trust in the shadow of Egypt! Therefore shall the strength of Pharaoh be your shame, and the trust in the shadow of Egypt your confusion." (Isa. xxx.1-3.)

48
Romans VI-VIII

No. 1. Seventh Chapter.

1. Paul's contrast. The law good, himself carnal.

   "For we know that the law is spiritual: but I am carnal, sold under sin." (Verse 14.)

2. Having sin in him, he is unable to do good.

   "Now then it is no more I that do it, but sin that dwelleth in me. For I know that in me (that is, in my flesh,) dwelleth no good thing: for to will is present with me; but how to perform that which is good I find not." (Verse 17, 18.)

3. Although he heartily approves the law, he is a slave to sin.

   "For I delight in the law of God after the inward man; but I see another law in my members, warring against the law of my mind, and bringing me into captivity to the law of sin which is in my members." (Verses 22, 23.)

4. Wretchedness results from this slavery.

"O wretched man that I am! who shall deliver me from the body of this death?" (Verse 24.)

5. Christ answers his cry for help.

"I thank God through Jesus Christ our Lord. So then with the mind I myself serve the law of God; but with the flesh the law of sin." (Verse 25.)

6. Death came by sin.

"For sin, taking occasion by the commandment, deceived me and by it slew me." (Verse 11.)

7. Christ gives life that we may bring forth fruit unto God.

"Wherefore, my brethren, ye also are become dead to the law by the body of Christ; that ye should be married to another, even to him who is raised from the dead, that we should bring forth fruit unto God." (Verse 4.)

8. In the flesh is slavery; in Christ is deliverance.

"For when we were in the flesh, the motions of sins, which were by the law, did work in our members to bring forth fruit unto death. But now we are delivered from the law, that being dead wherein we were held; that we should serve in newness of spirit, and not in the oldness of the letter." (Verses 5, 6.)

9. The law may not be condemned; it is good.

"Wherefore the law is holy, and the commandment holy, and just, and good." (Verse 12.)

No. 2. Eighth Chapter.

1. Condemnation gone from all who are in Christ.

"There is therefore now no condemnation to them which are in Christ Jesus, who walk not after the flesh, but after the Spirit." (Verse 1.)

2. The Spirit of life in Christ makes free from sin.

"For the law of the Spirit of life in Christ Jesus hath made me free from the law of sin and death." (Verse 2.)

3. The law could not make free from sin, but Christ does.

"For what the law could not do, in that it was weak through the flesh, God sending his own Son in the likeness of sinful flesh, and for sin, condemned sin in the flesh." (Verse 3.)

4. Through Christ the righteousness of the law may be maintained.

"That the righteousness of the law might be fulfilled in us, who walk not after the flesh, but after the Spirit." (Verse 4.)

5. Which has dominion, the flesh or the Spirit?

"For they that are after the flesh do mind the things of the flesh; but they that are after the Spirit, the things of the Spirit." (Verse 5.)

6. The carnal mind an implacable foe of the Almighty.

"Because the carnal mind is enmity against God: for it is not subject to the law of God, neither indeed can be." (Verse 7.)

7. The dominion of the carnal mind is death.

"For to be carnally minded is death; but to be spiritually minded is life and peace." (Verse 6.)

8. The Spirit breaks the dominion of the carnal mind.

"So then they that are in the flesh cannot please God. But ye are not in the flesh, but in the Spirit, if so be that the Spirit of God dwell in you." (Verses 8, 9.)

9. By the Spirit we may mortify sin and live unto God.

"But if the Spirit of him that raised up Jesus from the dead dwell in you, he that raised up Christ from the dead shall also quicken your mortal bodies by his Spirit that dwelleth in you. Therefore, brethren, we are debtors, not to the flesh, to live after the flesh. For if ye live after the flesh, ye shall die: but if ye through the Spirit do mortify the deeds of the body, ye shall live." (Verses 11-13.)

10. The children of God are led by the Spirit.

"For as many as are led by the Spirit of God, they are the sons of God." (Verse 14.)

No. 3. Sixth Chapter.

1. Sin's dominion is broken by grace.

"For sin shall not have dominion over you: for ye are not under the law, but under grace." (Verse 14.)

2. By the crucifixion of the old man, we are free.

"Knowing this, that our old man is crucified with him, that the body of sin might be destroyed, that henceforth we should not serve sin. For he that is dead is freed from sin." (Verses 6, 7.)

3. Christ died unto sin, but liveth unto God.

"Now if we be dead with Christ, we believe that we shall also live with him." "For in that he died, he died unto sin once, but in that he liveth, he liveth unto God." (Verses 8, 10.)

4. We must therefore reckon (count, consider) ourselves dead to sin.

"Likewise reckon ye also yourselves to be dead indeed unto sin, but alive unto God through Jesus Christ our Lord." (Verse 12.)

5. Hence let no sin reign in our mortal bodies.

"Let not sin therefore reign in your mortal body, that ye should obey it in the lusts thereof." (Verse 12.)

6. We must yield (surrender, submit) ourselves to God, not to sin.

"Neither yield ye your members as instruments of unrighteousness unto sin: but yield yourselves unto God, as those that are alive from the dead, and your members as instruments of righteousness unto God." (Verse 13.)

7. In Christ we are free from (victorious over) sin.

"Being then made free from sin, ye became the servants of righteousness." (Verse 18.)

8. We may be free from sin and bring fruit to holiness.

"But now being made free from sin, and become servants to God, ye have your fruit unto holiness, and the end everlasting life." (Verse 22.)

9. We should be as truly holy as we were once sinful.

"I speak after the manner of men because of the infirmity of your flesh: for as ye have yielded your members servants to uncleanness and to iniquity unto iniquity; even so now yield your members servants to righteousness unto holiness." (Verse 19.)

10. This is not simply legal (imputed) holiness, but real, living holiness.

"What shall we say then? Shall we continue in sin, that grace may abound? God forbid. How shall we, that are dead to sin, live any longer therein?" (Verses 1, 2.)

I. The seventh chapter teaches the condition not simply of Paul or any other individual, but of humanity as a race, as a whole, without the assistance of grace. The law of God — holy, just, and good — requires of man perfect obedience. "Be ye holy," "be ye perfect." Man's judgment approves the law, acknowledges its purity and justice, even delighting in it as the expression of the Divine mind. But in contrast with this pure and holy law he sees his own sinfulness of nature and consequent inability to meet the standard required in God's law. So he cries out:

1. "The law is spiritual: but I am carnal, sold under sin." That is, the law is exactly right, but I am all wrong — a slave to sin and unable to keep God's law.

2 and 3. Though I see a beauty in God's law — yea, though "I delight in the law of God after the inward man" — yet there is in myself a contrary principle, a law of my fallen nature which is at war with the law of God, though my judgment heartily approves it as just and good. I am fettered with the "carnal mind," which is enmity against God, and thus, while "to will is present with me," "how to perform that which is good I know not." This gives me much trouble.

4. "O wretched man that I am! What!" God's holy law makes you wretched and miserable? No; not the law, but my own carnal, disobedient nature which renders me so helpless to keep the law, though approved by my judgment. Sin dwells within me, and wars against what I know is pure and good. O what a wretched slave to sin I am! Is there no remedy? Is there no relief? "Who shall deliver me from the body of this death?" Look up, my brother; there is help on high. God hath laid help on One that is "mighty to save." Now we hear him who was just crying, "O wretched man that I am! who shall deliver me?"

shouting with glorious triumph, "I thank God through Jesus Christ our Lord." Though my mind accepted God's law, I could not keep it, because of my flesh (carnal mind), till Christ came to my rescue. Now that Christ is come he has reached in him the solution of all his difficulties. Hear his exultant shout of victory as he goes on telling of freedom from his former bondage to sin; and see how he ascribes all his triumphs to Christ.

II. Eighth chapter.

1 and 2. "There is therefore now no condemnation to them which are in Christ Jesus." Without Christ "I am carnal, sold under [bondage to] sin," but in Christ I have freedom from sin, and justification before God. "For the law of the Spirit of life in Christ Jesus hath [not will, but *hath*] made me free from the law of sin and death." The power of sin dwelling in him made him do the things he condemned; for "sin, taking occasion by the commandment, slew him." (Rom. vii.11.) But now the law of spiritual life in Christ makes him free from this soul-destroyer, sin, and he no longer cries, "O wretched man!" but shouts in holy triumph of freedom from sin by Christ Jesus.

Hear his explanation:

3 and 4. "What the law could not do in that it was weak through the flesh [the condition described in the seventh chapter], God sending his own Son in the likeness of sinful flesh, and for sin [*i.e.*, an offering or sacrifice for sin], condemned sin in the flesh." We do not have to die to get freedom from sin, for by Christ it is *now* condemned *in the flesh*. "That [in order that] the righteousness of the law might be fulfilled in us" — that is, that the holy law of God, which is in antagonism to our carnal nature, might accomplish its intended results in the destruction of sin, so that our lives may become conformed to the holiness of God's law. The condition is that we walk not after the flesh (the "carnal mind"), but after the Spirit — the Holy Spirit of God.

5 to 7. The term "flesh" here means that "carnal mind" or evil principle in the nature of man which is said to be not "at enmity" toward God, but "is enmity against God." It is not subject to God's holy law, but is an inveterate, uncompromising, implacable foe to God and his righteousness. "To be carnally minded [that is, to be under the dominion of the carnal mind] is death." The Corinthian Christians were carnal. "I, brethren, could not speak unto you as unto [wholly] spiritual, but as unto carnal, even as unto babes in Christ." (1 Cor. iii.1.) A person may be "yet carnal," and still not be under the dominion of the carnal mind. *To be* carnally minded is death. The dominion of the carnal mind of the carnal mind is a fact in every unconverted soul; while babes in Christ, though "yet carnal," have in Christ "the power to have victory over the world, the flesh [*carnal mind*], and the devil."

8. "Ye are not in [slavery to] the flesh, but in [under the influence of] the Spirit, if so be that the Spirit of God dwell in you."

9. To live after the flesh brings death; but to follow the Spirit— crucify the flesh, thus living only to God— brings peace and holiness here and heaven hereafter.

III. The lesson of the sixth chapter confirms the ideas given on the seventh and eighth chapters.

"Sin shall not have dominion over you: for [because] ye are not under the law, but under grace." The seventh chapter portrays a man under the law without grace, hence in bondage to sin. His helpless wail is: "I am carnal, sold under sin." "When I would do good evil is present with me." "It is no more I that do it, but sin that dwelleth in me." "O wretched man that I am! who shall deliver me from the body of this death." Without the aid of grace (by Christ) how helpless! With the Divine aid, the freedom of grace, how triumphant! "Sin shall not have dominion." Publish the good news everywhere, preach it in every language; proclaim it on every hill-top; sing it in every tongue; shout it to earth and heaven; confuse all hell with the ringing notes of victory. To the trusting child of God it may be said: "Sin shall not have dominion over you." His glad response may be: "For the law of the Spirit of life in Christ Jesus hath made me free from the law of sin and death."

2 to 4. "Dead to sin," "crucified with Christ." That is, by the power of grace, through the indwelling Spirit, "our old man is crucified," our "carnal mind" is so completely destroyed that righteousness reigns within, love floods the soul, and the inner man, abiding in Christ, triumphs over all sin, "perfecting holiness in the fear of God." "Dead to sin" means that we have no more to do with sin than our dead in their graves have to do with the walks of daily life. St. Paul personally professed this deadness to sin: "I am crucified with Christ: nevertheless I live; yet not I, but Christ liveth in me: and the life which I now live in the flesh I live by the faith of the Son of God, who loved me, and gave himself for me. I do not frustrate the grace of God: for it righteousness come by the law, then Christ is dead in vain." (Gal. ii.20, 21.) He says in this profession of holiness, deadness to sin, life only in, to, and for Christ, he does "not frustrate the grace of God"— that is, he claims this victory by grace through faith and not of himself. "Likewise [in the same way— viz., by grace and faith] reckon [count, consider] yourselves dead indeed unto sin, but alive unto God through Jesus Christ." By nature we are dead *in* sin; by grace we may be dead *to* sin.

5. "Let not sin therefore reign in your mortal body." Notice that these triumphs of grace are conditional. We have our part to perform: "*Reckon* yourselves dead to sin." "*Let not* sin reign in your mortal body." Our victory over sin may be complete, but is actually only in proportion to our consecration and faith. Many there are who are

themselves converted, and yet they cannot say with Paul: "I am crucified with Christ;" "it is not I that liveth, but Christ which liveth in me;" "I am dead indeed unto sin;" "for the law of the Spirit of life in Christ Jesus hath made me free from the law of sin and death."

6 to 8. "Being made free from sin," by the grace of God in Christ, ye may "yield yourselves unto God" and "bring forth fruit unto holiness" and receive in "the end everlasting life."

9 and 10. "Shall we continue in sin, that grace may abound?" Shall we expect the results of grace in judgment, that we may reach heaven at last, though we have continued in sin here? "God forbid. How shall we, that are dead to sin, live any longer therein?" Many are thinking that God's grace will avail to save them in heaven, though they continue in sin on earth. They say they are not under the law, but under grace; meaning that grace operates against the law, thus saving the lawless as well as the obedient. Imputed holiness rests on this dogma; and men believe that in accepting Christ, by a single act of faith, they are ever after exempt from the claims of the law. Hence they claim to be good Christians, while confessing that they "sin every day, in word, thought, and deed." No wonder they sing, lustily: "Free from the law, O happy condition!" But Paul, by the Spirit, teaches differently. He says: "The law is holy," "the law is spiritual; but I am carnal." Where is the wrong, in the law or in the man? In the man. The law is all right. If God makes a change, where will it be? In the law? Surely not! It is "holy;" and God, who himself is holy, cannot change the law. Where is the wrong then? In the man. He is "carnal," sinful. Change him. How? Let him die to sin, but live unto God. "Shall we continue in sin," and trust to grace to abolish God's holy law, saving us in spite of it? God forbid; rather, let us "reckon ourselves dead indeed unto sin, but alive unto God, through Jesus Christ our

Lord." "Do we then make void the law through faith? God forbid: yea, we establish the law." (Rom. iii.31.) If we establish the law through faith, we do so by the results of grace in our lives— namely, the destruction of sin in us, "that the righteousness of the law might be fulfilled in us, who walk not after the flesh, but after the Spirit."

Three interpretations of the seventh of Romans are prevalent among expositors.

1. Some say it describes the best estate of the Christians in this life; that St. Paul here gave his experience as a Christian. That this is a false view we think we have established in this reading. Compare Romans vii.24, 25 with viii.1-4 and vi.14, 1, 2, 11, 22.

2. Another interpretation is that it represents a converted person who has not reached the experience of entire sanctification.

3. Many commentators tell us it represents a convicted but unconverted sinner; and if taken as Paul's personal experience, it represents his struggles under conviction before he was converted.

The real meaning seems to be a description of the depravity or carnality of the human race, of man as a whole, and of his utter dependence on grace. It shows how helpless we would all be, facing the holy law of God, if we were unaided by the gospel grace, which, however, is shown in the sixth and eighth chapters to be our sufficiency.

The three chapters together teach: (1) The holiness of God's law; (2) the depravity and consequent helplessness of man; (3) the all-sufficiency of the grace of God, in Christ Jesus. No individual need remain a day in the seventh chapter state of bondage to sin.

Does the freedom given in the eighth chapter come with conversion, or not till entire sanctification, as a second blessing? I think this lesson does not deal in *methods*, but simply gives the great *fact* of freedom from sin, and perfect holiness in Christ. There is nothing more clearly taught in the Scriptures, I think, than entire sanctification as a second experience of grace, a "second blessing," as taught by the Wesleys and others. But this lesson, I think, simply teaches the glorious fact of entire victory over sin, leaving the methods of grace to other lessons of Scripture. "Be ye holy." (1 Pet. i.15, 16.) "Blessed are the pure in heart: for they shall see God." (Matt. v.8.) "Holiness, without which no man shall see the Lord." (Heb. xii.14.)

49
KINGDOM OF HEAVEN, OF GOD

1. What it is, and what it is not.

    "For the kingdom of God is not meat and drink; but righteousness, and peace, and joy in the Holy Ghost." (Rom. xiv.17.)

2. To enter into his kingdom we must be converted.

    "And said, Verily I say unto you, Except ye be converted, and become as little children, ye shall not enter into the kingdom of heaven." (Matt. xviii.3.)

3. We should first seek the kingdom of God.

    "But seek ye first the kingdom of God, and his righteousness; and all these things shall be added unto you." (Matt. vi.33.)

4. Greatness in the kingdom of God is by humility.

    "Whosoever therefore shall humble himself as this little child, the same is greatest in the kingdom of heaven." (Matt. xviii.4.)

5. They who *trust* in riches cannot enter the kingdom.

"Children, how hard is it for them that trust in riches to enter into the kingdom of God!" (Mark x.24.)

6. God's kingdom shall have no end.

"And he shall reign over the house of Jacob forever; and of his kingdom there shall be no end." (Luke i.33.) See 2 Peter i.11.

7. The kingdom is come nigh unto us.

"And heal the sick that are therein, and say unto them, The kingdom of God is come nigh unto you. But into whatsoever city ye enter, and they receive you not, go your ways out into the streets of the same, and say, Even the very dust of your city, which cleaveth on us, we do wipe off against you: notwithstanding, be ye sure of this, that the kingdom of God is come nigh unto you." (Luke x.9-11.)

8. Christ's kingdom is not of this world.

"Jesus answered, My kingdom is not of this world: if my kingdom were of this world, then would my servants fight, that I should not be delivered to the Jews: but now is my kingdom not from hence." (John xviii.36.)

9. This kingdom is not in word — *i.e.*, form only — but in power.

"For the kingdom of God is not in word, but in power." (1 Cor. iv.20.)

10. One must be born of the Spirit to enter the kingdom.

"Jesus answered and said unto him, Verily, verily, I say unto thee, Except a man be born again, he cannot see the kingdom of God." (John iii.3.) See John iii.7, 8.

50
CHRISTIAN TRAINING OF CHILDREN

1. Train— catechise— them up in the way of the Lord.

> "Train up a child in the way he should go: and when he is old, he will not depart from it." (Prov. xxii.6.)

2. Nurture and admonition, education and reproof of the Lord.

> "And, ye fathers, provoke not your children to wrath: but bring them up in the nurture and admonition of the Lord." (Eph. vi.4.)

3. Teach them the holy Scriptures: they reveal the way of salvation.

> "And that from a child thou hast known the holy Scriptures, which are able to make thee wise unto salvation through faith which is in Christ Jesus." (2 Tim. iii.15.)

4. The child needs correction; if so raised, he brings joy to the home.

"Correct thy son, and he shall give thee rest; yea, he shall give delight unto thy soul." (Prov. xxix.17.)

5. Eli failed in this, and his home was cursed.

"Now the sons of Eli were sons of Belial; they knew not the Lord." "I will perform against Eli all things which I have spoken concerning his house: when I begin, I will also make an end. For I have told him that I will judge his house forever for the iniquity which he knoweth; because his sons made themselves vile, and he restrained them not." (1 Sam. ii.12; iii.12, 13.)

6. Abraham trained his children, and God blessed him.

"For I know him, that he will command his children and his household after him, and they shall keep the way of the Lord, to do justice and judgment; that the Lord may bring upon Abraham that which he hath spoken of him." (Gen. xviii.19.)

7. The curse of God is upon him who turns a child from God.

"But whoso shall offend one of these little ones which believe in me, it were better for him that a millstone were hanged about his neck, and that he were drowned in the depth of the sea." (Matt. xviii.6.)

8. But to receive them religiously is to receive Christ.

"And whoso shall receive one such little child in my name receiveth me." (Matt. xviii.5.)

9. Personal qualification for this duty.

"And thou shalt love the Lord thy God with all thine heart, and with all thy soul, and with all thy might." (Deut. vi.5.)

10. The way of success in teaching children for the Lord.

"And these words, which I command thee this day, shall be in thine heart: and thou shalt teach them diligently unto thy children, and shalt talk of them when thou sittest in thine house, and when thou walkest by the way, and when thou liest down, and when thou risest up." (Deut. vi.6, 7.)

51
INFANT BAPTISM

I. Proposition: God's Church was in the world before the coming of Christ.

1. The Church in the wilderness in the days of Moses.

"This is he, that was in the church in the wilderness with the angel which spake to him in the mount Sina, and with our fathers: who received the lively oracles to give unto us." (Acts vii.38.) See Acts vii.37.

2. David sung praise unto God in the midst of the Church.

"Saying, I will declare thy name unto my brethren, in the midst of the church will I sing praise unto thee." (Heb. ii.12.) See Psalm xxii.22-25.

3. The kingdom of God — the Church — was taken from the Jews and given to us.

"Therefore say I unto you, The kingdom of God shall be taken from you, and given to a nation bringing forth the fruits thereof." "And when the chief priests and Pharisees had heard his parables, they perceived that he spake of them." (Matt. xxi.43, 45.) See Matthew xxi.33-46.

4. They had the gospel— hence a Church— earlier, even in Abraham's day.

> "And the Scripture, foreseeing that God would justify the heathen through faith, preached before the gospel unto Abraham, saying, In thee shall all nations be blessed." (Gal. iii.8.)

5. The gospel then, as now, was appropriated by faith.

> "For unto us was the gospel preached, as well as unto them: but the word preached did not profit them, not being mixed with faith in them that heard it." (Heb. iv.2.) See Hebrews iii.16-iv.2.

II. Proposition: Infants were long ago made members of this Church, by an unchangeable law.

1. God established an everlasting covenant with Abraham. Circumcision was its sign.

> "And I will establish my covenant between me and thee and thy seed after thee in their generations, for an everlasting covenant, to be a God unto thee and to thy seed after thee." "This is my covenant, which ye shall keep, between me and you and thy seed after thee; Every man child among you shall be circumcised." "And the uncircumcised man child whose flesh of his foreskin is not circumcised, that soul shall be cut off from his people; he hath broken my covenant." (Gen. xvii.7, 10, 14.) See Genesis xvii.1-14.

2. This covenant, confirmed in Christ, was not made void by Mosaic law.

> "And this I say, that the covenant, that was confirmed before God in Christ, the law, which was four hundred and thirty years after, cannot disannul, that it should make the promise of none effect." (Gal. iii.17.) See Galatians iii.16-18.

3. This covenant promise is now sealed by baptism.

"For ye are all the children of God by faith in Christ Jesus. For as many of you as have been baptized into Christ have put on Christ. There is neither Jew nor Greek, there is neither bond nor free, there is neither male nor female: for ye are all one in Christ Jesus. And if ye be Christ's, then are ye Abraham's seed, and heirs according to the promise." (Gal. iii.26-29.)

4. The change from circumcision to baptism made at Pentecost.

"Then Peter said unto them, Repent, and be baptized every one of you in the name of Jesus Christ for the remission of sins, and ye shall receive the gift of the Holy Ghost. For the promise is unto you, and to your children, and to all that are afar off even as many as the Lord our God shall call." (Acts. ii.38, 39.)

III. The unlimited character of the commission.
1. It requires the baptizing of *nations*.

"Go ye therefore, and teach all nations, baptizing them in the name of the Father, and of the Son, and of the Holy Ghost." (Matt. xxviii.19.)

2. God set us an example. He baptized a nation.

"Moreover, brethren, I would not that ye should be ignorant, how that all our fathers were under the cloud, and all passed through the sea; and all were baptized unto Moses in the cloud and in the sea." (1 Cor. x.1, 2.)

IV. Apostolic practice — household baptism.
1. Lydia and her household were baptized under Paul's teaching.

"And a certain woman named Lydia, a seller of purple, of the city of Thyatira, which worshiped God, heard us: whose heart the Lord opened, that she attended unto the things which were spoken of Paul. And when she was baptized, and her household, she besought us, saying, If ye have judged me to be faithful to the Lord, come into my house, and abide there. And she constrained us." (Acts xvi.14, 15.)

2. Paul's definition of households.

"One that ruleth well his own house, having his children in subjection with all gravity; (for if a man know not how to rule his own house, how shall he take care of the Church of God?)" (1 Tim. iii.4, 5.) See 1 Timothy iii.2.

There are many who question the right of infants to baptism. We think God's word clearly teaches that they should be baptized. If our two first propositions can be established, their right to Christian baptism follows.

I. God's church was in the world before the days of Christ.

1. Our first proposition is settled by the scriptures adduced. Stephen *says* there was a church in the wilderness in the days of Moses. Moses lived before the coming of Christ. Therefore Stephen says, by inspiration, that my first proposition is true.

2. Paul has David confessing Christ in the Church. David also lived before the coming of Christ. Therefore if Paul, inspired, is a good witness, there was a Church in David's day. If they spoke of different Churches, then there were *two* Churches before Christ, and my proposition is still true that there was a Church before Christ.

3. This Jewish Church — of Moses and David — Christ called the "kingdom of God." He further declares that, for unfaithfulness and sin, it should be taken from them and given to others who would bring forth fruit. Notice (1) it is *God's* kingdom; (2) he prizes it, and, instead of destroying it, takes it from the Jews to put it in better

hands, who will cultivate it and render him the fruits. Therefore God's kingdom— the Church— is the same today it was then. Christ is its chief corner-stone, and, though rejected by the Jewish builders, he is become the head of the corner.

4. The gospel is preached to build up the kingdom of God, to advance the work of the Church. They had the gospel in Abraham's day. The presence of the Church is implied in the preaching of the gospel, and as the gospel was preached unto Abraham there must have been a Church also in his day. Further: God called him the father of the faithful. (Gal. iii.7; Rom. iv.11.) It is by the same kind of faith he exercised that we have become the children of God. So our gospel is of faith, as was the gospel in Abraham's day. Hence

5. It did not profit those to whom it was preached in the olden time except they received it by faith. Neither will membership in the Church save us, unless we receive the gospel by faith, for thereby we are justified. (Rom. v.1.) This shows the identity of the Church— the same then as now— having the same condition of salvation, viz., *faith*. Having found, according to my first proposition, a Church before the days of Christ, which preached the gospel of salvation by faith, as now, and that this Church Christ called the "kingdom of God," and said that it should be taken from the Jews and given to others, we proceed to our second proposition.

II. Infants were members of that Church by an unchangeable law.

If the Church was here at any given time, and infants were members of it by a law that was *unchangeable*, it follows necessarily that as long as the Church continues to exist the unchangeable law will continue to make infants members of it.

1. God calls it *"an everlasting* covenant." If everlasting, it is still in force. If it be objected that Canaan was given

as an everlasting possession, and the Jews have been cast out long ago, we reply: A covenant requires two parties, and the Jews broke the covenant and thus forfeited Canaan. They also forfeited the Church, or the kingdom of God, and it is taken from them and given to others. But God established an everlasting covenant with his people, and where his kingdom (his Church) is, there the everlasting covenant is in force. Now this abiding covenant embraces the children, the little ones, and consequently the seal or token of the covenant, circumcision, is given to children as early as eight days of age. Circumcision, though called the covenant, was necessarily only the token or *sign* of it, as we learn from Genesis xvii.11.

2. It has been contended that circumcision was simply a rite in the Mosaic ritual, and that it passed away when Christ came. But St. Paul heads off this very objection here. He says this Abrahamic everlasting covenant was confirmed (established) in Christ four hundred and thirty years before the Mosaic law, so that though that law perish, it cannot disannul this everlasting covenant. My objector says: "Then circumcision is yet binding." I say, No! but the covenant once sealed by circumcision, now sealed by baptism, is yet binding, *and that covenant yet includes the children.* "For of such is the kingdom of God." (Mark x.14.) "The kingdom of God shall be taken from you [the Jews] and given to a nation bringing forth the fruits." (Matt. xxi.43.)

3. As many as have been baptized into Christ have put on Christ. "If ye be Christ's, then are ye Abraham's seed, and heirs according to the promise." In this there is neither Jew nor Greek, male nor female, but all one in Christ. Still we must be the children of God by faith. Notice: It is not the baptism that saves; we must become children of God by faith. So it was not circumcision that saved us, for the gospel of faith was preached unto Abraham. Yet circumcision was the token or sign that sealed the cov-

enant and claimed the promise. As they accepted the promise of God they ratified it by circumcision, the token of the covenant. We are now baptized in the name of Christ, in token of our acceptance of the covenant, our claim upon the promise. "As many of you as have been baptized into Christ have put on Christ." "And if ye be Christ's, then are ye Abraham's seed, and heirs according to the promise." Some object that circumcision was only for males, whereas in infant baptism we baptized both male and female. Certainly, for in baptism Paul says: "There is neither Jew nor Greek, there is neither bond nor free, there is neither male nor female: for ye are all one in Christ Jesus."

4. I am asked when the change was made from circumcision to baptism. I reply: At Pentecost. "Be baptized every one of you in the name of Jesus Christ;… for the promise is unto you, and to your children." The reason here assigned for their baptism is *the promise is unto you.*" Is that a sufficient reason for their baptism? Peter, an inspired apostle, thought so. Very well! if "the promise is unto you" was a sufficient reason for the baptism of three thousand Jews at Pentecost, it will be a sufficient reason for the baptism of any one else to whom it applies. And lo! Peter applies "the promise" to "you, and to your children." Thus the promise, the Abrahamic covenant, heretofore sealed by circumcision and always applied to the children, is now by divine direction to be ratified and confirmed by baptism and special mention is made that it still includes the children. "Suffer the little children to come unto me, and forbid them not; for such is the kingdom of God." (Jesus)

III. We argue infant baptism from the Great Commission.

1. "Go ye therefore, make disciples of all nations, baptizing them," etc. (R.V.) It is utterly impossible to carry out this commission without baptizing the children. (1)

Many die before years of accountability, and therefore unbaptized unless in infancy. (2) Many, when they reach years of accountability, will refuse to be baptized. Thus you will have a large part of the nation unbaptized till the end of time. The cradle, like the grave, is a great leveler, and nowhere else can you baptize a nation.

2. God's own practice confirms this view. He baptized the nation of the Jews, entire, without excluding "the little crying babies," as many teachers now do. Shall his example be followed? Then receive the little ones in his name. "Whoso shall receive one such little child in my name receiveth me." (Matt. xviii.5.)

IV. The Apostle Paul practiced infant baptism.

1. Notice the passage closely: (1) "A certain woman." How many women? *One*. (2) "Which worshiped God." How many worshiped God? A certain woman— one. (3) "Heard us." How many heard the apostles? A certain woman— one. (4) "Whose heart the Lord opened?— converted. How many hearts did the Lord open? *One*. (5) "That she attended unto the things which were spoken of Paul"— obeyed his teaching. How many followed Paul's instructions? One— "she attended," etc. Now *so far as the record goes* there is but one actor or agent here introduced. One person— a certain woman— worships God, hears the apostles, has her heart opened of the Lord, attends the things spoken of Paul. "And when she was baptized." Now if Paul had been like some teachers, there would have been no other baptisms that day. But there were others. "When she was baptized, and her household, she besought us, saying, If ye have judged me to be faithful," etc. She alone claimed to be "faithful to the Lord," as she only is recorded to have worshiped God, had her heart opened, and attended to the things spoken of Paul. But while she only is represented as acting, some others are baptized, and they are hers— her household. The objector says: "They may not have been children."

Very well; be their age what it might, *they were baptized on her faith* so far as the record goes. It is not said of them, as of her, that their hearts were opened, they were faithful, they worshiped God, etc., but it is said that they were her household, and they were baptized.

2. But let Paul tell us what household means: "A bishop then must be blameless,... one that ruleth well his own house, having his children in subjection with all gravity; (for if a man know not how to rule his own house [children], how shall he take care of the Church of God?)" We submit: If ruling the "house" means controlling the children, surely baptizing the "household" means baptizing the children. Further: Even if there were no children in Lydia's household, we have authority here for baptizing households, and if this be practiced commonly, many little ones will seal the promise in the rite of Christian baptism.

52
THE SIN OF NEGLECT

1. No escape if we neglect the offered salvation.

   "How shall we escape, if we neglect so great salvation; which at first began to be spoken by the Lord, and was confirmed unto us by them that heard him." (Heb. ii.3.)

2. A woe against such as are at ease in God's cause.

   "Woe to them that are at ease in Zion, and trust in the mountain of Samaria, which are named chief of the nations." (Amos vi.1.)

3. For doing nothing, Meroz was bitterly cursed.

   "Curse ye Meroz, said the angel of the Lord, curse ye bitterly the inhabitants thereof; because they came not to help of the Lord, to the help of the Lord against the mighty." (Judg. v.23.)

4. The slothful soul will sleep, and suffer want.

   "Slothfulness casteth into a deep sleep; and an idle soul shall suffer hunger." (Prov. xix.15.)

5. The man who buried but *one* talent was lost.

"But he that had received one went and digged in the earth, and hid his Lord's money." "And cast ye the unprofitable servant into outer darkness: there shall be weeping and gnashing of teeth." (Matt. xxv.18, 30.)

6. God's ministers must cry aloud, and spare not.

"Cry aloud, spare not, lift up thy voice like a trumpet, and show my people their transgression, and the house of Jacob their sins." (Isa. lviii.1.)

7. They are but as dumb dogs who fail in warning men.

"His watchmen are blind: they are all ignorant, they are all dumb dogs, they cannot bark; sleeping, lying down, loving to slumber." (Isa. lvi.10.)

8. The watchman who neglects duty is condemned himself.

"When I say unto the wicked, O wicked man, thou shalt surely die; if thou dost not speak to warn the wicked from his way, that wicked man shall die in his iniquity; but his blood will I require at thine hand." (Ezek. xxxiii.8.)

9. Your sin will be sure to come out.

"But if ye will not do so, behold, ye have sinned against the Lord: and be sure your sin will find you out." (Num. xxxii.23.) See Numbers xxxii.20-22.

53
SIN MUST NOT BE COVERED, BUT CONFESSED

1. Whoso covereth his sin shall not prosper.

   "He that covereth his sin shall not prosper: but whoso confesseth and forsaketh them shall have mercy." (Prov. xxviii.13.)

2. Sin, being against God, must be confessed to him.

   "For I acknowledge my transgressions: and my sin is ever before me. Against thee, thee only, have I sinned, and done this evil in thy sight: that thou mightest be justified when thou speakest, and be clear when thou judgest." (Ps. li.3, 4.)

3. A refusal to confess sin gives us trouble.

   "When I kept silence, my bones waxed old through my roaring all the day long. For day and night thy hand was heavy upon me: my moisture is turned into the drought of summer. Selah." (Ps. xxxii.3, 4.)

4. When David confessed his sin God forgave it.

"I acknowledged my sin unto thee, and mine iniquity have I not hid. I said, I will confess my transgressions unto the Lord; and thou forgavest the iniquity of my sin. Selah." (Ps. xxxii.5.)

5. If we confess our sins, he is faithful to forgive.

"If we confess our sins, he is faithful and just to forgive us our sins, and to cleanse us from all unrighteousness. If we say that we have not sinned, we make him a liar, and his word is not in us." (1 John i.9, 10.)

6. The publican confessed, and prayed for mercy.

"And the publican, standing afar off, would not lift up so much as his eyes unto heaven, but smote upon his breast, saying, God be merciful to me a sinner. I tell you, this man went down to his house justified rather than the other: for every one that exalteth himself shall be abased; and he that humbleth himself shall be exalted. (Luke xviii.13, 14.)

7. The returning prodigal confessed his sin.

"I will arise and go to my father, and will say unto him, Father, I have sinned against heaven, and before thee, and am no more worthy to be called thy son: make me as one of thy hired servants." (Luke xv.18, 19.)

8. Daniel prayed, and confessed his sin and that of his people.

"And while I was speaking, and praying, and confessing my sin and the sin of my people Israel, and presenting my supplication before the Lord my God for the holy mountain of my God." (Dan. ix.20.)

54
DANCING

1. To whom we belong: the life we should live.

   "What! know ye not that your body is the temple of the Holy Ghost which is in you, which ye have of God, and ye are not your own? For ye are bought with a price: therefore glorify God in your body, and in your spirit, which are God's." (1 Cor. vi.19, 20.)

2. Every tree is known by its fruit. What of the dance?

   "Ye shall know them by their fruits. Do men gather grapes of thorns, or figs of thistles? Even so every good tree bringeth forth good fruit; but a corrupt tree bringeth forth evil fruit." (Matt. vii.16, 17.)

3. Is dancing of the flesh or the Spirit? As we sow we reap.

   "Be not deceived; God is not mocked: for whatsoever a man soweth, that shall he also reap. For he that soweth to his flesh shall of the flesh reap corruption; but he that soweth to the Spirit shall of the Spirit reap life everlasting." (Gal. vi.7, 8.)

4. How shall we walk, in the flesh or in the Spirit?

"This I say then, Walk in the Spirit, and ye shall not fulfill the lust of the flesh. For the flesh lusteth against the Spirit, and the Spirit against the flesh: and these are contrary the one to the other; so that ye cannot do the thing that ye would." (Gal. v.16, 17.)

5. Reveling among the works of the flesh.

"Now the works of the flesh are manifest, which are these, Adultery, fornication, uncleanness, lasciviousness, idolatry, witchcraft, hatred, variance, emulations, wrath, strife, seditions, heresies, envyings, murders, drunkenness, revelings, and such like: of the which I tell you before, as I have also told you in time past, that they which do such things shall not inherit the kingdom of God." (Gal. v.19-21.)

6. The children of the wicked are they who dance.

"Wherefore do the wicked live, become old, yea, are mighty in power?" "They send forth their little ones like a flock, and their children dance." (Job xxi.7, 11.)

7. Behold the insults they offer to God.

"Therefore they say unto God, Depart from us; for we desire not the knowledge of thy ways. What is the Almighty, that we should serve him? and what profit should we have, if we pray unto him?" (Job xxi.14, 15.)

8. God calls for our separation from the world.

"And what agreement hath the temple of God with idols? for ye are the temple of the living God; as God hath said, I will dwell in them, and walk in them; and I will be their God, and they shall be my people. Wherefore come out from among them, and be ye separate, saith the Lord, and touch not the unclean thing; and I will receive you, and will be a Father unto you, and ye shall be my sons and daughters, saith the Lord Almighty." (2 Cor. vi.16-18.)

To the question, Is it wrong to dance? it seems that to attempt a sober answer were almost folly, since the dance is so notoriously immoral and destructive of piety. But we turn on a little Bible light.

1. We are here taught: (1) That we do not belong to ourselves, but to God; (2) that we must therefore glorify him in both body and spirit, for they are his; (3) that we are temples for God to dwell in. We must not simply consult our pleasure, but the will of God; for we are his creation and by redemption. Our bodies as well as our souls belong to him, and must be used for his glory. Since God dwells in us, we must never go we cannot expect him to accompany us. No one can ask God's blessing upon the dance and his fellowship with it; hence, none should attend the dance. If each person would say, "I am the Lord's, soul and body, and will not go where I cannot ask his presence to accompany me, and his blessing to attend me," the question of dancing would be fully settled.

2. Every tree is to be judged by its own fruit. If the dance is a good tree, its fruit will be pure, noble, good; but if a corrupt tree, the fruit will be bad, pernicious. Remember that God's word is the arbiter of all questions, the tester of all fruits. Does the dance get people converted to God? does it make them purer in their lives holier in their walk and conversation? Does the ball induce people to read the Scriptures more earnestly, or to pray more fervently? Does it open the springs of virtue and purity, and bring forth righteousness and peace? If it does these things, let ministers, Churches, and all good people join heartily in the dance, till they multiply its fruit a hundredfold. But, on the other hand, if the dance is found to produce the bitter, poisonous fruits, contentions, strife, wrangling, quarrelings, fightings, murders; if it breeds

drunkenness, riots, and discord; if it causes jealousy, envy, and hatred; if it inflames passion, feeds lust, and destroys virtue— then let every voice be lifted against it, and every hand be raised for its destruction, till this foul demon of the pit— this base enemy of God and home and virtue— shall be banished to the hell of its deservings.

3. Be not deceived. How liable men are to be deceived on questions involving, as this does, fleshly pleasures! But God is not to be mocked in this matter. You will face the dancing record, as well as others, at his bar. Remember, too, as you sow so you *must* reap. "He that soweth to the flesh [seeking its pleasures outside of God's will] *shall of the flesh reap corruption."* If the dance is of God, its sowing is to the Spirit, and its reaping everlasting life; but if it is of the devil, its sowing is to the flesh, and its harvest is *corruption*. Again we say: *"Be not deceived."*

4. A question: Shall we walk (live) in (under the dominion of) the flesh or the Spirit? "The flesh [carnal nature of man] lusteth [warreth] against the Spirit." The casting vote is in the will. We may give the dominion of our lives to the flesh or to the Spirit. If we give the Spirit control in our lives, we will never dance, but will live for God and the right. If we give the flesh unbridled rein, we will dance, and perhaps contend that there is no harm in it. But this sowing to the flesh will bring its harvest; a corrupt tree will bring bad fruit, and in the end we will reap— corruption. A Catholic priest reports that "the confessional revealed the fact that nineteen-twentieths of the fallen women owe their fall to the dance." This writer has publicly challenged the men who dance, in a number of congregations, if there were any who could say that they were pure in their thoughts and hearts while in the ballroom, and he has never seen a man rise yet. The dance is nothing in all its tendencies but an open door-way to hell, a hot-house of lust and corruption. If we walk in the Spirit, we shall not fulfill the lusts of the flesh.

5. In this enumeration of the works of the flesh we have along with envyings and murders "revelings, and such like." This clearly includes the dance, which is certainly to be called a species of reveling, and is condemned as of the flesh— that corrupt tree which bringeth forth fruit unto death. The apostle adds: *"They which do such things shall not inherit the kingdom of God."* Thus by the word of God, the doom of the dance "and such like" is sealed.

6. If we ask of Job, "Whose children are they that dance?" he answers: "The children of the wicked." In many places the children of Church-members are regular participants in the dance; sometimes, with shame be it said, they are even leaders in the ball. Parents have failed to do their duty when their children are so far forgetful of God and eternity as to be found in the giddy throng which is speeding its way, through the "dance of death," to the wide-spread gates of hell. There the only music that will ever greet the ear will be the "weeping and gnashing of teeth" mingled with the unutterable groans of the damned. O my God, save the people from dancing their way to perdition!

7. "Therefore," therefore what, Job? Because they spend their days in wealth (margin, "mirth") in dancing and revelry, therefore they say unto God: "Depart from us; for we desire not the knowledge of thy ways. What is the Almighty, that we should serve him? and what profit should we have, if we pray unto him?" Thus the dance is exposed by the pen of inspiration; and its fearful fruit is hung up to the gaze of every Bible student. The children of the wicked dance, "therefore they say unto God, Depart from us; for we desire not the knowledge of thy ways." Thus it was in Job's time, is now, and ever shall be. The dance causes its thousands to turn their hearts against God, their backs upon heaven, and their feet into the broad road to death. By its baneful influence multitudes depart from God, backslide from the Church, and

die without hope; while other multitudes stop their ears to the gospel call, refuse the precious invitations of mercy, and the sun of their life sets behind the dark clouds of condemnation to rise no more, and the murky night of their eternal despair sets in.

8. If we would have God as our Father, we must separate ourselves from every unclean thing, of which the dance is one and chief, and come forth into the light of God's love and holiness, that we may be temples for his indwelling.

Reader, do you dance? If so, be done with it forever. May our God bless, guide, and save you! and may it be our happy lot to meet in heaven with all the sanctified! See Acts xxvi.18.

55
MOURNING FOR SIN

1. Submit to God; mourn and weep.

   "But he giveth more grace. Wherefore he saith, God resisteth the proud, but giveth grace unto the humble. Submit yourselves therefore to God. Resist the devil, and he will flee from you. Draw nigh to God, and he will draw nigh to you. Cleanse your hands, ye sinners; and purify your hearts, ye double-minded. Be afflicted, and mourn, and weep: let your laughter be turned to mourning, and your joy to heaviness. Humble yourselves in the sight of the Lord, and he shall lift you up." (Jas. iv.6-10.)

2. Humble yourself, and be exalted.

   "And whosoever shall exalt himself shall be abased; and he that shall humble himself shall be exalted." (Matt. xxiii.12.)

3. The mourner and the impenitent contrasted.

   "Surely he scorneth the scorners: but he giveth grace unto the lowly." (Prov. iii.34.)

4. Christ pronounces his blessing on the mourner.

"Blessed are they that mourn: for they shall be comforted." (Matt. v.4.)

5. The oil of joy instead of mourning; the Spirit's gift.

"The Spirit of the Lord God is upon me; because the Lord hath anointed me to preach good tidings unto the meek; he hath sent me to bind up the brokenhearted, to proclaim liberty to the captives, and the opening of the prison to them that are bound; to proclaim the acceptable year of the Lord, and the day of vengeance of our God; to comfort all that mourn; to appoint unto them that mourn in Zion, to give unto them beauty for ashes, the oil of joy for mourning, the garment of praise for the spirit of heaviness; that they might be called Trees of righteousness, The planting of the Lord, that he might be glorified." (Isa. lxi.1-3.)

6. David as a mourner. He confesseth his sin.

"When I kept silence, my bones waxed old through my roaring all the day long. For day and night thy hand was heavy upon me: my moisture is turned into the drought of summer. Selah. I acknowledged my sin unto thee, and mine iniquity have I not hid. I said, I will confess my transgressions unto the Lord; and thou forgavest the iniquity of my sin. Selah." (Ps. xxxii.3-5.)

7. The people of Nineveh in mourning for sin.

"So the people of Nineveh believed God, and proclaimed a fast, and put on sackcloth, from the greatest of them even to the least of them. For word came unto the king of Nineveh, and he arose from his throne, and he laid aside his robe from him, and covered him with sackcloth, and sat in ashes. And caused it to be proclaimed and published through Nineveh by the decree of the king and his nobles, saying, Let neither man nor beast, herd nor flock, taste any thing: let them not feed, nor drink water: but let man and beast be covered with sackcloth, and cry mightily unto God: yea, let them turn every one from his evil way, and from the violence that is in their hands. Who can tell if God will turn and repent, and turn away from his fierce anger, that we perish not?" (Jon. iii.5-9.)

8. God saw their penitence and saved them.

"And God saw their works, that they turned from their evil way; and God repented of the evil, that he had said that he would do unto them; and he did it not." (Jon iii.10) See David's experience, Psalm cxvi.1-9.

56
THE DOCTRINE OF THE LORD TRUE— A DEMONSTRATION

1. Jesus says, "Do his will," and *know* of the doctrine.

> "If any man will do his will, he shall know of the doctrine, whether it be of God, or whether I speak of myself." (John vii.17.)

2. God has a secret that he reveals to those who obey him.

> "The secret of the Lord is with them that fear him; and he will shew them his covenant." (Ps. xxv.14.)

3. This is not through the eye and ear, but to the inner consciousness.

> "But as it is written, Eye hath not seen, nor ear heard, neither have entered into the heart of man, the things which God hath prepared for them that love him. But God hath revealed them unto us by his Spirit: for the Spirit searcheth all things, yea, the deep things of God." (1 Cor. ii.9, 10.)

4. Our spirits must receive this witness of God's Spirit.

"The Spirit himself beareth witness with our spirit, that we are the children of God." (Rom. viii.16. R. V.)

5. God's Spirit in our hearts enables us to call him Father.

"And because ye are sons, God hath sent forth the Spirit of his Son into your hearts, crying Abba, Father." (Gal. iv.6.)

6. This witness, demonstrating the doctrine, is *in the believer*.

"If we receive the witness of men, the witness of God is greater: for this is the witness of God which he hath testified of his Son. He that believeth on the Son of God hath the witness in himself: he that believeth not God hath made him a liar; because he believeth not the record that God gave of his Son." (1 John. v.9, 10.)

7. The witness was never revealed by the natural senses.

"For since the beginning of the world men have not heard, nor perceived by the ear, neither hath the eye seen, O God, besides thee, what he hath prepared for him that waiteth for him." (Isa. lxiv.4.)

8. God's revealed secret is only for the righteous.

"For the forward is abomination to the Lord: but his secret is with the righteous." (Pro. iii.32.)

9. Job's triumph over the skeptic.

"For I know that my Redeemer liveth, and that he shall stand at the latter day upon the earth." (Job xix.25.)

57
DRUNKENNESS

1. Drunkenness causes poverty and brings want.

   "For the drunkard and the glutton shall come to poverty: and drowsiness shall clothe a man with rags." (Prov. xxiii.21.)

2. Drunkenness hides for shame under the cover of night.

   "For they that sleep, sleep in the night; and they that be drunken are drunken in the night." (1 Thess. v.7.)

3. By drinking God is forgotten, and justice perverted.

   "It is not for kings, O Lemuel, it is not for kings to drink wine; nor for princes strong drink: lest they drink, and forget the law, and pervert the judgment of any of the afflicted." (Prov. xxxi.4, 5.)

4. Drunkenness is so heinous as to be classed with theft and murder.

   "Know ye not that the unrighteous shall not inherit the kingdom of God? Be not deceived: neither fornicators, nor idolaters, nor adulterers, nor effeminate, nor abusers of themselves with mankind, nor thieves, nor covetous, nor drunkards, nor revilers, nor extortioners, shall inherit the kingdom of God." (1 Cor. vi.9, 10.)

5. Drunkards have even sold girls for wine to drink.

"And they cast lots for my people; and have given a boy for a harlot, and sold a girl for wine, that they might drink." (Joel iii.3.)

6. The day of God will come unawares upon some in drunkenness.

"And take heed to yourselves, lest at any time your hearts be overcharged with surfeiting, and drunkenness, and cares of this life, and so that day come upon you unawares." (Luke xxi.34.)

7. Drunkards shall not inherit the kingdom of God.

"Envyings, murders, drunkenness, revelings, and such like: of the which I tell you before, as I have also told you in time past, that they which do such things shall not inherit the kingdom of God." (Gal. v.21.)

8. So God's curse is pronounced upon the drunkard-maker.

"Woe unto him that giveth his neighbor drink, that puttest thy bottle to him, and makest him drunken also, that thou mayest look on their nakedness!" (Hab. ii.15.) See Habakkuk ii.12, 16.

It is estimated that there are in the United States two hundred thousand saloons— drunkard-factories. The outcome is an "army of six hundred thousand habitual drunkards, with a militia of one and a half millions of moderate drinkers to recruit their ranks. The average life of a confirmed drunkard does not exceed ten years, hence we have sixty thousand drunkards dropping into graves of infamy and despair every year; but the militia come forward and join the 'regulars,' and the ghastly ranks are kept full. And another sadder army of one hundred and thirty thousand widows and orphans of drunkards file past these sixty thousand graves, as an army of ghosts to follow the ghosts departed. Rum kills more, all told, every year, than any year of our civil war killed. But there is no arithmetic for the computation of tears, shames, heart-breaks, infamy, despair, and damnation We cannot tabulate these, but there is *one book* in which they are all written down; and that account must one day be faced by those who are responsible for it." (George Lansing Taylor, D.D.)

1. "The drunkard... shall come to poverty." How many homes are standing illustrations of the truth of the text! Old, broken, decayed houses; the winter winds whistling through cracks and crevices, or blowing in chilling gusts through the open windows (panes all gone); the rain pouring in torrents, almost, through the rotten roof; the chimney smoky, the fire gone down; and this the only shelter over the heads of a pure, virtuous woman and tender, lovely children. Broken chairs, beds of straw, a few old boxes; a board table, with rough, coarse food some days, some days none; the clothing in rags and tatters; and when to all this you add cruelty indescribable from him who should give a husband's love, a father's care and protection, still add the heartaches, the sighs and tears, the groans and agony, the remorse, the infamy, disgrace, and shame inseparable from such a life and facts— and you have the drunkard's home. Words are lame and unequal to the task of portraying the life and home of the victim of intemperance in this world. But could the veil be lifted for just a glimpse into the unseen world, that a slight view might be had of the eternal horrors that hang in black damnation over the future of the drunkard and the drunkard-maker— the liquor-vender— every soul would shriek

with pain, and every heart stand still with horror.

2. "They that be drunken are drunken in the night." It would seem that with all the squalor, misery, and wretchedness attendant on the life of the drunkard, it would be always literally true that men would hide away under cover of the shades of night to even touch the cup of death and hell, much less drinking to drunkenness. He should hang his head in shame and confusion before all decent people who ever touches the bowl of intoxicants.

3. "Not for kings to drink wine; nor for princes strong drink; lest they... forget the law, and pervert the judgment." Kings and princes are named here, but the meaning is rulers, officers of the law of any station. They must not drink wine or strong drink; but in many places legislators, judges, and executives in high and low places are such as come under God's curse as pronounce by the prophet: "Woe unto them that rise up early in the morning, that they may follow strong drink; that continue until night, till wine inflame them!" (Isa. v.11.) Men in official positions pander to the demands of the accursed liquor traffic, which has done more to rob heaven, pollute earth, and people hell than any other agency in the devil's employ. The man who will attempt to secure office through bribery and the use of whisky is lower, doubtless, in the moral scale than a poor, benighted Hottentot, and about as base as the cannibals of the South Sea Islands. And he who in office will sell out the weal of his country and fellow-men to the insatiate blood-hounds of the demon of intemperance is doubtless doomed to dwell in fiery billows, surrounded by gnashing fiends, while the wailings of his whisky-cursed fellows drive arrows of remorse into his trembling, terrorized conscience forever. The prophet quoted above continues: "And the harp and the viol, the tabret and pipe, and wine, are in their feasts: but they regard not the work of the Lord, neither consider the operation of his hands. Therefore my people are gone into

captivity, because they have no knowledge: and their honorable men are famished, and their multitude dried up with thirst. Therefore hell hath enlarged herself, and opened her mouth without measure: and their glory, and their multitude, and their pomp, and he that rejoiceth, shall descend into it." (Isa. v.12-14.)

4. "Be not deceived: neither fornicators, nor idolaters, nor adulterers, nor effeminate, nor abusers of themselves with mankind, nor thieves, nor covetous, nor drunkards, nor revilers, nor extortioners, shall inherit the kingdom of God." What a long, black catalogue is here given! and right in the midst of it all, with adulterers, thieves, and extortioners, stands the poor drunkard — his conscience seared, his heart hardened, his eyes blood-shot, his whole being corrupted, his manhood — made to bear the image of God — completely wrecked, and wrecked forever.

5. The utter ruin of manhood has never been more complete, I reckon, than when, frenzied by drink, the poor, besotted, licentious wretches would give "a boy for a harlot, and sell a girl for wine, that they might drink." Drunkenness and licentiousness are twin evils that in combination have wrought more ruin upon earth, and wrecked eternally more blood-bought souls than any other allies of the pit.

6. "The day" of the Lord will "come unawares" upon some, because they allow their hearts overcharged with "surfeiting and drunkenness." Thus they waste the precious privileges of life, trample under foot its golden opportunities, and in gluttony and drunkenness sink into their graves amidst the deepening shades of a starless night.

7. "Envyings, murders, drunkenness, revelings, and such like:... they which do such things shall not inherit the kingdom of God." Men allow envyings, revelings, etc., to be very small affairs; while drunkenness is considered as "an unfortunate occurrence." But when God speaks of these things

he tears away the thin veil of respectability, and shows them to be crimes against God and the soul. Drunkenness not only fires the nerves, maddens the brain, and thereby stirs up strife and contention, but it turns over the keys to man's inner self to the black hosts of hell. The result is that he who was made in the image of God, and whose body was for a temple of the Holy Ghost, becomes as a cage of unclean birds; and the vile demons of envy, jealousy, anger, hatred, malice, lust, theft, murder, and such like, hold high and hellish carnival over the havoc that has been wrought. In the complete wreck of all the good the man possessed — his mental perceptions blurred, his physical powers prostrated, his last anchor to God and heaven cut — the poor lost soul beats out on a stormy sea, devils in hold, on deck, in the sails and the rigging, all hissing, raving, gnashing, till the poor, wearied, frenzied mortal realizes the horrors of hell on earth, and in all wild despair welcomes the approach of death which ushers him into the presence of his holy Judge, from whence he is driven with an abiding consciousness of self-ruin, into the unending horrors and sufferings of a devil's awful hell. My God, put the fearful picture into the minds and consciences of men, if perchance they may learn the folly of drink, the wisdom of total abstinence. The task is too great for man; words fail, and pen is powerless.

8. "Woe unto him that giveth his neighbor drink!" (1) This "woe" will apply to the vender of intoxicants, the liquor-seller. He gives his neighbor the drink that may pauperize his family, degrade his manhood, dethrone his reason, and *demonize* the whole spiritual being. But the bottle will never sink the drunkard deeper under God's burning curse than it will sink the criminal who gave him drink. If it is not a crime to sow the seeds of drunkenness in a man's life, what is a crime? (2) Similar to the selling is the very pernicious habit of *"treating,"* of social drinking. O how many noble men have learned through the aid of this abominable habit their first taste for intoxicants! Reader, if, in the

choice between heaven and hell, between the happiness of yourself and family and the probable utter ruin of all, you decide to drink, let me beg you by your manhood, your respect for others, and your fear of God's wrath and judgments, never, never under any circumstances ask any living mortal to drink with you; for God says: "Woe to him that giveth his neighbor drink, that puttest thy bottle to him," etc. *Think on this*! (3) A third application of the text is to him who gives his influence to the support of the liquor traffic. This Christian (?) nation is to-day engaged in the wholesale and retail liquor traffic. You ask: "How?" By its government license. *License* means "liberty granted, authority given;" so, when the county, State, nation, or other form of government licenses a business it thereby assumes partnership, giving the legal authority as its stock, or investment, for a division of the spoils. In republics the government is in the hands of the people. When therefore such government sells liquor license, it is tantamount to the people becoming whisky-sellers. As a consequence, the blood of the whisky-slain will be required at their hands. "Woe unto him that giveth his neighbor drink!" During a campaign for prohibition I met a Church-member, who said: "Brother Pickett, I'm an Anti." "You're what?" "I'm an Anti-prohibitionist." "You are?" "Yes!"

"Well, so is the devil." No man who fears God can afford to support a license system for the sale of intoxicating liquors; nor should he support a candidate for office, or a political party that favors such license. The attitude of every Christian and true citizen ought to be one of uncompromising and relentless war upon the ungodly traffic. The national and political hope of our country, under God, is in the Prohibition party. May the day soon come when the angel of temperance will spread her downy wings over a land of peace, purity, and plenty; while our sunny land of freedom sweeps heavenward, a beacon light for the nations!

58
PRAYER
No. 1

I. Commands to pray.
1. Continue in prayer and give thanks.

"Continue in prayer, and watch in the same with thanksgiving." (Col. iv.2.)

2. Never cease— *i.e.,* quit, give up, or stop— praying.

"Pray without ceasing." (1 Thess. v.17.)

II. Promises to answer prayer.
1. Ask, and receive; seek, and find, etc.

"Ask, and it shall be given to you; seek, and ye shall find; knock, and it shall be opened unto you: for every one that asketh receiveth; and he that seeketh findeth; and to him that knocketh it shall be opened." (Matt. vii.7, 8.)

2. Let there be united prayer.

"Again I say unto you, That if two of you shall agree on earth as touching any thing that they shall ask, it shall be done for them of my Father which is in heaven." (Matt. xviii.19.)

III. Some conditions of successful prayer.
1. No compromise with sin.

"If I regard iniquity in my heart, the Lord will not hear me." (Ps. lxvi.18.)

2. Abide in Christ, ask in faith.

"If ye abide in me, and my words abide in you, ye shall ask what ye will, and it shall be done unto you." (John xv.7.) "And all things, whatsoever ye shall ask in prayer, believing, ye shall receive." (Matt. xxi.22.)

IV. Some Bible prayers answered.
1. A sinner converted in answer to prayer.

"And he said unto Jesus, Lord, remember me when thou comest into thy kingdom. And Jesus said unto him, Verily I say unto thee, To-day shalt thou be with me in paradise." (Luke xxii.42, 43.)

2. Peter delivered when the Church prayed.

"Peter therefore was kept in prison: but prayer was made without ceasing of the Church unto God for him." "And, behold, the angel of the Lord came upon him, and a light shined in the prison: and he smote Peter on the side, and raised him up, saying, Arise up quickly. And his chains fell off from his hands. And the angel said unto him, Gird thyself, and bind on thy sandals: and so he did. And he saith unto him, Cast thy garment about thee, and follow me. And he went out, and followed him; and wist not that it was true which was done by the angel; but thought he saw a vision. When they were past the first and second ward, they came unto the iron gate that leadeth unto the city; which opened to them of his own accord: and they went out, and passed on through one street; and forthwith the angel departed from him. (Acts xii.5, 7-10.)

59
PRAYER
No. 2

1. The praying soul shall be saved.

   "For there is no difference between the Jew and the Greek: for the same Lord over all is rich unto all that call upon him. For whosoever shall call upon the name of the Lord shall be saved." (Rom. x.12, 13.)

2. Our prayers should not be for show.

   "And when thou prayest, thou shalt not be as the hypocrites are: for thy love to pray standing in the synagogues and in the corners of the streets, that they may be seen of men. Verily I say unto you, They have their reward." (Matt. vi.5.)

3. The Saviour himself went alone to pray.

   "And when he had sent them away, he departed into a mountain to pray." (Mark vi.46.)

4. The Saviour prayed all night before choosing his apostles.

   "And it came to pass in those days, that he went out

into a mountain to pray, and continued all night in prayer to God. And when it was day, he called unto him his disciples: and of them he chose twelve, whom also he named apostles." (Luke vi.12, 13.)

5. **Jesus prayed with agony, in Gethsemane.**

"And he was withdrawn from them about a stone's cast, and kneeled down, and prayed, saying, Father, if thou be willing, remove this cup from me: nevertheless, not my will, but thine, be done. And there appeared an angel unto him from heaven, strengthening him. And being in an agony he prayed more earnestly: and his sweat was as it were great drops of blood falling down to the ground." (Luke xxii.41-44.)

6. **He prayed with submission.**

"And he went forward a little, and fell on the ground, and prayed that, if it were possible, the hour might pass from him. And he said, Abba, Father, all things are possible unto thee; take away this cup from me: nevertheless, not what I will, but what thou wilt." (Mark xiv.35, 36.)

7. **A river-side prayer-meeting.**

"And on the Sabbath we went out of the city by a river-side, where prayer was wont to be made; and we sat down, and spake unto the women which resorted thither." (Acts xvi.13.)

8. **Daniel prayed three times a day, though death faced him.**

"Now when Daniel knew that the writing was signed, he went into his house; and, his windows being open in his chamber toward Jerusalem, he kneeled upon his knees three times a day, and prayed, and gave thanks before his God, as he did aforetime." (Dan. vi.10.)

60
PRAYER
No. 3

1. We should never become discouraged in prayer.

   "And he spake a parable unto them to this end, that men ought always to pray, and not to faint." (Luke xviii.1.)

2. Pray for the Holy Spirit.

   "If ye then, being evil, know how to give good gifts unto your children; how much more shall your heavenly Father give the Holy Spirit to them that ask him?" (Luke xi.13.)

3. Pentecost came through united prayer.

   "These all continue with one accord in prayer and supplication, with the women, and Mary the mother of Jesus, and with his brethren." (Acts i.14.)

4. The place was shaken where the disciples prayed.

   "And when they had prayed, the place was shaken where they were assembled together; and they were all filled with the Holy Ghost, and they spake the word of God with boldness." (Acts iv.31.)

5. Pray everywhere, lifting up holy hands.

"I will therefore that men pray everywhere, lifting up holy hands, without wrath and doubting." (1 Tim. ii.8.)

6. Pray in the exercise of present faith.

"Therefore I say unto you, What things soever ye desire, when ye pray, believe that ye receive them, and ye shall have them." (Mark xi.24.)

7. When we pray, we *must* forgive.

"And when ye stand praying, forgive, if ye have aught against any; that your Father also which is in heaven may forgive you your trespasses. But if ye do not forgive, neither will your Father which is in heaven forgive your trespasses." (Mark xi.25, 26.)

8. Sometimes we must fast while praying.

"Howbeit this kind goeth not out but by prayer and fasting." (Matt. xvii.21.)

9. Secret prayer will bring open reward.

"But thou, when thou prayest, enter into thy closet, and when thou hast shut thy door, pray to thy Father which is in secret; and thy Father which seeth in secret shall reward thee openly." (Matt. vi.6.)

10. The penitent publican's prayer answered.

"And the publican, standing afar off, would not lift up so much as his eyes unto heaven, but smote upon his breast, saying, God be merciful to me a sinner. I tell you, this man went down to his house justified rather than the other: for every one that exalteth himself shall be abased; and he that humbleth himself shall be exalted." (Luke xviii.13, 14.)

61
PRAYER
No. 4

1. Pray for all men— for rulers, sinners, etc.

"I exhort therefore, that, first of all, supplications, prayers, intercession, and giving of thanks, be made for all men; for kings, and for all that are in authority; that we may lead a quiet and peaceable life in all godliness and honesty. For this is good and acceptable in the sight of God our Saviour." (1 Tim. ii.1-3.)

2. Solomon's prayer at the dedication of the temple.

"And Solomon stood before the altar of the Lord in the presence of all the congregation of Israel, and spread forth his hands toward heaven: and he said, Lord God of Israel, there is no God like thee, in heaven above, or on earth beneath, who keepest covenant and mercy with thy servants that walk before thee with all their heart." (1 Kings viii.22, 23.)

3. Though said to be standing, he was really kneeling.

"And it was so, that when Solomon had made an end of praying all this prayer and supplication unto the Lord, he arose from before the altar of the Lord, from kneeling on his knees with his hands spread up to heaven." (1 King viii.54.) See 1 Kings viii.22-53.

4. The apostles desired to give themselves wholly to prayer and the ministry.

"But we will give ourselves continually to prayer, and to the ministry of the word." (Acts vi.4.)

5. The Church should pray for her ministers.

"Praying always with all prayer and supplication in the Spirit, and watching thereunto with all perseverance and supplication for all saints; and for me, that utterance may be given unto me, that I may open my mouth boldly, to make known the mystery of the gospel." (Eph. vi.18, 19.)

6. Paul and Silas prayed at midnight, in jail.

"And at midnight Paul and Silas prayed, and sung praises unto God: and the prisoners heard them. And suddenly there was a great earthquake, so that the foundations of the prison were shaken: and immediately all the doors were opened, and every one's bands were loosed." (Acts xvi.25, 26.)

7. The prayer of the thief and its answer.

"And he said unto Jesus, Lord, remember me when thou comest into thy kingdom. And Jesus said unto him, Verily I say unto thee, To-day shalt thou be with me in paradise." (Luke xxiii.42, 43.)

8. Our confidence that God will answer prayer.

"And this is the confidence that we have in him, that, if we ask any thing according to his will, he heareth us: and if we know that he hear us, whatsoever we ask, we know that we have the petitions that we desired of him." (1 John v.14, 15.)

9. Pray about every thing; be anxious for nothing.

"Be careful for nothing; but in every thing by prayer and supplication with thanksgiving let your requests be made known unto God. And the peace of God, which passeth all understanding, shall keep your hearts and minds through Christ Jesus." (Phil. iv.6, 7.)

62
WOMAN'S MINISTRY

1. Let your women keep silence — a difficulty.

   "For God is not the author of confusion, but of peace, as in all churches of the saints. Let your women keep silence in the churches: for it is not permitted unto them to speak; but they are commanded to be under obedience, as also saith the law. And if they will learn any thing, let them ask their husbands at home: for it is a shame for women to speak in the church." (1 Cor. xiv.33-35.)

2. Directions for women to pray and prophesy — some relief.

   "Every man praying or prophesying, having his head covered, dishonoreth his head. But every woman that prayeth or prophesieth with her head uncovered dishonoreth her head: for that is even all one as if she were shaven." (1 Cor. xi.4, 5.)

3. Prophesying defined — the difficulty gone.

   "But he that prophesieth speaketh unto men to edification, and exhortation, and comfort." (1 Cor. xiv.3.)

4. Women to prophesy — Joel's prediction.

"And it shall come to pass afterward, that I will pour out my Spirit upon all flesh; and your sons and your daughters shall prophesy, your old men shall dream dreams, your young men shall see visions: and also upon the servants and upon the handmaids in those days will I pour out my Spirit." (Joel ii.28, 29.)

5. The time fulfilled — Peter's testimony.

"But this is that which was spoken by the prophet Joel; And it shall come to pass in the last days, saith God, I will pour out of my Spirit upon all flesh: and your sons and your daughters shall prophesy, and your young men shall see visions, and your old men shall dream dreams: and on my servants and on my handmaidens I will pour out in those days of my Spirit; and they shall prophesy." (Acts ii.16-18.)

6. A woman who judged (ruled) Israel — a prophetess.

"And Deborah, a prophetess, the wife of Lapidoth, she judged Israel at that time." (Judg. iv.4.)

7. Four sisters who prophesied — daughters of an evangelist.

"And the next day we that were of Paul's company departed, and came unto Caesarea; and we entered into the house of Philip the evangelist, which was one of the seven; and abode with him. And the same man had four daughters, virgins, which did prophesy." (Acts xxi.8, 9.)

8. There were some women who helped Paul in the gospel.

"And I entreat thee also, true yokefellow, help those women which labored with me in the gospel, with

Clement also, and with other my fellow-laborers, whose names are in the book of life." (Phil. iv.3.)

There is abroad a queer opinion, that women must not preach, exhort, or even pray in public. It is argued that the Scriptures positively forbid such exercises in public.

1. "Let your women keep silence in the churches: for it is not permitted unto them to speak." This is the passage used in opposition to woman's ministry. But let us see. Notice the verses before and after: "God is not the author of confusion, but of peace." If your women "will learn any thing, let them ask their husbands at home: for it is a shame for women to speak in the church." Has this "speaking" which is liable to cause "confusion," disturb the "peace," and show the spirit of insubordination of "disobedience," any of the characteristics of preaching, exhorting, or praying? The speaking objected to had all these features in it; so the women were told, if they would "*learn* any thing, let them ask their husbands at home: for it is a shame for women to *speak*," etc. The thing objected to is evidently either questioning the preacher in the midst of his sermon, or speech-making, disputing, debating, wrangling. The points guarded are: They must not cause "confusion;" must be under "obedience;" must "learn" of "their husbands at home." God has the salvation of the world so at heart "that he gave his only begotten Son" for its redemption: commanded that his gospel be preached "to every creature;" and, since "the harvest truly is great," we are told to pray "for more laborers." In the face of these urgent demands for workers, if a consecrated, gifted woman presents herself to go forth bearing precious seeds of gospel truth for the salvation of men; or if she should lift her voice in earnest tones of importunate prayer, is she to be coolly told to "keep silence: for it is a shame for women" to pray or preach? Some of the most useful and gifted evangelists now living are women.

Holy, earnest, gifted, their conversions are numbered by the thousands, while earth rejoices in the blessings attending their labors, and heaven exults in their God-given triumphs. But many would stop their labors. Would St. Paul? Let us see.

2. "Every man praying or prophesying;... every woman that prayeth or prophesieth," etc. What, Paul! A woman to pray or prophesy? Why, they "must keep silence!" Yes, where confusion would result, as in debating mooted, unsettled questions; but they may pray and prophesy; for were there not women who prophesied under the law? Was not Anna a prophetess who welcomed the infant Jesus with thanksgiving at his appearance in the temple? Since women are authorized by Paul (the Holy Ghost, rather, through Paul) to prophesy, let him define prophesying for us.

3. "He that prophesieth *speaketh* unto men to edification, exhortation, and comfort." Women may *pray* and they may *prophesy* — *i.e.,* speak unto men, not to "confusion," but to edification, exhortation, and comfort. To edify means to build up. The gospel is preached to edify the Church, and this is prophesying; and the women are allowed to do it as well as the men. To prophesy means to exhort. Women are authorized to prophesy. Therefore women are authorized to exhort. If the women exhort — speak unto men to edification and comfort (and Paul plainly directs that it be so) — then it is clearly a fact that, whatever is meant in the requirement that they "keep silence," it is not intended to interfere with their praying, preaching, etc., in real evangelistic work.

4. "It shall come to pass afterward, that I will pour out my Spirit upon all flesh; and your sons and your daughters shall prophesy." By the Spirit's inspiration the prophet looked out through the vista of coming centuries till his eye caught the glories of the Pentecostal dispensation, when, under mighty baptisms of the Holy Ghost, both

the sons and the daughters should catch the prophetic fire and go forth as heralds of mercy and truth.

5. Peter leaves us in no doubt as to the fulfillment of Joel's prophecy. "This is that which was spoken by the prophet Joel; And it shall come to pass in the last days, saith God, I will pour out of my Spirit upon all flesh: and your sons and your daughters shall prophesy." Under the inspiration of that wonderful day, when tongues of fire from the upper world rested upon the assembled disciples, Peter declares the time to have come when the daughters and the handmaidens shall receive the Spirit and shall prophesy— *i.e.,* "speak unto men to edification, and exhortation, and comfort." This is the order of the Holy Ghost; but the fogs of superstition from mediaeval errors have beclouded the minds of Christendom till the people, seizing on the opening passage in this chapter, have effectually shut the mouths of godly women, teaching them to believe the public ministry of the word by themselves a sin against God; and thus the devil has reaped a rich harvest from the fields of the Lord. "God giveth the word, and the women who publish it are a great host." (Ps. lxviii.11. R.V.) Dr. Godbey, commenting on this passage, says: An everlasting stigma rests upon the escutcheon of King Jame's translators for concealing the feminine gender, which is actually unmistakable — *oth* being the Hebrew termination, *basaroth* in the Hebrew positively and unequivocally meaning *preaching women*. Glory to God for this prophetic vision of hosts and armies of women going forth preaching the gospel to all nations! The fulfillment of this vision is to bring the millennium." ("Victory," p. 27.)

6. Deborah was a prophetess in Israel, and she also "judged Israel." So many are afraid of woman's ministry and woman suffrage that they might do well to take a lesson here from the word of God.

7. "Philip the evangelist [some preachers of this age

call evangelists 'tramps;' but the Lord recognized at least this one. See also Ephesians iv.11-13; 2 Timothy iv.5]... had four daughters, virgins, which did prophesy." Let an evangelist with four preaching daughters come along now, and O how many would raise a cry, "Let your women keep silence!" forgetful that when God's Spirit is poured out "your sons and your daughters shall prophesy."

8. "Help those women which labored with me in the gospel." So even St. Paul had some women assisting him in his gospel ministrations.

Deborah, Anna, Philips four daughters, Phoebe, Priscilla, "those women which labored with Paul in the gospel," and a host of women from all countries and ages will doubtless join with prophets, apostles, pastors, evangelists, teachers and other workers in the great harvest home, giving praises and glory and thanksgiving unto Him in whose name they preached, and by whose grace they had salvation and their successes. Let us labor with them in weeping here, that we, as well as they, may come with rejoicing, bringing our sheaves.

63
The Sabbath

1. **We are commanded to keep the day holy.**

    "Remember the Sabbath-day, to keep it holy." (Ex. xx.8.)

2. **We must neither work ourselves nor make others do it.**

    "Six days shalt thou labor, and do all thy work: but the seventh day is the Sabbath of the Lord thy God: in it thou shalt not do any work, thou, nor thy son, nor thy daughter, thy man-servant, nor thy maid-servant, nor thy cattle, nor thy stranger that is within thy gates: for in six days the Lord made heaven and earth, the sea, and all that in them is, and rested the seventh day: wherefore the Lord blessed the Sabbath-day and hallowed it." (Ex. xx.9-11.)

3. **God sanctified the seventh day in the beginning.**

    "And on the seventh day God ended his work which he had made; and he rested on the seventh day from all his work which he had made. And God blessed the seventh day, and sanctified it: because that in it he had rested from all his work which God created and made." (Gen. ii.2, 3.)

4. Nehemiah worked a great reform in Sabbath-keeping.

"In those days saw I in Judah some treading winepresses on the sabbath, and bringing in sheaves, and lading asses; as also wine, grapes, and figs, and all manner of burdens, which they brought into Jerusalem on the Sabbath-day: and I testified against them in the day wherein they sold victuals." "Did not your fathers thus, and did not our God bring all this evil upon us, and upon this city? yet ye bring more wrath upon Israel by profaning the Sabbath." "When I testified against them, and said unto them, Why lodge ye about the wall? if ye do so again, I will lay hands on you. From that time forth came they no more on the Sabbath." (Neh. xiii.15, 18, 21.)

5. The Sabbath must not be simply a pleasure day, but a holy day.

"If thou turn away thy foot from the Sabbath, from doing thy pleasure on my holy day; and call the Sabbath a delight, the holy of the Lord, honorable; and shalt honor him, not doing thine own ways, nor finding thine own pleasure, nor speaking thine own words: then shalt thou delight thyself in the Lord; and I will cause thee to ride upon the high places of the earth, and feed thee with the heritage of Jacob thy father: for the mouth of the Lord hath spoken it." (Isa. lviii.13, 14.)

6. Jesus Christ is Lord of the Sabbath.

"And he said unto them, That the Son of man is Lord also of the Sabbath." (Luke vi.5.)

7. Called by St. John the Lord's-day.

"I was in the Spirit on the Lord's-day, and heard behind me a great voice, as of a trumpet." (Rev.i.10.)

"It is manifest that redemption has a marvelous influence on the prosperity, intelligence, health, safety, and happiness of a people. But the Sabbath is the only door through which, by faith in Christ, they can enter the goodly land and become possessed of its blessings. It is the sheet-anchor that fastens redemption to the earth. Hence the public desecration of the Sabbath strikes at the dearest interests of society, and undermines the peace, welfare, happiness, and prosperity of any land. Surely such an institution cannot be too highly prized and too carefully guarded. Every one should know that the hopes of the world are linked in with the redemption, and if they are to be gratified it is imperative that the Sabbath be kept a day of rest, and that on that day earthly cares be laid aside, and that it be observed as a holy day. Give the people a Sabbath and a faithful ministry of the word of God, and there is no evil which can attack them, or shape that sin can assume, either in the State or the act of an individual, or in a nation in the form of the unhallowed commerce of the liquor traffic, or corruption in the courts of justice, or a bad social order and form of government, that redemption will not antagonize... Remove the Sabbath from a nation, and you strangle among that people the very life of the things that are true, things that are pure, things that are just, things that are honest, and things that are lovely and of good report. Rob a nation of the Sabbath, and you leave it in its sins, with the only door of escape shut and barred against it." (Rev. T.M.C. Birmingham, in "National Salvation." J.D. Barbee, Agent, Nashville, Tenn. Price twenty-five cents. A splendid little book.)

1. "Remember the Sabbath-day to keep it holy." The

tendency to forget the Sabbath as a holy day seems general. Man is so depraved that he forgets God and the things of God. God gave the Sabbath not only as a day of rest, but also as a day for spiritual development, a day for the cultivation of an unworldly, a spiritual, heavenly life. Its authority will last and its obligations continue while time endures and the government of God abides over man.

2 and 3. "Six days shalt thou labor and do all thy work." This teaches us to labor in the six days. Laziness is no part of Christian character. A man has no right to idle through the six working-days of the week, but he must labor at something that will make the world better or better off. "The seventh day is the Sabbath of the Lord thy God." It is the consecrated, holy day that God has set apart from worldly to heavenly uses. As God has devoted it to such high and holy use, man should never degrade it to a lower and meaner use. It is the *seventh day*— but not *of the week*. An extensive battle is being fought here. There are some who, with great zeal and diligence, are striving to get the people to observe Saturday for the Sabbath instead of our present Sunday. But the command does not say the seventh day *of the week*, thus giving a definite starting-point for the count, but simply the *seventh day*; by which can only be meant that the people must labor six days, and then rest and worship must follow for man's physical and spiritual good. Give us these two things— (1) every seventh day in order, (2) unanimity in its observance, it being regularly kept as a *holy day by all the people*— and I have little idea that Almighty God would care whether the day kept be Saturday, Monday, Wednesday, or Sunday. Our monthly and yearly calendar are not the same as that of the Jews; and why need the weekly be, further than to attain the objects of the fourth commandment— viz., every seventh day for spiritual, holy, heavenly uses, that we may be advanced

in spiritual life, and consequent glory be given to God. The Seventh-dayism of this generation distracts communities, disbands Churches, arouses controversy, wrecks families— between the father keeping Saturday and the mother Sunday, the children get no day: all this over the nonsensical idea that somebody knows, even yet, the *seventh day of the week* since creation dawned, a thing preposterous and absurd. All in the name of the holy day, it has become a prolific source of Sabbath desecration, enkindling strife and breeding infidelity. In our present calendar enumeration Sunday is the first, Saturday the seventh day of the week; but if the enumeration begin with Monday, Sunday will be the seventh. Does the keeping of God's commandment, which is as wide as the world and as long as time, hinge on the national arrangement of a calendar? God has sanctified a day regularly in seven— a seventh day— for spiritual purposes. Let us so use our present Sabbath.

4. We need a Nehemiah in our age to work a sweeping reform in the Sabbath observance. Thousands are sufficiently orthodox in creed, as to the day to be observed, who are fearfully heterodox in practice, as to the manner of keeping the Sabbath. No work or business of any kind should ever be performed on the Sabbath, except in cases of necessity. Any business use of the day should not be only objected to, but uncompromisingly opposed and fought, by every friend of God and the Sabbath. If a thing is wrong in me, it is wrong in another; and if I encourage another in doing an evil, I am party with him to the crime. Sin is a unit; so that each man, when a number combine in doing a wicked thing, is guilty of the whole, as though he had done the deed alone. If forty men engage in murdering a man, you have forty murderers; if ten men swear falsely about one thing, you have ten perjured men. Whoever, therefore, willingly participates in a wrong thing, though many others may join him in it, he is nevertheless guilty of the whole. Now to ap-

ply this principle: There is in this land of Bibles and Churches a wholesale system of Sunday travel and commerce on the highways of the nation, both by water and land. The steamboats ply our lakes and rivers on the Sabbath-day as if we were a nation of heathens; and our railroads run freight and passenger trains as though this were a land of godless atheists. Hundreds of thousands of poor, hard-worked men toil away through weariness and pain day after day, year in and year out, with no sweet Sabbath of rest and worship to lift their minds to a higher and holier realm. Thus they forget God; associate with sin till it becomes familiarly pleasant; contract habits of drinking, gambling, licentiousness; and thus, living without God, they die without hope, the sun of their lives setting behind the murky clouds of despair, to know no rising forever. O how many of my fellow-men have sunk into the yawning abysms of an endless hell through these godless corporations, which move on for gain over the holy commandments of my God, with high hand desecrating his holy day! But the principle announced above finds there a broad application. No business will run without patronage, and the steam-boats and railroads are not exceptions to the rule. Every patron of a train or boat running on the Sabbath-day is an abettor of the evil, a party to the wholesale ruin and demoralization that follow in its wake. It is probable that not a Sabbath passes in the year but that thousands of professing Christians, some even preachers (?) of the gospel, may be found rushing through the land on railroad trains— the devil's carriages— as though they were totally oblivious of the commandments of God, and utterly regardless of the present and eternal welfare of the thousands of railroad employees who have no Sabbath rest and worship. The man who will lend his sanction, support, and patronage to a Sunday train or steam-boat needs to learn anew the Ten Commandments, dwelling at length upon the fourth. There are men who would not witness a dance, play a game of cards, take a drink of wine, or set foot inside a saloon (shame on him who will do these things); there are men who would not do these things; they would not buy or sell a yard of dry goods, a pound of sugar, or a box of matches on the Sabbath; they would not swap a two-bit pocket-knife, nor give change under other ordinary circumstances, perhaps, for a five-dollar bank-note; yet they will go to the station agent on Sunday, buy a ticket, deposit a bill, receive their change, get on board the train, and ride any distance to suit their convenience, while conductors, engineers, firemen, agents, etc., are thus robbed of their Sabbath, their God, and their souls. We have even known some instances in which preachers would go on a Sunday train to their appointments. A sermon on keeping the Sabbath from such a preacher would doubtless be answered with: "Physician, heal thyself." He who preaches to others to forsake sin ought to forsake his own sins; and if Sabbath desecration is not sin, where may sin be found? If thus selling out five hundred thousand men, soul and body, to the devil is not sinful, then we had best quit talking of influence and moral responsibility. In this same catalogue might be mentioned other similar, but perhaps smaller, agencies of Sabbath desecration; but which, nevertheless, should receive a steady fire from the ranks of the army of Christ. (1) Sunday mails. If the post-office should be opened on the Sabbath, mail should never be put in or taken out by Christians. (2) Sunday newspapers. No Christian can afford, as a soldier of Jesus Christ, to patronize a daily paper that has seven issues per week. Nor should any one spend the sacred hours of the holy day in reading secular newspapers, even when they are decent— which we are sorry to say many are not, but are rather filled with the venomous, polluted scrapings of creation. (3) Street-cars and livery teams ought not to be used on the Sabbath. How Christian men can consent to run or to patronize— which is the same— these things which take from man and beast the day which God appointed for rest and worship is beyond our comprehension.

5. "Turn away thy foot… from doing thy pleasure on my holy day." There is a tendency in many places to foreignize— rather, to devilize— the Sabbath of our country by making it simply a day for pleasure and pastime. The sad spectacle is already presented of thousands attending beer-gardens, *base*-ball games, picnics, etc., on the holy day of God. Saloons too frequently are allowed to do a thriving business in our cities; and in many places, if front doors are closed, side and back entrances admit the motley crowd of sons of Belial, who seem to live only for the pleasures of sense and time. Others there are, more refined in their sins, who make the holy Sabbath a day for pleasure-drives, big dinners, social visits, with gossiping, etc. We would not in every case unqualifiedly discountenance and condemn visiting on the Sabbath, but would say that it should be in the fear of God and should be turned to spiritual profit. Simple pleasure-seeking should never be allowed on the Sabbath, for it should be to us "the holy of the Lord, honorable;" we should not find our own pleasure nor speak our own words, that the Lord may bless us.

6. "The Son of man is Lord also of the Sabbath." We should respect it therefore as we love and honor him. Let it be a day of approach unto him, that we may become by its precious aids more and more conformed to the Divine image.

7. It is the Lord's day. Keep it, beloved reader, as such; and may "the Lord of the Sabbath" be always your Lord and mine until we meet around "the great white throne," where heaven's eternal Sabbath will swallow up the Sabbaths of earth, and the saints of the Lord bid us welcome to the mansions prepared!* (*See the "Holy Day," by author of this book.)

64
THE HOLY SPIRIT

1. The Spirit is a personality, not simply an influence.

"Go ye therefore, and teach all nations, baptizing them in the name of the Father, and of the Son, and of the Holy Ghost." (Matt. xxviii.19.) See 2 Corinthians xiii.14.

2. He reproves the world of sin.

"And when he is come, he will reprove the world of sin, and of righteousness, and judgment." (John xvi.8.)

3. He regenerates the soul that was dead in sin.

"Marvel not that I said unto thee, Ye must be born again. The wind bloweth where it listeth, and thou hearest the sound thereof, but canst not tell whence it cometh, and whither it goeth: so is every one that is born of the Spirit." (John iii.7, 8.)

4. The Spirit of truth. He testifies of Christ.

"But when the Comforter is come, whom I will send

unto you from the Father, even the Spirit of truth, which proceedeth from the Father, he shall testify of me." (John xv.26.)

5. He teaches in the school of Christ.

"But the Comforter, which is the Holy Ghost, whom the Father will send in my name, he shall teach you all things, and bring all things to your remembrance, whatsoever I have said unto you." (John xiv.26.)

6. His presence more important than that of Christ.

"Nevertheless I tell you the truth; It is expedient for you that I go away: for if I go not away, the Comforter will not come unto you; but if I depart, I will send him unto you." (John xvi.7.)

7. He abides in the believer, but being unseen the world will not receive him.

"And I will pray the Father, and he shall give you another Comforter, that he may abide with you forever; even the Spirit of truth; whom the world cannot receive, because it seeth him not, neither knoweth him: but ye know him; for he dwelleth with you, and shall be in you." (John xiv.16, 17.) "But as it is written, Eye hath not seen, nor ear heard, neither have entered into the heart of man, the things which God hath prepared for them that love him. But God hath revealed them unto us by his Spirit: for the Spirit searcheth all things, yea, the deep things of God." (1 Cor. ii.9, 10.)

8. We must not grieve the Holy Spirit.

"And grieve not the Holy Spirit of God, whereby ye are sealed unto the day of redemption." (Eph. iv.30.) See 1 Thessalonians v.19.

9. In olden times some, by rebellion, vexed the Holy Spirit.

> "But they rebelled, and vexed his Holy Spirit: therefore he was turned to be their enemy, and he fought against them." (Isa. lxiii.10.)

This is a lesson of great importance. Only let the Church be filled with the Spirit, and she will shake the world for Christ. May the blessed Holy Spirit, whom we seek to honor in this lesson, use it to his own glory in the salvation and spiritual advancement of his people! Amen.

1. The personality of the Spirit and his oneness with the Father and the Son are here recognized. In our baptism we own the Father as Ruler, the Son as Redeemer, and the Holy Ghost as Regenerator and Sanctifier. If the Spirit has no personality, but is simply an impersonal influence, then we may not baptize in his name, for there is no one to be recognized as thus co-equal with the Father and the Son. But the Saviour himself recognized the Spirit as a person and associated him with the Father and himself, and bade us honor him in every baptism administered.

2. In this passage the important work of conviction is assigned to the Spirit. He will reprove or convict — *i.e.*, convince — the world of sin, of righteousness, and of judgment. That is, he will make men realize the truth that they are sinners, that they can and must be righteous, and that they must be brought into the judgment. The results of the judgment will depend on our characters, whether we be righteous or sinners; and this lesson the Spirit imparts to the world.

3. When men are awakened by the voice of the Spirit, and find themselves dead in sin — that is, without a life of love for God — and when they cry out in anguish of soul for the mercy of God, mourning heartily over their sins (Jon. iii.8-10), then the Holy Spirit is ready to give

comfort (Matt. v.4) and joy to the aching heart. Yea, he gives life to the dead. He steals upon the sin-burdened heart as softly as the gentle breeze. He is as the wind which "bloweth where it listeth, and thou hearest the sound thereof, but canst not tell whence it cometh, and whither it goeth." Though unseen, his presence gives life and peace, for he regenerates the sin-dead soul, and imparts a heavenly life.

4. He is the Comforter. There is no comfort like that which the aching heart finds at the cross by the coming of the Comforter. Further, he is the Spirit of truth, and he testifies of Christ. His messages to the penitent are filled with mercy and peace, while to the faithful believer he brings the strength of the Lord, testifying of him who saves to the "uttermost," that their joy may be full. (John xvii.13.)

5. He becomes our teacher — Christ his theme, the Bible his text-book. And O beloved reader, what a schooling is here offered us! This is truly the training-school of the Almighty preparatory to the college of the skies, the university of the New Jerusalem. Under his tuition, if faithful students, how rapid our advancement in a knowledge of heavenly things, of the "life hid with Christ in God!" "If any of you lack wisdom, let him ask of God, that giveth to all men liberally." (Jas. i.5.)

6. Jesus here tells us that the Spirit's presence is worth more to us than his own. Many think: "O if I could only see Jesus as the disciples did, it would be so much easier to live right!" But the Master says: "No! the Comforter's presence is worth more to you than mine. 'It is expedient for you that I go away.'" One reason is that the Spirit may dwell in us; another, that he can be everywhere at once, which Christ could not in human form. We may each one of us have the Comforter wherever we may be, whatever sorrows or temptations may befall us. Thanks be unto the Holy Spirit, with the Father and the Son!

7. The indwelling of the Spirit is the safety of the believer. But the world wants to see that which it accepts. As God the Spirit is invisible, there are many who reject his counsel. Unbelief says: "Show me the Spirit." Faith opens wide the door of the heart, and turns over to the heavenly Guest the key to every chamber of the soul. He hears the injunction, "Acquaint now thyself with him, and be at peace," for "the secret of the Lord is with them that fear him." "Ye know him; for he dwelleth with you, and shall be in you."

8. The work of the Spirit includes a personal knowledge of salvation and divine things by the revelation of the things of God to the soul; "for the Spirit searcheth all things, yea, the deep things of God."

9 and 10. We must not grieve (resist, rebel against) the Spirit of God as many have done in the times of the past. O how many have cursed their own souls and blighted their lives forever by quenching the Spirit, resisting his impressions, and grieving him by their obstinate rebellion and persistence in sin!

It is a very sad fact that we do not generally honor the Spirit as we should. Very few churches continually lean on his mighty arm, invoke his abiding presence, and trust continually in his power for victory. In some quarters his existence is even denied, his personality disputed, and his presence and direct work in salvation ridiculed. We hear of so-called preachers of the gospel (breeders of infidelity they are, instead of ministers of Christ Jesus) who pour contempt upon the personal character, the office, and work of the blessed Holy Spirit. These scoffers even sneeringly look about the church and under the benches for the Holy Ghost. Let such hypocrites know that the sin "against the Holy Ghost hath never forgiveness."

65
SUPPLEMENT TO BIBLE-READING ON THE HOLY SPIRIT

The doctrine of the Trinity, or three persons in the God-head, one only God, has been a great puzzle to many people. Let us see if there is any thing so very unreasonable in the doctrine of the Trinity.

Man is himself a trinity. He is composed of body, soul, and spirit. The body, being the visible and tangible part, is made most of by many, when it is in fact the weakest personage in the trinity of man.

But under sin the tendency with man is to materialize every thing. "The natural man receiveth [or understandeth] not the things of the Spirit of God: for they are foolishness unto him: neither can he know them, because they are spiritually discerned." (1 Cor. ii.14.) "I will pray the Father, and he shall give you another Comforter, that he may abide with you forever; even the Spirit of truth, whom the world cannot receive, because it seeth him not, neither knoweth him: but ye know him; for he dwelleth with you, and shall be in you." (John xiv.16, 17.) This blindness to spiritual things is, as we here see, the result of sin; for it characterizes the world and the natural man, but not the believer, the spiritual. "Ye know him."

How may man thus know God? Physically? No, indeed; for "no man hath [thus] seen God at any time." (1 John iv.12.) But if man is a spirit as well as a body, he may know God spiritually.

Man physically consists of a body, with all its members or parts — eyes, ears, hands, feet, etc. Man's soul consists of the indwelling life, which gives vitality to the physical man. The soul sees through the body's eyes, hears through the body's ears, walks with its feet, strikes with its hands, etc. You call a man from a distance. He hears you, and, answering your call, comes running toward you and extends his hand to clasp yours; but before you catch his hand death strikes him and he falls lifeless — soulless — at your feet. He yet has ears, and they seem as before; but though you call ever so loudly he answers not: the man inside the body, who used the ear for hearing, has gone. Your sweetest strains of music stir no chord in his soul; your loudest thunders awaken no response therein; for, although the ear is there, there is no man — the soul — at hand to use it: consequently it hears not. You ask: "Where is he?" One answers, "There!" pointing to his body stretched out upon the ground; but your better judgment says: "No! he who answered my call and came at my bidding has gone; he is not here." His wife stands before him, but his eye lights up no more with the glow of love: the man who loved is gone. Put the most delicious food in his mouth, but he tastes it not; pour the richest perfume around him, he smells it not; pierce him with the sharpest instrument, he feels it not. The man who saw, heard, felt, smelled, tasted, sees, hears, feels, smells, tastes no more, though the physical organs with which he did these things are all yet there. So far we have man in the dual or twofold elements of body and soul.

Now let us consider man as a spirit. Let the body be the material, visible, tangible man — simply that which we consign to the tomb when life has departed. Let the soul be the man that inhabits the body and gives sight to the eye, hearing to the ear, and general life to the man, that he may be "a living soul." (Gen. ii.7.) There remains a real man, yet unmentioned, in man the triunity — viz., man the spirit. And here is that mental quality of man that you cannot confine, which, having its home in the body, its throne or central office in the brain, traverses the earth; yea, visits other worlds. What is thought, but the movements and workings of the spirit?

In preaching, speaking, singing, conversing, who preaches, speaks, sings, converses? Is it not man the spirit? A speaker stands before an audience of thousands. He speaks humorously, they laugh; pathetically, they cry. Seeing their tears you say: "He has hurt those people, has abused or struck them, and they cry for pain." I say: "No; he is not within reach of them, and has nothing in his hand." Still they cry freely. He — man the spirit — formulates a thought, and by the use of the tongue clothes it in a word, by which he applies it to his audience, and they are affected by it. His spirit goes out by sound, and comes in contact with the thousand spirits before him; and they all move at his bidding, weep or laugh at his words. Or, he may reproduce his thoughts on paper, print them by thousands, and send them abroad to affect thousands whom he never saw. Kind reader, this writing is an illustration. There may be hundreds of miles between us, or while you read this I may be in heaven with God, the angels, and redeemed ones; still you read, and agree or disagree with me. And it is a real agreement or disagreement upon the subject under consideration, although it is not all physical.

Alexander ruled the world. Washington gave independence to his country. How did they do it? Physically? Certainly not. By their soul-powers? No; but by their spirit or mind power. There were men of stronger muscular power than Washington; there were men of better soul-power or goodness than Alexander; but still these were men of power in their generations. At this writing I am two or three hundred miles from my family, and yet I am with them. I see the faces of my children, hear the prattle of my babe, and fondle the little ones upon my knees. Of course this is not done physically, but in the spirit it is a matter of frequent occurrence. I have never visited New York or London, and yet have been in these cities often. Contradictory, is it? Yes! No! I am understood. My eyes have never seen either city; and yet in my mind, or spirit, I have walked their streets, scrambled through their surging masses, and pitied their poor in want and squalor, while urging their wealthy to be rich in good works. By this same spirit-power man rises up to heaven, hard by the throne of God, or sinks down amidst the wailings of lost souls into the region of the damned. The spirit of man, like the Spirit of God, is (at least in a measure as a finite being) omnipresent. And here is the power of man in the earth; by this he perpetuates himself, and lives on to eternity. Paul said of Abel: "He being dead yet speaketh." (Heb. xi.4.) Of the righteous it is said, after they die in the Lord: "They rest from their labors and their works [their influences] do follow them." (Rev. xiv.13.)

"That Christ may dwell in your hearts by faith." (Eph. iii.17.) "Christ in you, the hope of glory." (Col. i.27.) The body of Christ may not dwell in our hearts; such a thing is impossible and absurd; and yet Christ may be formed in us the hope of glory. The real Christ, the Christ of power in the earth, is Christ the Spirit— *i.e.,* the Spirit or word of Christ. The father and mother, by their precept and example, live themselves over in the life of the child, the teacher in the life of the pupil. Wesley yet lives in six millions of Methodists, Luther in all Protestants, Bunyan in every reader of his immortal "Pilgrim's Progress." So Christ lives to-day, thank God, in the hearts of all his true and humble followers in all lands. "Let this mind be in you, which was also in Christ Jesus." (Phil. ii.5.) How does the ruler govern, or the general manage his armies? Is it not by imparting to them his spirit? So God rules the world in righteousness by imparting to it his Spirit.

But some will say: "I can't see God's Spirit, and I don't believe in what I can't see." This objection is exceedingly foolish. You cannot see your own spirit. You read a book and cry over it: it is simply the writer imparting to you his spirit, which is his real self, though you have no access to him by any of the five senses — as seeing, hearing, etc. You cannot see the wind, though it may sweep down every thing around you. You cannot see, feel, or hear, etc., the force of gravitation; and yet this unseen and intangible force binds you to this globe in spite of your mightiest efforts to rise. Oppose and resist it if you will; but defy and control it you cannot. So the mightiest forces of earth are unseen, and many of them outside the range of your five senses.

Man is a trinity — body, soul, and spirit — yet the force in man is his spirit; by this he multiplies himself and makes himself felt in many places. So God is a trinity; and by his Spirit he moves the world, convicts the sinner, regenerates the penitent seeker, and sanctifies the consecrated, trusting believer. "It is expedient for you that I go away: for if I go not away, the Comforter will not come unto you; but if I depart, I will send him unto you." "Now if any man have not the Spirit of Christ, he is none of his." (Rom. viii.9.)

Now let every believer "tarry... until ye be endued with power from on high." (Luke xxiv.49.) "Ye shall receive power, after that the Holy Ghost is come upon you: and ye shall be witnesses unto me," etc. (Acts i.8.)

> Holy Spirit, faithful Guide,
> Ever near the Christian's side,
> Gently lead us by the hand,
> Pilgrims in a desert land.

66
FULL SALVATION
No. 1

1. Jesus' name denotes his mission, to save from sin.

   "And she shall bring forth a son, and thou shalt call his name JESUS: for he shall save his people from their sins." (Matt. i.21.)

2. Can we be justified if we sin? No.

   "He that committeth sin is of the devil; for the devil sinneth from the beginning. For this purpose the Son of God was manifested, that he might destroy the works of the devil. Whosoever is born of God doth not commit sin; for his seed remaineth in him: and he cannot sin, because he is born of God." (1 John iii.8, 9.)

3. If we claim to know Christ, and yet sin, we lie.

   "And hereby we do know that we know him, if we keep his commandments. He that saith, I know him, and keepeth not his commandments, is a liar, and the truth is not in him." (1 John ii.3, 4.)

4. It is cleansing — not pardon — from all sin.

"But if we walk in the light, as he is in the light, we have fellowship one with another, and the blood of Jesus Christ his Son cleanseth us from all sin." (1 John 1. 7.)

5. By nature we are all sinners; hence need cleansing.

"If we say that we have no sin, we deceive ourselves, and the truth is not in us." "If we say that we have not sinned, we make him a liar, and his word is not in us." (1 John i.8, 10.)

6. Paul himself had it. He was crucified, but lived by faith.

"For the law of the Spirit of life in Christ Jesus hath made me free from the law of sin and death." (Rom. viii.2.) "I am crucified with Christ: nevertheless I live; yet not I, but Christ liveth in me: and the life which I now live in the flesh I live by the faith of the Son of God, who loved me, and gave himself for me. I do not frustrate the grace of God: for if righteousness come by the law, then Christ is dead in vain." (Gal. ii.20, 21.)

7. No one can maintain fellowship with God, and live in sin.

"This then is the message which we have heard of him, and declare unto you, that God is light, and in him is no darkness at all. If we say that we have fellowship with him, and walk in darkness, we lie, and do not the truth." (1 John i.5, 6.)

8. Our state under the law without grace.

"For we know that the law is spiritual: but I am carnal, sold under sin." "O wretched man that I am! who shall deliver me from the body of this death?" (Rom. vii.14, 24.)

9. Deliverance from this state by grace.

"I thank God through Jesus Christ our Lord. So then with the mind I myself serve the law of God; but with the flesh the law of sin." (Rom. vii.25.) "There is therefore no condemnation to them which are in Christ Jesus, who walk not after the flesh, but after the Spirit." "For they that are after the flesh do mind the things of the flesh; but they that are after the Spirit, the things of the Spirit." (Rom. viii.1, 5.)

67
HOLINESS
No. 2

1. God requires us to be *holy*.

    "But as he which hath called you is holy, so be ye holy in all manner of conversation; because it is written, Be ye holy; for I am holy." (1 Pet. i.15, 16.)

2. We can never see God without holiness.

    "Follow peace, with all men and holiness, without which no man shall see the Lord." (Heb. xii.14.)

3. As God's children we should cleanse away all filthiness, perfecting holiness.

    "Having therefore these promises, dearly beloved, let us cleanse ourselves from all filthiness of the flesh and spirit, perfecting holiness in the fear of God." (2 Cor. vii.1.)

4. The first tabernacle "the holy," the second "the holiest."

    "For there was a tabernacle made; the first, wherein was the candlestick, and the table, and the showbread; which is called the sanctuary. And after the second veil, the tabernacle which is called the holiest of all." (Heb. ix.2, 3.)

5. We have liberty to enter this "holiest" by the blood of Jesus.

"Having therefore, brethren, boldness to enter into the holiest by the blood of Jesus, by a new and living way, which he hath consecrated for us, through the veil, that is to say, his flesh; and having a high-priest over the house of God; let us draw near with a true heart in full assurance of faith, having our hearts sprinkled from an evil conscience, and our bodies washed with pure water." (Heb. x.19-22.)

6. This victory of faith must be unwaveringly professed.

"Let us hold fast the profession of our faith without wavering; for he is faithful that promised; and let us consider one another to provoke unto love and to good works." (Heb. x.23, 24.)

7. We are to worship God because of his holiness.

"Exalt ye the Lord our God, and worship at his footstool; for he is holy." "Exalt the Lord our God, and worship at his holy hill; for the Lord our God is holy." (Ps. xcix.5, 9.)

8. If we would have everlasting life, we must bear the fruit of holiness.

"But now being made free from sin, and become servants to God, ye have your fruit unto holiness, and the end everlasting life." (Rom. vi.22.)

9. God's people are to be a peculiar, a holy people.

"For thou art a holy people unto the Lord thy God, and the Lord hath chosen thee to be a peculiar people unto himself, above all the nations that are upon the earth." (Deut. xiv.2.) "But ye are a chosen generation, a royal priesthood, a holy nation, a peculiar people; that ye should shew forth the praises of him who hath called you out of darkness into his marvelous light." (1 Pet. ii.9.)

10. It is not by death, but for all of life.

"The oath which he sware to our father Abraham, that he would grant unto us, that we, being delivered out of the hand of our enemies, might serve him without fear, in holiness and righteousness before him, all the days of our life." (Luke i.73-75.)

68
Perfect Love
No. 3

1. Perfect love is for such as know Jesus and keep his word.

> "But whoso keepeth his word, in him verily is the love of God perfected: hereby know we that we are in him." (1 John ii.5.)

2. We are required to be perfect (in love).

> "Be ye therefore perfect, even as your Father which is in heaven is perfect." (Matt. v.48.)

3. It enables us to love our enemies.

> "But I say unto you, Love your enemies, bless them that curse you, do good to them that hate you, and pray for them which despitefully use you, and persecute you." (Matt. v.44.)

4. It is God who makes us perfect (in love).

> "Now the God of peace, that brought again from the dead our Lord Jesus, that great Shepherd of the sheep, through the blood of the everlasting covenant, make

you perfect in every good work to do his will, working in you that which is well pleasing in his sight, through Jesus Christ; to whom be glory forever and ever. Amen." (Heb. xiii.20, 21.)

5\. And the Holy Spirit bears witness to that perfection.

"For by one offering he hath perfected forever them that are sanctified. Whereof the Holy Ghost also is a witness to us." (Heb. x.14, 15.)

6\. St. John professed perfect love.

"Herein is our love made perfect, that we may have boldness in the day of judgment: because as he is, so are we in this world. There is no fear in love; but perfect love casteth out fear: because fear hath torment. He that feareth is not made perfect in love." (1 John iv.17, 18.)

7\. It is after conversion, we leave the principles and go on to it.

"Therefore leaving the principles of the doctrine of Christ, let us go on unto perfection; not laying again the foundation of repentance from dead works, and of faith toward God." (Heb. vi.1.)

8\. The object of preaching Christ is that men may be made perfect.

"To whom God would make known what is the riches of the glory of this mystery among the Gentiles; which is Christ in you, the hope of glory: whom we preach, warning every man, and teaching every man in all wisdom; that we may present every man perfect in Christ Jesus." (Col. i.27, 28.)

9\. The object of the various orders of the ministry is the perfection of the saints.

> "And he gave some, apostles; and some, prophets; and some, evangelists; and some, pastors and teachers; for the perfecting of the saints, for the work of the ministry, for the edifying of the body of Christ: till we all come in the unity of the faith, and of the knowledge of the Son of God, unto a perfect man, unto the measure of the stature of the fullness of Christ." (Eph. iv.11-13.)

10. Job's is a case to the point. God pronounced him perfect.

> "There was a man in the land of Uz, whose name was Job; and that man was perfect and upright, and one that feared God, and eschewed evil." (Job i.1.)

69
SANCTIFICATION
No. 4

1. God wills our sanctification.

"For this is the will of God, even your sanctification." (1 Thess. iv.3.)

2. We ought therefore to seek it earnestly in life.

"Whatsoever thy hand findeth to do, do it with thy might; for there is no work, nor device, nor knowledge, nor wisdom, in the grave, whither thou goest." (Eccl. ix.10.)

3. If we are children of God and hope for heaven, we must purify ourselves.

"Behold, what manner of love the Father hath bestowed upon us, that we should be called the sons of God: therefore the world knoweth us not, because it knew him not. Beloved, now are we the sons of God, and it doth not yet appear what we shall be: but we know that, when he shall appear, we shall be like him; for we shall see him as he is. And every man that hath this hope in him purifieth himself, even as he is pure. (1 John iii.1-3.)

4. Atonement means at-one-mind with God— that is, sanctification.

"For both he that sanctifieth and they who are sanctified are all of one: for which cause he is not ashamed to call them brethren." (Heb. ii.11.)

5. Jesus gives us his second testament for our sanctification by his broken body.

"Then said he, Lo, I come to do thy will, O God. He taketh away the first, that he may establish the second. By the which will we are sanctified through the offering of the body of Jesus Christ once for all." (Heb. x.9, 10.)

6. Christ died to sanctify us. He wants his Church without spot.

"Husbands, love your wives, even as Christ also loved the Church, and gave himself for it; that he might sanctify and cleanse it with the washing of water by the word, that he might present it to himself a glorious Church, not having spot, or wrinkle, or any such thing; but that it should be holy and without blemish." (Eph. v.25-27.)

7. Sanctification is by the blood of Christ.

"Wherefore Jesus also, that he might sanctify the people with his own blood, suffered without the gate." (Heb. xiii.12.)

8. It is by faith.

"To open their eyes, that they may turn from darkness to light, and from the power of Satan unto God, that they may receive remission of sins and an inheritance among them that are sanctified by faith in me." (Acts xxvi.18. R. V.)

9. Called heart-purity

"Blessed are the pure in heart: for they shall see God." (Matt. v.8.)

10. Jesus prayed for the sanctification of his disciples.

"Sanctify them through thy truth: thy word is truth." (John xvii.17.)

11. Also for all believers, but not for the world.

"Neither pray I for these alone, but for them also which shall believe on me through their word." "I pray for them: I pray not for the world, but for them which thou hast given me; for they are thine." (John xvii.20, 9.)

12. The Thessalonians were Christians— examples to believers.

"Remember without ceasing your work of faith, and labor of love, and patience of hope in our Lord Jesus Christ, in the sight of God and our Father." "So that ye were ensamples to all that believe in Macedonia and Achaia." (1 Thess. i.3, 7.)

13. They were not wholly sanctify; Paul prayed that they might be.

"And the very God of peace sanctify you wholly; and I pray God your whole spirit and soul and body be preserved blameless unto the coming of our Lord Jesus Christ. Faithful is he that calleth you, who also will do it." (1 Thess. v.23, 24.)

14. Sanctification twofold— we consecrate, God purifies.

"Sanctify yourselves therefore, and be ye holy: for I

am the Lord your God. And ye shall keep my statutes, and do them: I am the Lord which sanctify you." (Lev. xx.7, 8.)

Though there are four different terms or titles used, the four last readings all pertain to one thing — namely, the higher life of faith, the rich and abiding fullness of salvation. Mr. Moody says: "There is a life of perfect peace, perfect joy, and perfect love; and that ought to be the aim of every child of God, that ought to be their standard, and they should not rest until they have attained to that position. That is God's standard, where he wants all his children." ("Secret Power," p. 77.)

Every traveling Methodist preacher answers the following questions affirmatively: "Have you faith in Christ? Are you going on to perfection? Do you expect to be made perfect in love in this life? (See Discipline.) (1) They are already Christians, they "have faith in Christ," and are preachers of his gospel. (2) Still they may not have yet experienced perfect love. (3) But they are groaning after it, and expect it in this life. Alas for those who deride this precious experience, after such questions as the above have been affirmatively answered before God and man!

1. The Scriptures tell us that God wills our sanctification; that Jesus died to sanctify us with his own blood; that his blood cleanseth from all sin; that we must be perfect (in love, in Christian life); St. John definitely professed perfect love, "Herein is our love made perfect;" while inspiration declares Job to have been "perfect."

2. The commands and promises pertaining to the grace of sanctification, the experience of perfect love, all set it forth as a present attainment. "*Be* ye therefore perfect." "Walk before me," said God to Abraham, "and *be* thou perfect." "*Be* ye holy." "He would grant unto us, that we, being delivered out of the hand of our enemies, might serve him without fear, in holiness and righteousness be-

fore him, *all the days of our life.*" Christ is the author of our sanctification, and we receive it by the merits of his blood, through "faith." There are extant several absurd, unscriptural theories of entire sanctification. (1) The Romanists say: "After death, in purgatory." See Ecclesiastes ix.10, with Hebrews xiii.12. (2) Many say: "We are sanctified in death." See 1 Corinthians xv.25, 26, with Hebrews x.19 and Luke i.73-75.

3. Some teach sanctification by growth. This is absurd and unscriptural. Growth is enlargement, addition; sanctification is an elimination, a subtraction. Growth makes larger and more vigorous our good principles; sanctification cleanses us from evil, impure elements. Sanctification, being wrought in us by the Holy Ghost, greatly facilitates growth in grace and usefulness. See 1 John i.7; iii.3; Leviticus xx.8; Hebrews ii.11; xiii.20, 21.

4. Others teach that we are sanctified when we are converted. We are partially sanctified at conversion, but *not wholly*. The disciples were certainly converted. (1) Their names were written in heaven. (Luke x.20.) (2) Christ ordained them as his preachers. (Mark iii.14, 15.) (3) Yet they were not sanctified, and he prays for their sanctification. (John xvii.17, with verses 14, 16.) The Corinthians, though sanctified in a measure, were "yet carnal." (1 Cor. i.2, with 1 Cor. iii.1-3.) Though "babes in Christ," they were "yet carnal," and were exhorted to "cleanse themselves of all filthiness, perfecting holiness," etc. The Thessalonians, though excellent working Christians, having the "joy of the Holy Ghost," and being "ensamples to all the believers," were not yet *sanctified wholly*. Paul prayed for them, however, and said God would sanctify them. From all of which we learn that there is an experience of grace higher than conversion. It is not for *sinners*, but for *believers*. Hence the common expression is: "The conversion of sinners, and the sanctification of believers." To sinners the word says: "Except ye repent," etc.; "ex-

cept ye be converted," etc., "ye must be born again." To believers we have: "Go on to perfection;" "if we walk in the light, the blood cleanseth," etc.; "the will of God, your sanctification;" "perfect holiness in fear of God;" "sanctify them;" the God of peace sanctify you wholly." Paul describes it all as two tabernacles— the first holy, the second holiest, and says we may enter *the holiest* by the blood of Jesus. (Heb. ix.2, 3, with Heb. x.19-23.) It is therefore, as Mr. Wesley calls it, "a second blessing." We do not thus enumerate the blessings of life, for they cannot be counted; they are more than the hairs of our head; but we thus state relatively the blessings of sanctification. Mr. Wesley says: "Men are converted before they are sanctified." And this may be learned from Paul, John, and the blessed Saviour. Finally: Let no Christian rest without the experience. It is the great need of the Church. When holiness fills the Church there is power in the pulpit and life in the pew. A holy Church has peace, full prayer-meetings, live class-meetings, glowing missionary zeal, and that "power from on high" that enables her to rout the armies of hell, drive the devil from the field a vanquished foe, and plant the banner of Immanuel on the fallen bulwarks of sin in the last field of conflict. Glory to God for such precious grace! Praise the Lord!

70
CHRIST AS FOUND IN THE OLD AND NEW TESTAMENTS

PROPHECY	FULFILLMENT
1. The place of his birth.	He was born in Bethlehem.
"But thou, Bethlehem Ephratah, though thou be little among the thousands of Judah, yet out of thee shall come forth unto me that is to be ruler in Israel; whose goings forth have been from of old, from everlasting." (Mic. v.2.)	"Now when Jesus was born in Bethlehem of Judea in the days of Herod the king, behold, there came wise men from the east to Jerusalem." (Matt. ii.1.) See Luke ii.4-7.
2. Christ as the prophet.	Jesus is that prophet.
"The Lord thy God will raise up unto thee a Prophet from the midst of thee, of thy	"For Moses truly said unto the fathers, A Prophet shall the Lord your God raise up unto

PROPHECY	FULFILLMENT
brethren, like unto me; unto him ye shall hearken." (Deut. xviii.15.)	me; him shall ye hear in all things whatsoever he shall say unto you." (Acts iii.22.) See also Acts vii.37, 38.

3. His birth of a virgin.

"Therefore the Lord himself shall give you a sign; Behold, a virgin shall conceive, and bear a son, and shall call his name Immanuel." (Isa. vii.14.)

Conceived of the Holy Ghost.

"Joseph, thou son of David, fear not to take unto thee Mary thy wife: for that which is conceived in her is of the Holy Ghost." (Matt. i.20.) See Matthew i.18-25.

4. John his harbinger.

"The voice of him that crieth in the wilderness, Prepare ye the way of the Lord, make straight in the desert a highway for our God."

John the Baptist fulfilled it.

"For this is he that was spoken of by the prophet Esaias, saying, The voice of one crying in the wilderness, Prepare ye the way of the Lord, make his paths straight." (Matt. iii.3.)

5. The Son of God with power.

"For unto us a child is born, unto us a son is given: and the government shall be upon his shoulder: and his name shall be called Wonder-

Son of God.

(John iii.16.) "And Jesus came and spake unto them, saying, All power is given unto me in heaven and in earth." (Matt. xxviii.18.)

PROPHECY	FULFILLMENT
ful, Counselor, The mighty God, The everlasting Father, The Prince of Peace." (Isa. ix.6.)	
6. His mission. The Spirit on him.	He had the Divine anointing.
"The Spirit of the Lord God is upon me; because the Lord hath anointed me to preach good tidings unto the meek; he hath sent me to bind up the brokenhearted, to proclaim liberty to the captives, and the opening of the prison to them that are bound." (Isa. lxi.1.)	"The Spirit of the Lord is upon me, because he hath anointed me to preach the gospel to the poor; he hath sent me to heal the brokenhearted, to preach deliverance to the captives, and recovering of sight to the blind, to set at liberty them that are bruised." (Luke iv.18.)
7. His miracles are foretold.	The blind, the deaf, the lame.
"Then the eyes of the blind shall be opened, and the ears of the deaf shall be stopped. Then shall the lame man leap as a hart, and the tongue of the dumb sing: for in the wilderness shall waters break out, and streams in the desert." (Isa. xxxv.5, 6.)	"The blind receive their sight, and the lame walk, the lepers are cleansed, and the deaf hear, the dead are raised up, and the poor have the gospel preached to them." (Matt. xi.5.)

Prophecy	Fulfillment
8. His suffering for us portrayed.	Crowned with thorns and buffeted.
"He is despised and rejected of men; a man of sorrows, and acquainted with grief: and we hid as it were our faces from him; he was despised, and we esteemed him not. Surely he hath borne our griefs, and carried our sorrows: yet we did esteem him stricken, smitten of God, and afflicted. But he was wounded for our transgressions, he was bruised for our iniquities: the chastisement of our peace was upon him; and with his stripes we are healed." (Isa. liii.3-5.)	"And when they had plaited a crown on thorns, they put it upon his head, and a reed in his right hand: and they bowed the knee before him, and mocked him, saying, Hail, King of the Jews! And they spit upon him, and took the reed, and smote him on the head." (Matt. xxvii.29, 30.) See Matthew xxvii.34, 35.
9. The price at which he was sold.	His betrayal—the price.
"And I said unto them, If ye think good, give me my price; and if not, forbear. So they weighed for my price thirty pieces of silver. And the Lord said unto	"And said unto them, What will ye give me, and I will deliver him unto you? And they covenanted with him for thirty pieces of silver. And from that time he sought opportunity

PROPHECY	FULFILLMENT
me, Cast it unto the potter: a goodly price that I was prized at of them. And I took the thirty pieces of silver, and cast them to the potter in the house of the Lord." (Zech. xi.12, 13.)	to betray him" (Matt. xxvi.15, 16.) See Matthew xxvii.3-8.
10. He was crucified with thieves, buried with the rich. "And he made his grave with the wicked, and with the rich in his death; because he had done no violence, neither was any deceit in his mouth." (Isa. liii.9.)	Between two thieves. His death. "Then were there two thieves crucified with him; one on the right hand, and another on the left." (Matt. xxvii.38.) His burial with the rich. "When the even was come, there came a rich man of Arimathea, named Joseph, who also himself was Jesus' disciples: he went to Pilate, and begged the body of Jesus. Then Pilate commanded the body to be delivered. And when Joseph had taken the body, he wrapped it in a clean linen cloth, and laid it

Prophecy	Fulfillment
	in his own new tomb, which he had hewn out in the rock: and he rolled a great stone to the door of the sepulcher, and departed." (Matt. xxvii.57-60.)
11. Complete dominion in earth.	His victories will even include death.
"He shall have dominion also from sea to sea, and from the river unto the ends of the earth." (Ps. lxxii.8.)	"For he must reign, till he hath put all enemies under his feet. The last enemy that shall be destroyed is death." (1 Cor. xv.25, 26.)

71
ENTIRE SANCTIFICATION
Rev. W.C. Dunlap

1. The God of peace sanctifies wholly.

"And the very God of peace sanctify you wholly; and I pray God your whole spirit and soul and body be preserved blameless unto the coming of our Lord Jesus Christ." (1 Thess. v.23.)

2. Being in God the Father and in Christ Jesus, they were converted.

"Paul, and Silvanus, and Timotheus, unto the Church of the Thessalonians which is in God the Father, and in the Lord Jesus Christ: Grace be unto you, and peace, from God our Father, and the Lord Jesus Christ." (1 Thess. i.1.)

3. They had working faith, laboring love, and patient hope.

"Remembering without ceasing your work of faith, and labor of love, and patience of hope in our Lord Jesus Christ, in the sight of God and our Father." (1 Thess. i.3.)

4. They had the gospel of power, of the Holy Ghost, and of assurance.

> "For our gospel came not unto you in word only, but also in power, and in the Holy Ghost, and in much assurance; as ye know what manner of men we were among you for your sake." (1 Thess. i.5.)

5. They had Holy Ghost joy under affliction— persecution.

> "And ye became followers of us, and of the Lord, having received the word in much affliction, with joy of the Holy Ghost." (1 Thess. i.6)

6. Their lives were examples to all the believers.

> "So that ye were ensamples to all that believe in Macedonia and Achaia." (1 Thess. i.7.)

7. They send the gospel abroad.

> "For from you sounded out the word of the Lord not only in Macedonia and Achaia, but also in every place your faith to Godward is spread abroad; so that we need not to speak any thing." (1 Thess. i.8)

8. They kept their faith and love.

> "But now when Timotheus came from you unto us, and brought us good tidings of your faith and charity, and that ye have good remembrance of us always, desiring greatly to see us, as we also to see you: therefore, brethren, we were comforted over you in all our affliction and distress by your faith: for now we live, if ye stand fast in the Lord." (1 Thess. iii.6-8.)

9. Their faith being imperfect, Paul greatly desired to see them.

> "Night and day praying exceedingly that we might see your face, and might perfect that which is lack-

ing in your faith Now God himself and our Father, and our Lord Jesus Christ, direct our way unto you. And the Lord make you to increase and abound in love one toward another, and toward all men, even as we do toward you: to the end he may stablish your hearts unblamable in holiness before God, even our Father, at the coming of our Lord Jesus Christ with all his saints." (1 Thess. iii.10-13.)

1. The very God of peace sanctify you wholly." (1) They were partially sanctified already; hence he prays that this partial sanctification, which is an accompaniment of regeneration, may be perfected in them. (2) It is to be done by "the very God of peace" — that is, the God who gave them peace at their justification is the one to whom they must look for their entire sanctification. It is therefore a blessing, and is to come from him from whom they received "peace" in their justification. (Rom. v.1.) This teaching comports exactly with that of Methodism — namely, when we are "born again" we are partially sanctified. "That a distinction exists between a regenerate state and a state of entire and perfect holiness will be generally allowed." (Watson's "Institutes," ch. xxix.p. 611. Publishing House of the M. E. Church, South. 1887.) "The regenerate state is also called in Scripture sanctification, though a distinction is made by the Apostle Paul between that and being 'sanctified *wholly.*'" (*Ibid.*, p. 510.) "Methodism differs from Moravianism in that it does not hold regeneration and entire sanctification to be identical." (Bishop Simpson, in "Encyclopædia of Methodism.") But were these Thessalonians converted? Let us see:

2. "Unto the Church of the Thessalonians." (1) Here Paul recognized them as constituting the Church. Would he consider as a "Church" those who were simply a band of unconverted people? (2) They were "in God the Fa-

ther, and in the Lord Jesus Christ." Are unconverted people in God, and in Christ Jesus? (3) They were not backsliders, for they were addressed as "the Church *which is in* God the Father," etc., thus using the present tense, and thereby declaring their state at the time of writing.

3. "Your work of faith, and labor of love, and patience of hope in our Lord Jesus Christ." Here are three characteristics of this "Church of the Thessalonians which is in God the Father, and in the Lord Jesus Christ," that will not be found or looked for in either unconverted sinners or backsliders. (1) "Work of faith." Their *faith* led to activity for God. (2) "Labor of love." Their *love* intensified their work till it became labor, toil. (3) "Patience of hope." Their heavenly hope was so clear and strong that it strengthened their patience under suffering and persecution. How bright will be the day of salvation when all our Churches may be described as "in God the Father, and in the Lord Jesus Christ;" having a "work of faith, a labor of love, and a patience of hope in our Lord Jesus Christ, in the sight of God an our Father!" But the secret of such conversions is given:

4. "For our gospel came not unto you in word only, but also in power, and in the Holy Ghost, and in much assurance." They had the gospel (good news); it came to them in power — *i.e.*, in the Divine presence was their strength. "All power is given unto me." "Go teach all nations... and lo! I am with you alway." Divine power was in that gospel, the Holy Ghost accompanied it, enforcing its truths, and it brought "much assurance" — certainly of salvation. Theirs was no "hope-so" religion, for they received the Holy Ghost witnessing with their spirits that they were "children of God." (Rom. viii.16.)

5. They "received the word in much affliction." It cost them much of persecution, suffering, affliction to become "followers" of the apostles "and of the Lord." They were no doubt hated, ridiculed, despised, even by their own

families and former friends, for their devotion to Jesus of Nazareth; but still they "received the word in much affliction, *with joy of the Holy Ghost.*" Thank God for a religion that can bring joy to the heart and sunshine to the soul, even amidst the storm of persecution and the muttering thunders of oppression which grind down the helpless "under much affliction!" Rich experiences of grace were given to these Thessalonian converts by the gospel of power, and the presence of the Holy Ghost. Such experiences in grace will affect the lives of the people correspondingly.

6. "Ye were ensamples [examples] to all that believe in Macedonia and Achaia." Examples to whom, Paul? To sinners? No; but rather to all believers in that whole country. That must have been a live, vigorous, spiritual Church when Paul was ready to commend it as a pattern to all the "believers" of the surrounding country. Some think sanctification synonymous with regeneration. Partial sanctification is; but entire sanctification is the subject of the apostle's prayer for these Thessalonian Christians whom he commends so highly "as being in God the Father, and in the Lord Jesus Christ;" as having "a work of faith, labor of love, and patience of hope in our Lord Jesus Christ;" as having "received the word in much affliction, with joy of the Holy Ghost;" as becoming "followers of us, and of the Lord;" all through the "word" which came "in power, and in the Holy Ghost, and in much assurance;" and finally he commends them as "ensamples to all the believers" in that section of country.

7. "From you sounded out the word of the Lord." Here we find the truest test of real Christian life— namely, missionary activity. That is but a shallow type of religion which sits down in ease and comfort, singing itself to sleep over the vain, delusive hope of reaching heaven, while the world all around is perishing for the gospel of salvation, and to us is given the standing order to "preach the

gospel to every creature." The missionary spirit is the Christly spirit and best thermometer of spiritual life.

8. "We were comforted over you in all our affliction and distress by your faith." Timothy "brought us good tidings of your faith and charity— [*i.e.*, love]." Has any one the disposition to call them unconverted or backslidden? Paul's latest news from them was very encouraging; their faith and love comforted him in afflictions and distress. "Well, Paul, they need nothing more than to hold on and grow in grace." Yes, they do. "The very God of peace sanctify them wholly [entirely]." Notice his interest in seeing them *perfected in faith, and established in holiness.*

9. "Praying exceedingly that we might see your face, and might perfect that which is lacking in your faith." They had a work of faith, and he was much comforted over their faith, yet he prayed day and night anxiously to see them and perfect that which was lacking in their faith. He has no complaint of their lives, no charge against them, but is deeply interested in seeing them and perfecting their faith. Salvation is through grace by faith. Their faith was not perfect; hence their salvation was not perfect; hence their salvation was not perfect. "To the end he may stablish your hearts unblamable in holiness." "This is the will of God, even your sanctification." (1 Thess. iv.3.) "God hath not called us to uncleanness, but unto holiness." (1 Thess. iv.7.) "The God of peace sanctify you wholly." "Faithful is he that calleth you, who also will do it." (1 Thess. v.23, 24.) They were not "sanctified wholly," though they were one of his model Churches. He desired greatly to see them and hold a "holiness meeting," that he might get their faith perfected, so the God of peace who willed their sanctification, and called them to it, might "sanctify them wholly," and "stablish them unblamable in holiness." O for Paul's to-day who will not let the Church rest till holiness shall sweep her borders, and with shout and song she will wave the banner of Jesus over the captured strongholds of hell! Amen and amen.

72
How Holy?
Rev. William M'Donald
Editor, *Christian Witness*

"But as he which hath called you is holy, so be ye holy in all manner of conversation; Because it is written, Be ye holy; for I am holy." (1 Pet. i.15, 16.)

"And the very God of peace sanctify you wholly; and I pray God your whole spirit and soul and body be preserved blameless unto the coming of our Lord Jesus Christ. Faithful is he that calleth you, who also will do it." (1 Thess. v.23, 24.)

"Mark the perfect man, and behold the upright: for the end of that man is peace." (Ps. xxxvii.37.)

"If I regard iniquity in my heart, the Lord will not hear me." (Ps. lxvi.18.)

"It is God that girded me with strength, and maketh my way perfect." (Ps. xviii.32.)

"Wherefore he is able also to save them to the uttermost that come unto God by him." (Heb. vii.25.)

WE ARE TOLD that it is preposterous to talk of being entirely holy in this life. If such an experience were possible, it would unfit the soul for earth. The heavenly attraction would be so great that earth could no longer retain us, but we should go at once to heaven. Entire holiness is reserved for the heavenly life. "We are to be holy [it is said], as we are commanded to be holy; but the notion that we are to be saved from all sin is a fruitful cause of much fanaticism."

If it be true that we are to be holy, there is an important question to be settled — viz., *how holy*? To what extent may we be saved from sin in this life? To say that we must be holy, and yet insist that we cannot be entirely holy, is to leave us in great doubt as to what is demanded.

What sins may we be saved from? and what sins must remain, from which we cannot be saved? To what extent may our love be made perfect? and in what respect must it be imperfect? How far may our humility be made perfect? and in what particular must it remain imperfect? To what extent may our faith be made perfect? and where does unbelief say: "Thus far shalt thou go, and no further?" These are questions which should be settled. Another question should be answered — viz., If we cannot be completely, fully saved in this life, why? Whose fault is it? Is it true that Jesus is not able to save us to the uttermost? Have we discovered that his blood does not cleanse us from all unrighteousness? If uttermost does not mean complete, fully, perfectly, how much does it mean? If cleansing from *all* unrighteousness does not mean *all*, then where is the limit? and who is responsible for the limitation? It is answered: "We, of course, are responsible. God is able, but we are so weak that we can never hope for such an experience in this life."

But who proposes to accomplish this great work, weak, feeble man, or Almighty God? Is it not "the God of peace *himself*" who is to sanctify you wholly?"

If a father commands his weak son to lift a hundred pounds, when he is only able to lift twenty, but at the same time assures him that he will take hold with him, and that wherein the son's strength is inadequate it shall be supplemented by his own, will any one say that with such assistance it is impossible for the son to do what the father commanded? And is the son justified in saying "I cannot lift such a burden; I am too weak?" To be sure *he* is, but with "the promise of the father" does his weakness justify him in not making the effort?

God commands us to love him with all the heart. Our reply is that we are too weak for so great a work. But has not God promised: "I will circumcise thy heart that thou mayest love the Lord thy God with all thy heart? God commands us to "cleanse ourselves from all filthiness of the flesh and spirit, perfecting holiness in the fear of God." But I have no power to cleanse myself to such an extent. True. But God has promised that "if we confess our sins, he is faithful and just to forgive us our sins, and to cleanse us from all unrighteousness."

If God's promise is to be depended upon, where is the failure? Who is to blame for the non-accomplishment of the work? Is it impossible for us to *be* what we are condemned for *not* being? Can we be blamed for failing to do what is impossible to be done? God commands us to "be holy," and to "be perfect," and to "love him with all the heart." Has a superior a right to command, or is a subject or subordinate under obligation to obey, in any matter which is not capable of his choice? If we cannot love God "with all the heart," then God has commanded an impossibility, and a law which is impossible to be observed cancels itself. If salvation from all sin is a subject capable of our choice, then we are held responsible for not being fully saved; but if it is not capable of our choice, then we are not responsible for not being fully saved. If we cannot be fully saved here and now, will some one tell us to what extent we may be saved? We should know what we have a right to expect, and when we are saved as fully as we may be in this life. The Scriptures insist on our being "saved to the uttermost," from "all sin," from "all unrighteousness," from "all filthiness of flesh and spirit." We are required not only to "love God," but to love him "with all our heart," and to have "our love made perfect;" not only to be holy, but to "perfect holiness."

In view of these scriptural utterances, where is the limit of salvation? If any thing short of the uttermost, how much short?

73
SANCTIFICATION DELIVERS FROM FEAR
REV. C.C. CARY

"There is no fear in love; but perfect love casteth our fear: because fear hath torment. He that feareth is not made perfect in love." (1 John iv.18.)

I. What fear is it from which sanctification delivers?

1. Not filial fear.

"Let us have grace, whereby we may serve God acceptably with reverence and godly fear." (Heb. xii.28.) "O that there were such a heart in them, that they would fear me, and keep all my commandments always." (Deut. v.29.) "Fear the Lord, ye his saints: for there is no want to them that fear him." (Ps. xxxiv.9.) "And I will make an everlasting covenant with them... I will put my fear in their hearts, that they shall not depart from me." (Jer. xxxii.40.)

2. Not that fear which is necessary to watchfulness and to urge us to duty.

"Work out your own salvation with fear and trembling." (Phil. ii.12.) "Let us therefore fear, lest, a promise being left us of entering into his rest, any of you should seem to come short of it." (Heb. iv.1.)

3. Both that filial fear and that fear which is necessary to watchfulness, exists in connection with and yet does not antagonize the following:
(1) Confidence in God.

"In the fear of the Lord is strong confidence." (Prov. xiv.26.)

(2) Trust in God.

"Ye that fear the Lord, trust in the Lord: he is their help and their shield." (Ps. cxv.11.)

(3) Gladness of heart.

"They that fear thee will be glad when they see me." (Ps. cxix.74.)

(4) Happiness.

"Happy is the man that feareth always." (Prov. xxviii.14)

(5) Leads to testimony.

"Then they that feared the Lord spake often one to another." (Mal. iii.16.)

II. It is a harassing, *tormenting fear* which interferes with peace of mind and composure of soul, and exists in connection with doubt or a measure of unbelief.

"There is no fear in love; but perfect love casteth out fear: because fear hath torment." (1 John iv.18.)

Hence the caution against that state of heart which produces this fear.

"Take heed, brethren, lest there be in any of you an

evil heart of unbelief, in departing from the living God." (Heb. iii.12.)

The "carnal mind" gives rise to this fear.

"There were they in great fear, where no fear was." (Ps. liii.5.) "If iniquity be in thine hand, put it far away, and let not wickedness dwell in thy tabernacles. For then shalt thou lift up thy face without spot; yea, thou shalt be steadfast, and shalt not fear." (Job. xi.14, 15.)

Consciousness of inward or outward sin, or of the remains of the carnal mind, occasions this slavish, tormenting fear.

"And the Lord God called unto Adam, and said unto him, Where art thou? and he said, I heard thy voice in the garden, and I was afraid. (Gen. iii.9, 10.)

III. A measure of this fear which hath torment is found in a converted state.

"And his disciples came to him, and awoke him, saying, Lord, save us: we perish. And he saith unto them, Why are ye fearful, O ye of little faith?" (Matt. viii.25, 26.)

1. These were converted men, for they had some faith. 2. They had that fear which hath torment. 3. This fear is of the nature of sin, and exists in connection with doubt and unbelief. 4. Converted people have in them, then, something of the nature of sin. 5. There is therefore sin in believers.

The sad case of Peter (Matt. xxvi.69-75), who through fear when accosted by a maid denied his Lord, is another case in point. 1. Peter was converted, for he was called to preach and sent out to heal the sick and cast out devils. 2. He was not backslidden, for an hour before he was ready to fight for his Master. 3. He had that evil principle within which is so common among the average Christians which makes it so easy to deny the Lord Jesus, and so hard to be bold in the face of opposition and danger.

IV. From this slavish, tormenting fear, God has promised a gracious and complete deliverance through sanctifying grace.

> "The Lord shall give thee rest from thy sorrow, and from thy fear, and from the hard bondage wherein thou wast made to serve." (Isa. xiv.3.) "The oath which he sware to our father Abraham, That he would grant unto us, that we, being delivered out of the hand of our enemies, might serve him without fear, in holiness and righteousness before him, all the days of our life." (Luke i.73-75.) "Perfect love casteth out fear." (1 John iv.18.)

As this fear is of the nature of sin, the broad promise covers it: "The blood of Jesus Christ his Son cleanseth us from all sin." "He is able to save unto the uttermost," even from fear and doubt and unbelief, and place us in the light of full assurance: "Let us draw near with a true heart in full assurance of faith, having our hearts sprinkled from an evil conscience." (Heb. x.22.)

This gracious salvation implies full deliverance from:
1. The slavish fear of God.

> "For ye have not received the spirit of bondage again to fear; but ye have received the Spirit of adoption, whereby we cry, Abba, Father. The Spirit itself beareth witness with our spirit, that we are the children of God." (Rom. viii.15, 16.) "For God hath not given us the spirit of fear; but of power, and of love, and of a sound mind." (2 Tim. i.7.)

If, therefore, this fear is detected in the converted heart, it is not of God, but belongs to our old nature.

2. Fear of man.

"The fear of man bringeth a snare." (Prov. xxix.25.)

Hence the need of deliverance from it, and watchfulness against it.

> "Ye shall not be afraid of the face of man." "Fear not, neither be discouraged." "Dread not, neither be afraid of them. The Lord your God which goeth before you, he shall fight for you." (Deut. i.17, 21, 29, 30.) "The Lord is on my side; I will not fear: what can man do unto me?" (Ps. cxviii.6.)

The evil fruits of his fear are seen in the doubts that disturb good people, and the distress of mind in those who pray in their families when strangers are present; when they attend prayer-meeting, and are uneasy lest they be called on to pray; and in keeping silence testimony meetings. Full salvation gives a happy deliverance from this slavish fear of man.

3. Fear of want.

> "Trust in the Lord, and do good; so shalt thou dwell in the land, and verily thou shalt be fed." "In the days of famine they shall be satisfied." (Ps. xxxvii.3, 19.) "O fear the Lord, ye his saints: for there is no want to them that fear him. The young lions do lack, and suffer hunger: but they that seek the Lord shall not want any good thing." (Ps. xxxiv.9, 10.) "He that walketh righteously, and speaketh uprightly;... he shall dwell on high; his place of defense shall be the munitions of rocks: bread shall be given him; his waters shall be sure." (Isa. xxxiii.15, 16.)

Two things are implied: (1) Deliverance from want; (2) from the *fear* of want. The sanctified soul has such a faith in God's overruling providence that he does not antici-

pate and give way to his fears by continually asking: "What shall I eat? what shall I drink? and wherewithal shall I be clothed?" (Matt. vi.25.) He is not afraid of want.
4. Fear of death.

> "And deliver them, who through fear of death were all their life-time subject to bondage." (Heb. ii.15.) "O death, where is thy sting? O grave, where is thy victory? The sting of death is sin; and the strength of sin is the law. But thanks be to God, which giveth us the victory through our Lord Jesus Christ." (1 Cor. xv.55-57.)

Sanctification does not propose to save from death. The righteous and the wicked alike die. But deliverance from the dread of death is what is promised.
5. Fears of evil, either imaginary or real. We speak of those fears which come in troops as well as singly — fears of future ills — many of which are never realized, and which like a thick cloud darken the sky, robbing of peace of mind, and causing distrust of Providence.

> "The righteous shall be in everlasting remembrance. He shall not be afraid of evil tidings: his heart is fixed, trusting in the Lord." (Ps. cxii.6, 7.) "But whoso hearkeneth unto me shall dwell safely, and shall be quiet from fear of evil." (Prov. i.33.)

Mark: It is one thing to be delivered from *evil*, and another to be saved from the *fear* of evil. Sanctification delivers from all evil which is of the nature of sin, but not from trouble. It does, however, deliver from the *fear* of evil or trouble. It saves also from the dread of storms and cyclones which render some persons so unhappy when a dark cloud arises.

BOLDNESS

While negatively full salvation implies complete deliverance from the fear that hath torment, positively it imparts boldness.

> "And when they had prayed, the place was shaken where they were assembled together; and they were all filled with the Holy Ghost, and they spake the word of God with boldness." (Acts iv.31.)

CONCLUSION

If these things be true, well may we exclaim with the Psalmist: "The Lord is my light and my salvation; whom shall I fear? the Lord is the strength of my life; of whom shall I be afraid?"

74
THE SANCTIFICATION OF THE DISCIPLES
REV. B.F. GASSAWAY

1. That they were converted or born of God all will admit.

> "He came unto his own, and his own received him not. But as many as received him, to them gave he power to become the sons of God, even to them that believe on his name: which were born, not of blood, nor of the will of the flesh, nor of the will of man, but of God." (John i.11-13.)

2. After this they were ordained and sent forth to preach, with power to work miracles.

> "And he ordained twelve, that they should be with him, and that he might send them forth to preach, and to have power to heal sicknesses, and to cast out devils." (Mark iii.14, 15.)

3. It was said of the "seventy" disciples after they returned from a special mission:

> "Notwithstanding, in this rejoice not, that the spirits are subject unto you; but rather rejoice, because your

names are written in heaven." (Luke x.20.)

Surely what is said of the "seventy" may be predicated of the "*twelve*" without violence to the sacred text.

4. Their promised exaltation— a promise which could only have been given to those truly born of God.

> "And Jesus said unto them, Verily I say unto you, That ye which have followed me, in the regeneration when the Son of man shall sit in the throne of his glory, ye also shall sit upon twelve thrones, judging the twelve tribes of Israel." (Matt. xix.28.)

And yet they were not sanctified wholly.

1. They were self-seeking and ambitious.

> "Then came to him the mother of Zebedee's children with her sons, worshiping him, and desiring a certain thing of him. And he said unto her, What wilt thou? She saith unto him, Grant that these my two sons may sit, the one on thy right hand, and the other on the left, in thy kingdom." (Matt. xx.20, 21.)

2. They were vindictive and revengeful.

> "And when his disciples James and John saw this, they said, Lord, wilt thou that we command fire to come down from heaven, and consume them, even as Elias did? But he turned, and rebuked them, and said, Ye know not what manner of spirit ye are of." (Luke ix.54, 55.)

3. They were bigoted and narrow.

> "And John answered him, saying, Master, we saw one casting out devils in thy name, and he followeth not us; and we forbade him, because he followeth not us." (Mark ix.38.)

4. They were deficient in moral courage and consecration.

"Then all the disciples forsook him, and fled." "Now Peter sat without in the palace: and a damsel came unto him, saying, Thou also wast with Jesus of Galilee. But he denied before them all, saying, I know not what thou sayest." "And again he denied with an oath, I do not know the man." "Then began he to curse and to swear, saying, I know not the man." (Matt. xxvi.56, 69, 70, 72, 74.)

But that they were truly converted cannot be denied. 1. They had received the revelation from God that Jesus was the Christ.

"And Simon Peter answered and said, Thou art the Christ, the Son of the living God. And Jesus answered and said unto him, Blessed art thou, Simon Bar-jona: for flesh and blood hath not revealed it unto thee, but my Father which is in heaven." (Matt. xvi.16, 17.)

2\. They had received the words of Jesus and had believed that he was sent from God.

"For I have given unto them the words which thou gavest me; and they have received them, and have known surely that I came out from thee, and they have believed that thou didst send me." (John xvii.8.)

3\. The world hated them because they were true to God.

"I have given them thy word; and the world hath hated them, because they are not of the world, even as I am not of the world." (John xvii.14.)

4\. And yet they had not been sanctified, for Jesus now prays that they may be.

"Sanctify them through thy truth: thy word is truth. As thou hast sent me into the world, even so have I also sent them into the world. And for their sakes I sanctify myself, that they also might be sanctified through the truth." (John xvii.17-19.)

5. This prayer was fulfilled at Pentecost, while the disciples were waiting for the fulfillment of the Father's promise— the baptism of the Holy Ghost, by which they were sanctified wholly.

> "And there appeared unto them cloven tongues like as of fire, and it sat upon each of them. And they were all filled with the Holy Ghost." (Acts ii.3, 4.)

6. The Apostle Peter declares this Pentecost baptism and the one received by Cornelius eight years after to be identical (Acts xi.15), and declares the result of these baptisms to be heart-purity, or entire sanctification.

> "And God, which knoweth the hearts, bare them witness, giving them the Holy Ghost, even as he did unto us; and put no difference between us and them, purifying their hearts by faith," (Acts xv.8, 9.)

Thus we find that the disciples were born of God, truly converted, called to the ministry, clothed with power to work miracles, and ordained to preach the gospel of repentance *before* Christ prayed for their sanctification, which followed at Pentecost.

75
SANCTIFICATION THE BIBLE STANDARD OF SALVATION
REV. W.B. GODBEY, A.M.

1. When God created human nature he created it just as he wanted it, "in his own image and likeness," which is "righteousness and true holiness." (Eph. iv.24.) When Satan invaded Eden he subjugated the race, and with it this world — *i.e.*, he destroyed spiritual life in the human race, and superinduced spiritual death — *i.e.*, utter depravity.

2. The race was not propagated in the unfallen state. Hence we are the children of fallen Adam; hence, "I was shapen in iniquity, and in sin did my mother conceive me." (Ps. li.5.) Or, as the immortal poet has it:

> Lord, I am vile, conceived in sin,
> Born unholy and unclean,
> Sprung from the man whose guilty fall
> Corrupts his race and taints us all.

Total depravity — *i.e.*, that the human race is totally deprived of spiritual life by the fall — is the great predominant truth without the due recognition of which all theology gets into an inextricable tangle. Hence the race is propagated destitute of the divine image.

3. Simultaneously with the removal of the divine image from the human heart Satan imparted his own filthy and polluted image, superinducing a state of indefatigable activity and conservatism to his own diabolical administration. Christ came to "destroy the works of the devil." (1 John iii.8.) Hence the work of Christ is not only to restore the divine, which he does in regeneration, but to destroy the Satanic image, which he does in sanctification. All salvation consists in two facts — *i.e.*, life and power. Regeneration gives you life, and sanctification gives you power. Since this world is a battle-field, and Satan is so much stronger than we are, it follows as a logical sequence that if we do not get power we will be conquered and slain — *i.e.*, if we do not get sanctified, we will certainly lose our regeneration. Hence the great utility of sanctification is to keep us from losing our religion. The Bible is clear and explicit. See Hebrews vi.1-6; xii.1-17. If we do not get sanctified, we are certain to backslide and ultimately lose our souls.

4. Sanctification is one of the plainest words in the Bible. The English word simply means to purify. The inspired Greek *hagiadzo* is from *gee*, the world, and *alpha*, not. Hence it simply means to take the world out of our hearts. 1 John ii.16 says: "All that is in the world, the lust of the flesh, and the lust of the eyes, and the pride of life" — *i.e.*, the Satanic image. The mind unreflectingly concludes that sanctification — *i.e.*, the removal of the Satanic image — should precede the impartation of the divine. But we must remember that vital phenomena are inseparable from the Holy Ghost — *i.e.*, wherever he goes he carries with him the divine image.

5. The regenerated state in all the Bible, and especially in the apostolic Epistles, as in Methodism and in all the-

ology, is recognized as a mixed state— e. g., James's double-minded man and Paul's double-tongued man represent the mixed state. Paul applies the double-tongued state to preachers (of course unsanctified). James's word for double-minded, *dipsuchai*— *i.e.*, double-minded— means the unsanctified Christian. The tongue is the exponent of the soul; hence when the soul is double the tongue is double. The Bible knows but two minds— *i.e.*, the carnal mind, which is the image of Satan, and the mind of Christ, which is the image of God. The sinner has the carnal mind alone, while the unsanctified Christian has the carnal mind subordinated to the mind of Christ. Hence his heart is the scene of civil war. "The flesh"— *i.e.*, the carnal mind— "lusteth against the Spirit, and the Spirit against the flesh;... so that ye cannot do the things that you would"— *i.e.*, you are awfully beset with sins of omission. "To will is present with you, but how to perform that which is good you find not." Your will is with God, but you lack the power. Justification brings us into the kingdom of peace, but sanctification into the kingdom of power.

6. Conquest invariably precedes destruction. A nation must be conquered before it can be exterminated. The American aborigines were first conquered and after exterminated. The first Adam is the great enemy of the human soul. He is conquered in regeneration, and taken away in sanctification. Hence regeneration stops us from committing sin, but it does not stop us from feeling sin, for, though conquered and dethroned, sin is still alive in our hearts. Hence we never can enjoy perfect rest till our enemies are all taken away. Reader, are you involved in this terrible heart-war with indwelling sin? Don't forget that this is a fight for life. If sin die first, you will live forever; if you die first, sin will live forever. Hurry up; end this war in the death of sin, or you die, world without end.

7. Justification is the antithesis of condemnation, sanctification of depravity, and glorification of infirmity. Many Christians ignorantly oppose sanctification because they compare it with glorification. As a result they put sanctification up to glorification, and would thus banish it from the earth. Sanctification renders you "holy" and "blameless" by taking away all your sins, but you may still have many innocent faults. Glorification, which you receive after you die and before you go to heaven, sweeps away all the collateral effects of sin through those fallen minds an bodies, so as to enable us to enter heaven in the angelic state. The supernatural radiance flashing from the countenance of the sainted dead in their coffins is but the splendor of the glorified soul reflected back on the vacated tenement as it retreats out of the body.

8. Justification cuts down the upas-tree [*sic*] of sin; sanctification digs out all the bitter roots, so that it will never sprout again. Regeneration plants and germinates your crop; sanctification cleans out the weeds, briers, and brambles, and gives the crop a chance to grow. Dr. Pierce says: "Sanctification is the tap-root striking straight down into the deep interior of the subsoil, and holding the tree in perfect security amid the wildest storms, while those having only lateral roots are all prostrated beneath the irresistible tempest; but those having that vertical root running deep down and winding round the everlasting rocks are constrained to strike deeper and deeper as every hurricane sweeps by." Thus sanctified people are strengthened and confirmed by every temptation, while the unsanctified fall on every side.

9. A standard of Bible salvation below sanctification would be utterly inadequate, because sanctification means the elimination of depravity — *i.e.*, inbred sin — from the heart. Probation ends with the present life; hence sin which survives this life must remain forever. The Bible positively states that "without holiness" — *i.e.*, sanctifi-

cation—"no man shall see the Lord." (Heb. xii.14.) Sanctification is from the Latin *sanctus*, holy, and *facio*, to make. As we are born unholy (Ps. li.5), we must all be made holy, or lost forever. Regenerated people are in *transitu*— i.e., in process of being saved— sanctified people are saved. John Wesley says: "Regeneration saves us from evil habits, and sanctification saves us from evil tempers. Unsanctified Christians are troubled with evil tempers. Of course they are not fully saved as long as they have them. The work of Christ is not to take us to heaven, but to destroy our sins; then heaven will come to us. Inbred sin is the seed and root from which all actual sins originate. Hence the great work of Christ is to destroy it." Thus it is the grand work of the second Adam to slay the first Adam— i.e., to kill inbred sin. Reader, is it dead in you? If not, turn it over to Christ without delay, lest tomorrow be eternally too late.

10. Some preachers very incorrectly make a difference between sanctification and perfection. You will see at once the utter futility of their position when you simply learn the meaning of the words. They are both of Latin origin: sanctification is from *facio*, to make, and *sanctus*, holy; perfection is from the same *facio*, to make, and *per*, complete. So you see that, though they sound differently, they have precisely the same meaning. Christ came to destroy sin— i.e., to make us holy. Whenever he has made us holy he has completed his work. Holiness and sanctification in the Bible are precisely synonymous, as they are translations of the same Greek, *hagiasmos*; Hebrew, *kadash*. So you see holiness, sanctification, and perfection all mean the very same gracious work.

11. It is lamentable indeed that the great body of the Church are so far beneath the Bible standard. In that way they have forfeited the Holy Ghost power, by which they would long ago have conquered the world for Christ, and brought on the millennium. Sadly shorn of her power,

she has been dragged captive at Satan's victorious chariot-wheels the last fifteen hundred years. But, glory to God, the day is breaking! Heathenism is floundering like the mighty leviathan of the deep, already in the gospel lasso, as the sanctified armies led on by Bishop Taylor and General Booth are even now going forth to conquer the world. This holiness movement is belting the globe with Pizarrean arms, and already shaking the world with the tread of a conquerer [sic]. Sluggards and carnalists will be left or run over. Look out, all, and be sure you board the train! This holiness revival is the van-guard of the millennium; we sing as we march along: "We never, never will give in." Sanctified people are fearless of men and devils, glad of an opportunity to go, under the commission, into the darkest jungles of heathendom, without a salary, and trust the Lord there as they do at home. Reader, are you saved from all sin, actual and original? This movement unties the Saviour's hands and gives him a chance. O consecrate and trust him now to sanctify. Consecrate— *i.e.*, return to God— then trust him to sanctify you; hold on till you establish a faith-habit, and there abide forever. Jesus is certain to shine through you, and ring the bells of heaven from the crown of your head to the soles of your feet.

12. An unfinished, roofless house speedily falls into dilapidation. Paul calls regeneration the foundation. (1 Cor. iii.11.) It takes the second blessing, through faith, to put us on standing ground. (Rom. v.) Consequently those who make justification the finality inadvertently exchange justification for a backslidden state, and make condemnation their standard. It is a lamentable fact that popular Christianity this day is the Christianity of condemnation, which is not the Christianity of Christ. "There is therefore now no condemnation to them which are in Christ Jesus." (Rom. viii.1.) That fatal dilemma supervenes upon the extreme difficulty, if not impossibility, of maintain-

ing uniformly the justified state. The truth of the matter is that justification is not the standing ground of Bible salvation (Rom. v.2.), but sanctification; while justification is the ingressive state, the Bible knows no standard but full salvation— *i.e.,* entire sanctification. The Zinzendorfian says he got full salvation in regeneration; then let him confess his sanctification, and abide in it. The attempt to maintain a standard below sanctification conduces to all irregularities of sinning and repenting, falling and rising, and ultimates in hopeless apostasy and damnation. We enter the heavenly state here or never. (Eph. vi.9.) These irregularities will never do for the heavenly state. With that collapsing religion, if even in heaven, O how quickly would you fall like Lucifer!

13. The Bible standard is full salvation— *i.e.,* entire sanctification— faithfully and persistently confessed with the mouth. See Romans x.10; Hebrews xiii.15. God will not be cheated. He is going to have your testimony. Sanctification turns the devil out, and confession locks the door. Whenever you get sanctified and decline to confess it, you leave the door ajar; the devil sees it, and comes back. Reader, are you a faithful witness to entire sanctification? If not, O fly this moment to the cleansing fountain, plunge beneath the crimson flood; in the twinkling of an eye Jesus' blood can sanctify! Consecration puts you on believing ground, and faith receives the prize. Be sure you always have faith in Jesus to sanctify you and keep you sanctified. If so, you will soon have the sweet consciousness that he sanctifies you.

Glory to the Father, Son, and Holy Ghost! Reader, live and die sanctified, and meet me in heaven. "Amen, and Amen."

76
ENCOURAGEMENTS TO SPIRITUAL JOY
REV. C.J. OXLEY

I. We are commanded to rejoice in the Lord.

"Be glad in the Lord, and rejoice, ye righteous: and shout for joy, all ye that are upright in heart." (Ps. xxxii.11.) "But let all those that put their trust in thee rejoice: let them ever shout thy name be joyful in thee." (Ps. v.11.) "Rejoice in the Lord always: and again I say, Rejoice." (Phil. iv.4.)

Much harm is done to the true spiritual life by the idea that a certain gloom, or restriction of the lively emotions, bears some relation to piety. Gloominess bears the same relation to piety that rust does to the sword-blade— eats into it. The command, "Be sober," does not mean be gloomy, morose, or uncheerful. Christ takes no more delight in a sad heart than we do to live in a dark house. Therefore let in the light of the Sun of righteousness, that all may be joy and gladness within. True joy is more than mirthfulness; laughing is not rejoicing. Joy is seated deeply within, and enables its possessor to be cheerful amid all the trials and difficulties of life. It comes from surrendering the heart entirely to the Lord, that it may be warmed by the genial rays of the Sun of righteousness.

II. Transientness of worldly joy,

> "That the triumphing of the wicked is short, and the joy of the hypocrite but a movement." (Job xx.5.)

Worldly pleasures are soon gone. The joy of the sinner is short, transient, feeble, uncertain. The Christian's joy is lasting, healing, healthful, precious.

III. The Christian's joy, being in God, is abiding.

> "Although the fig-tree shall not blossom, neither shall fruit be in the vines; the labor of the olive shall fail, and the fields shall yield no meat; the flock shall be cut off from the fold, and there shall be no herd in the stalls: yet I will rejoice in the Lord, I will joy in the God of my salvation." (Hab. iii.17, 18.)

Worldly prosperity is needful to the sinner's joy. Not so with the true Christian; adversity drives him nearer to the Lord. For examples, take Job, with his loathsome affliction; Joseph, sold into bondage by his jealous brothers; Daniel, cast into the den of lions for his fidelity to God; and Paul, enduring persecutions almost unbearable through his unswerving devotion to Christ. These all triumphed through grace and were "more than conquerors." A heart fixed on God stand and outride the raging storms of life, and will be cheerful amid life's worst calamities. As the sunflower turns in the direction of the sun, though the clouds may hide it from view, so the true child of God knows that behind the clouds of earthly sorrow there shines on forever the sun of heavenly joy, and thither he turns his face.

IV. Christ the source of unspeakable joy.

> "Whom having not seen, ye love; in whom, though

now ye and see him not, yet believing, ye rejoice with joy unspeakable and full of glory." (1 Pet. i.8.)

We may know Christ as really as did Peter, James, or John. The world gave nothing to the Redeemer but sorrow and suffering. He gave us in return joy and blessings. How great the joy of the convert when Christ is revealed in his heart! He is the comfort and joy of the believer; and the higher the Christian life, the more its joy and gladness. Heart-emptiness is the plague of millions. They try to fill the heart with pleasure, wealth, and fame; but yet the void remains. When Jesus fills the heart there is then a treasure to rejoice over continually. The Christian's joy is in fellowship with Christ, and in bringing others to him.

V. Joy is perfected in heaven.

> "Thou wilt show me the path of life: in thy presence is fullness of joy; at thy right hand there are pleasures forevermore." (Ps. xvi.11.) "And God shall wipe away all tears from their eyes; and there shall be no more death, neither sorrow, nor crying, neither shall there be any more pain: for the former things are passed away." (Rev. xxi.4.)

There is no sorrow in heaven. Unfading joy is the portion of the sanctified, in that blest world forever.

> Joy is a fruit that will not grow
>   In nature's barren soil:
> All we can boast, till Christ we know,
>   Is vanity and toil.

Members of Schmul's Wesleyan Book Club buy these outstanding books at 40% off the retail price.

Join Schmul's Wesleyan Book Club by calling toll-free:
800-S$_7$P$_7$B$_2$O$_6$O$_6$K$_5$S$_7$
Put a discount Christian bookstore in your own mailbox.

Visit us on the Internet at
www.wesleyanbooks.com

You may also order direct from the publisher by writing:
Schmul Publishing Company
PO Box 776
Nicholasville, KY 40340

www.ingramcontent.com/pod-product-compliance
Lightning Source LLC
Chambersburg PA
CBHW071315150426
43191CB00007B/629